CANDY FROM STRANGERS

CANDY FROM STRANGERS

Kids and Consumer Culture

Stephen Dale

NEW STAR BOOKS
Vancouver

NEW STAR BOOKS LTD.
107 – 3477 Commercial Street   1574 Gulf Road, #1517
Vancouver, British Columbia   Point Roberts, Washington
Canada V5N 4E8   USA 98281

info@NewStarBooks.com   NewStarBooks.com

Publication of this work is made possible by grants from the Canada Council,
the British Columbia Arts Council, and the Department of Canadian Heritage
Book Publishing Industry Development Program.

Cover design by Rayola Graphic Design
Interior design by Solo Corps
Printed and bound in Canada by Friesens
First printing, August 2005

LIBRARY AND ARCHIVES CANADA
CATALOGUING IN PUBLICATION

Dale, Stephen, 1958–
        Candy from strangers : kids and consumer culture / Stephen Dale.

Includes index.
ISBN 1-55420-015-6

1. Child consumers. 2. Advertising and children. 3. Consumption
(Economics)—Social aspects. I. Title.

HF5415.32.D34 2005   305.23   C2005-900839-3

This one's dedicated to Ben and Matthew,
who contributed to this book more than they might realize.

Acknowledgments

I'm grateful to a number of people who helped get this book into print. For their initial encouragement and enthusiasm, I'd like to thank Don Bastian and Angel Guerra. Among those who helped me with things like access and advice, I'll mention two key people: Matthew Behrens and Ted Mumford. Erika Shaker's CCPA email updates on educational and marketing issues were of terrific help to me during the research stage. Thanks to Dean Cooke for his fairness and understanding. For providing this book with a good home, I am profoundly appreciative of the wonderful people at New Star Books: Rolf Maurer, Carellin Brooks, Karin Konstantynowicz and Mel McLean. I'm also grateful to Audrey McClellan, a talented and sensitive editor whose grasp of big philosophical matters and small grammatical details immeasurably improved the prose on the pages that follow.

This book could not have been written without the generous financial assistance of the Canada Council for the Arts and the Ontario Arts Council, for which I am grateful.

Finally, for their ongoing support, good humour and great company, I offer my heartfelt thanks to Laura Macdonald, Ben Macdonald-Dale, and Matthew Macdonald-Dale.

PART ONE

Childhood For Sale

CHAPTER I

The World Is a Shopping Mall

*"I have a good car and a wide assortment of excellent hair-care
products. I know what I want from life; I have ambition."*
— Douglas Coupland, *Shampoo Planet*

As I crawl through the late rush hour traffic, the sightlines down Bay
Street provide a clear view of the clock tower on Toronto's old city
hall: big hand on the XI, meaning that it's exactly five to nine. On
the dashboard, my digital timepiece begs to differ. It says 8:53—a
little more lenient, but still confirmation that the question of the
moment is not whether I'm going to be late, but by how much.

To the left and the right, ahead and behind, there are people in
business attire planted behind steering wheels, making the same
kind of calculation. This is the way of the adult world. The wheels
of commerce turn so that mortgages can be paid and obligations
met. Just about everyone in that slow-moving parade of metal and
petrochemical effluent, winding its way along an asphalt ribbon
past the cut-rate suburban hotel where I stayed last night and towards the heart of the city, is living the same story. Lives measured
not in coffee spoons, but in the blinks of LED timepieces on dash-
boards, in minutes late for work. And somewhere in the back of all

their minds, the remembrance of a mythical time when it wasn't like this ... when you travelled by skateboard or as part of a pack on the subway, when getting someplace on time wasn't really the point. Childhood, it's called—a time of self-discovery, of learning and leisure—a concept so appealing in principle (if not always in practice) that over time it has become the focus of a multibillion-dollar industry.

The traffic eventually eases and I'm able to find an underground parking space and sprint through the drizzle towards the basement conference room at the Toronto Hilton, where I wanted to be twenty minutes ago. For the next two days this will be the site of a conference called Understanding Youth, one of several big-ticket North American trade shows (other giants of the genre are TeenPower in Chicago and KidPower in Orlando, which have spawned separate events for marketing to kids online and marketing to kids in Latin America) where practitioners of the art of persuasion share tips on how to infiltrate the insular kingdom called Youth Culture, the better to liberate some of its citizens' spare change.

It's hard to show up at one of these events with an unjaundiced eye, given the kind of reviews the kid-marketing industry has been receiving lately. About eight months before this conference, for instance, members of the American Psychological Association (APA) had picketed outside New York's Grand Hyatt Hotel, where Brunico Communications (the same trade magazine/trade show outfit that is producing Understanding Youth here in Toronto) had staged the Golden Marble Awards, a kind of Academy Awards for children's advertisers. The psychologists' basic complaint was that the kid-focused ads being honoured that night represented an unethical use of the psychologist's craft. They contend that advertisers have not bought the profession's insight into children's aspirations and fears with the aim of making kids stronger, better human beings, but rather in order to pry money out of their pockets by feeding them the false promise that laying down their allowance at the shopping mall cash register will somehow make them whole, happy, and self-fulfilled.[1]

Some APA members also believe that the increased sophistication and volume of marketing to kids has had a broadly negative social impact, helping to diminish the idealism that was once taken as a hallmark of childhood. For instance, Allen Kanner, a psychologist from Berkeley, California, told the APA's Monitor on Psychology that while kids used to tell him they wanted to grow up to be nurses or astronauts, today they are most likely to say that their goal is to "make money." [2] In October 2000, this negative view of the youth-marketing industry gained a national spotlight in the United States when the Center for Media Education (CME)—backed by 50 distinguished co-signers including parenting author T. Berry Brazelton, Nobel laureate Roald Hoffman, and children's advocate Marian Wright Edelman—wrote to all the U.S. presidential candidates, urging them to commit to strong actions to limit the "unprecedented and unethical assault" carried out by children's marketers, which the CME saw as a contributor to rising rates of violence, obesity, and anorexia and, as such, a threat to public health. [3]

But if those critics are brutally blunt in their characterization of kid marketing as toxic to children and corrosive to the concept of childhood, the practitioners of this maligned trade respond with an equally ferocious joviality. Two days of listening to relentlessly upbeat speakers at the Understanding Youth conference—their sales pitches and best-case scenarios often reinforced by quick-cut video pastiches on the giant screen overhead—was as wearying as attending a Dale Carnegie weekend retreat or being trapped in a marathon high-school pep rally. High school is actually a good analogy for a gathering like this, largely because the delegates seemed a lot younger than your typical convention crowd. Not that this event bore much resemblance to my high school, which I recall through the murky filter of time as being populated by a fair number of cynics and pessimists, losers and hoodlums. No, this was more like a high school where any trace of negative thinking had been genetically engineered out of the student body, leaving only candidates for student council, smooth-talking keeners (think of what Ferris Bueller might have been like if he had bought the establishment ethos) who are as likely to hold down an after-school job selling real estate as flipping burgers at McDonald's.

You get a sense of how dramatically this group differs from the common denizens of the workaday world when the pager sales guys meeting in an adjacent room—let's call them "the control group"—bolt for the coffee urn resting on a common expanse of beige broadloom in the hallway. The control group all wear dark suits, dark frowns, and conservative ties. They provide the neutral background that highlights the Understanding Youth delegates on a break nearby, most of them talking intently into cellphones accessorized to match their clothes—a sea of hundred-dollar haircuts, sometimes in metallic blue or Day-Glo red, and nary a jacket and tie in sight. The hidden message in this panorama of business operatives who dress and talk like kids is that, in the minds of these delegates, at least, that sad line separating the repressive world of commerce from the carefree zone of youth—the same psychic divide which had presented itself to me in the frozen line of traffic that morning—can be eradicated. Sure, they talked money—megabucks, in fact—but the unspoken law here was that nobody should seem more concerned with business than with the abstract pursuit of cool, with the sheer joy of alighting upon the indefinable essence of hip, of finding tomorrow's big trend and riding it to shore like a champion surfer balanced on a boiling wave. It's all very esoteric, with most of the experts who presented here exuding a certain aura of the wizard or the alchemist—their principal skill being the ability to attain Oneness with the Youth Mind, to defy the laws of nature by remaining kids themselves even though their biological casing and the cars they drive might suggest that they do indeed carry passports from Planet Grownup.

Speaking of people occupying the dual worlds of youth and adulthood, I'd like to introduce you to Max Valliquette, the twenty eight year old president of Youthography, a Toronto-based market research and advertising firm, who additionally served as MC for the duration of Understanding Youth. I called Valliquette on the phone a few days after the conference, hopeful that he could put the details that arose in two days of sessions into some wider historical and social perspective for me. I figured he'd be good at this, having witnessed his able performance introducing speakers, directing delegates to breakout sessions, and providing pointed little off-the-cuff synopses of the prior proceedings. His polished delivery and good timing I put down to the impressive career sidelines noted in Valliquette's self-penned bio in the conference binder: his experience as part of the celebrated Second City comedy troupe, and a stint as host of a youth-oriented TV chat show called Mr. Jones, which ran briefly on public television in Ontario. Yet when I mention these achievements in the course of our debriefing session, Valliquette turns the acknowledgement around—downplaying his credits on stage and TV so as to advance the idea that his current advertising work is no less authentic, no less important an accomplishment, both as a cultural endeavour and an expression of self.

"Even when I was doing the TV show and working on sketch comedy, I was still in the ad game at the same time," he recalls. His first foray into advertising, at the age of twenty-three, was with a company called Bozell Worldwide, working on "youth brands" such as Taco Bell, Hershey and Budweiser. "I was in the future planning department—what most people would call a strategic planning department—and I was essentially responsible for making sure that new culture came in." Valliquette says it was a good fit, since most of the requirements of the job just happened to be his hobbies. "My friends all laughed because I still watched twenty hours of television a week, I read probably, honestly, I read forty or fifty magazines a month. My friends joked that it seemed like I was doing exactly what I had always done, but now I was getting paid for it. I tend to always do more than one thing; I'll be watching TV and reading a magazine. I mean, I really like consuming current culture. I see every film, I listen to every piece of music that I can."

This habit of plugging into more than one medium at the same time is popularly (and all too frequently) known as "multitasking," and to many commentators on youth culture it is a defining characteristic of the Internet generation. So in case you haven't noticed what's happening here, let me spell it out: Max Valliquette is positioning himself as a youth-culture insider, a kindred spirit rather than an interloper, a marketer whose approach to the target is based on empathy rather than the impulse to conquer. It's a message he drives home with the insistence of a sledgehammer as he describes the team assembled by his company, Youthography, formerly a division of a larger firm called NRG Solutions, which Valliquette and three partners (also in their twenties) bought and spun off as an independent entity about four months earlier. "Our designer is twenty," he recites. "Our videographer is twenty-two. Our researcher is nineteen or twenty. Our chief programmer, our online community engineer, is twenty years old. I'm not twenty-one so I don't live like a twenty-one year old. I consume some of those things but not all of them. But having actual young people here keeps us very fresh, keeps us very honest."

Even Valliquette himself—the elder statesman of his corporate clan at a ripe old twenty-eight—still fits within the marketing world's current definition of what constitutes "youth." That fact is in itself highly significant, and it provides a convenient platform for Valliquette's neat synopsis of current marketing scholarship that details how the changing life cycle of North Americans—remade by technology and the new roles it has forced upon us—has recast the basic assumptions of this business. Where before there were kids, teenagers, and adults, explains Valliquette, a series of profound sociological shifts in the latter part of the twentieth century have made younger children more worldly wise, while simultaneously pushing the borders of non-adulthood upwards to roughly age thirty. So while crusaders against the youth-marketing machine wring their hands at how younger kids are being bombarded with images that were once the province of teens and young adults, the marketing experts more sanguinely accept the blurring of prior age distinctions as an inevitable adjustment to some major social changes.

This helps to explain the wide spectrum of content on display at the Understanding Youth conference. On one hand, there were a number of speakers who waxed philosophical about the phenomenon known to the cognoscenti as KAGOY—short for Kids Are Getting Older Younger, a syndrome many critics blame on Britney Spears and the TV programmers who run adult sitcoms in family hour, but which Valliquette feels has more to do with kids being enlisted at a younger age to microwave dinner and load the dishwasher for their busy, dual-income families. On the other hand, however, many of those same delegates trying to tap into the *Weltschmerz* of today's ten year olds were also pitching to a group of twenty-somethings (I heard no catchy anagram to describe them) living in a state of dependantless, mortgage-free quasi-kidhood that didn't exist thirty years ago.

So a company president pushing thirty and an elementary school tyke have more in common than you might think. Today "there is, like, this prolonged period of pre-adult life stage," Valliquette says, "where you can be thirteen years old and you live at home and you make dinner for your family every night and you have some kind of part-time work and you hang out with your friends and you spend time online and you go to school. But you can be twenty-three years old and do all of those exact same things. You know, people are getting married later, they are having kids later, even leaving school later, because a general undergraduate arts degree doesn't have the cachet it once did. Yet they are taking care of themselves at an even earlier age. That's a great paradox."

It's also great for business, and not just because this bulging demographic has, as a group, unprecedented disposable income. The extra change in their pockets, ventures Valliquette, is the product of a number of changes in the way that work and family life are now organized—including an increase in the number of dual-income professional families, the boom in part-time after-school employment in fast food and retail, and even the rising divorce rates, which result in more guilt-driven gift-giving and bequeath kids extra sets of parents and grandparents. As James U. McNeal wrote in his landmark book *Kids as Customers*, these and other sociological shifts began to dramatically boost kids' status as consumers in the 1980s.[4] Add to all this the fact that the carefree days of youth—in the marketers' imagination a huge void begging to be filled with beer and soda pop, CDs, junk food, and hours spent scouring the shelves at Blockbuster—last about a decade longer than they used to, and you've got a bonanza for youth-directed businesses that may well dwarf the youth-culture explosion of the 1960s. "Even when the boomers came of age, you still had a significantly smaller period of time to be a young person," says Valliquette.

So it's obvious why these "selling to youth" conferences are a big draw (at $1,500 a pop, this one attracted about three hundred people, representing enterprises from convenience store chains to cosmetics companies to government agencies) and why there is such enthusiasm here (no, it's not just the constant flow of sample lollipops and frozen fruit bars boosting participants' blood sugar levels). The lure is economic. Matthew Diamond, CEO of the teen-marketing phenomenon Alloy Online, got straight to the heart of the matter in his keynote address, recounting that the 56 million ten to twenty-four year olds in the United States (a demographic that's growing 19.5 percent faster than the overall population) spent over $150 billion in 1999, a total that was set to grow to $250 billion in the year 2000. Diamond had a few more statistical morsels to tickle the salivary glands of his audience: 66 percent of U.S. teens have savings accounts; 44 percent have access to their parents' credit cards; 14 percent have a credit card in their own name.[5] The year 2000 YTV *Kid and Tween Report* tells a similar story in Canada. Canadian kids in the nine to fourteen age bracket alone—that doesn't include older teens—enjoy $1.8 billion in discretionary income (up from $1.1 billion in 1995) and influence an additional $20 billion in parental spending.

How far are marketers willing to go to get their piece of the pie? As McNeal notes in *Kids as Customers*, the techniques that children's advertisers have used to mesmerize and cajole children into parting with their allowance (or pressuring Mom or Dad to fork over) have raised such a storm in the short history of children's marketing that in 1978 the U.S. Federal Trade Commission came close to banning ads aimed at children.[6] The standard image driving such initiatives—of child marketers as a band of nefarious con artists, out to trick gullible kids—has been reinforced by the periodic candour of ad execs, like the one who muttered to a reporter that "advertising at its best is making people feel that without their product, you're a loser." She went on to explain that "kids are very sensitive to that. If you tell them to buy something, they are resistant. But if you tell them that they'll be a dork if they don't, you've got their attention. You open up emotional vulnerabilities, and it's very easy to do with kids because they are the most emotionally vulnerable."[7]

Although there were no statements remotely like that one at Understanding Youth, one naturally wonders what hidden agenda lurks behind the carefully chosen words and collective happy face worn by conference participants. Did the delegates actually believe all those statements about how the marketing industry is empowering kids, allowing them to assume their new role as self-directed free agents in the great candy store of life? Or was this more like a confab of Moonies, with all of the adrenalized enthusiasm a mask for a sinister form of mind control?

Indeed, many features of the industry that make its critics apoplectic were on open display at Understanding Youth. Those who believe that the marketing onslaught has taken some (or all) of the innocence out of childhood, for instance, might well have blanched at the sight of the World Wrestling Federation logo,[8] prominently displayed around the conference hall and on flyers to denote the WWF's status as a major sponsor of this youth-focused event. There's also been a huge outcry against corporations trying to plug their products in schools—whether through sponsored events, ads on school property, or exclusive vending contracts. Critics argue that this commercialization of education delivers a captive audience to advertisers, blunts free inquiry, and gives commercial propaganda the unfair advantage of an implicit endorsement by teachers and school officials.[9] Their protests seem to have had an impact, with school boards in places like Seattle (where half of the public high schools and most middle schools had required students to sit attentively through the two minutes of commercials that accompany the ten-minute newscast piped into classrooms by Channel One) backing away from deals with commercial outfits.[10] Sure enough, a session at Understanding Youth dealt with how campus marketers can refine their pitch to retain their access to the schoolyard audience in the face of such pressure.

But some critics see the colonization of schools by advertisers as part of a more general malaise, in which it's become next to impossible for kids to find sanctuary from the incessant assault of marketing. In this view of the world, there is practically no aspect of childhood that isn't conquered and controlled by the commercial imperative; no experience that comes without a sponsor's tag or an opportunity for a little covert market research. There was plenty at Understanding Youth to support this perspective.

Take the now-defunct website Curve.com—launched in Great Britain by the Toronto office of the multinational marketing firm Modem Media—which on the surface was an electronic playground where kids, mostly between the age of thirteen and nineteen, visited chat rooms and bantered with their peers on subjects like fashion, music, sports, and friends. In reality the site was an advertising appendage of General Motors (GM), which used Curve.com to collect data—by tracking traffic flows and personal information collected when kids signed in—on the likes, dislikes and cultural proclivities of its future customers, and to lay some of the groundwork for revamping GM's currently uninspiring image among youth. Specifically, the site was supposed to tell GM what advertising themes were likely to appeal to its target group and which venues would put its advertising in the target group's line of vision. Though many of the site's fans were way too young to drive, GM apparently felt it was worth the expense of keeping these kids squarely in its crosshairs until it was time to pull the trigger (at least, it did feel that way until, in a fitting acknowledgement of the temporal nature of the Internet, GM yanked the site off the web). I felt a melancholy sense of inevitability listening to Modem Media account manager Elizabeth Crothers describe what is expected of these kids in the years to come. Despite the assertion of some demographers that environmental issues are top of mind for today's kids, GM expects this principle to be sacrificed on the altar of personal comfort. According to Crothers, the company is confident that the target consumer, by the time she is twenty-four, "will forsake the stress of taking public transit and buy her own car."

What Curve.com had in common with a lot of the other enterprises touted at Understanding Youth is that it was an advertising tool that didn't appear to be an advertising tool. Companies are starting to camouflage their marketing campaigns because young people, particularly teens, are expressing rising skepticism at the messages broadcast to them through conventional means. The result is a trend to supplement traditional media buys by taking the message to the street, opting for "guerrilla" marketing techniques that sometimes take the form of travelling road shows carted off to dance clubs, skateboard parks, and cinema queues. Often there is an attempt to cultivate an anti-establishment sheen with this kind of campaign. Consider, for instance, the two presenters at an Understanding Youth panel on guerrilla marketing, who have forged a new partnership known as "Girlrilla Girls." Although they work for mainstream corporations, the name is no doubt intended to, um, borrow some of the streetwise feel of the Guerrilla Girls, a group of women artists whose specialty is dressing up in gorilla suits and plastering New York City with politically pointed posters. Similar vibe, but different purpose. While the NYC original concerned itself with issues like women's rights, homelessness, rape, and the Gulf War, the partners behind the Canadian knock-off have a background publicizing things like cellphones and candy.

The fact that one can encounter guerrilla marketing in three-dimensional form in the course of one's day—say, by being approached by a costumed cartoon character giving away samples in a cinema queue, or by walking around an artist drawing an elaborate scene on a sidewalk in chalk—is just one more confirmation that advertising is everywhere, having spread across the broadcast waves and through cyberspace, across the landscape on billboards, and back into the fabric of real life. The optimum strategy in this age of fragmentation, apparently, is mutual reinforcement—to bombard the target from as many different angles as possible so that resistance becomes futile.

At his company, explains Alloy Online CEO Matthew Diamond, this is known as "the comprehensive convergence approach" and it has worked like a charm, helping to transform Alloy from a firm comprising "two guys and a dog," as Diamond puts it, to a marketing titan with $80 million in annual revenues that commands the attention of 10 to 12 million kids (the bulk of them in the United States). Alloy, Diamond explains, will not just hype a product on its website (a cyberspace version of the amusement park, where kids can play games, discover trivia about their favourite pop stars, and win prizes ... making it another example of marketing by stealth, with the site's commercial purpose camouflaged by an outer layer of frivolity and fun). It can also feature the product in one of its advertorial magazines, perhaps by associating the product with a hot musical star (in the past, Alloy has used the pop group Cleopatra to plug Covergirl cosmetics and Britney Spears to hype Herbal Essence shampoo). It can push the product in its catalogue or in its line of books. It can send out ads by e-mail. It can even beam its "deal of the day" plugs to young cellphone users through its Alloy Wireless division. It all adds up to a kind of psychic carpet bombing, where little turf is left untouched by the message from our sponsor.

Many of the complaints that this type of saturation advertising elicits—most of which resolve into the single grievance that marketing is taking over the world, leaving kids little space to grow up where they won't be badgered to buy something—can be seen (if one spins it a certain way) as a result of the industry's own overwhelming success. It's a bit like the rap against the car, which people have embraced with such fervour that the world has been remade in its image, with roads obliterating the countryside and auto exhaust helping to chew a hole in the earth's atmosphere. Or against humanity as a species, which has thrived so wonderfully well that we have crowded out many of the planet's other inhabitants. Likewise, the advertising industry was such a brilliant hit that it has grown and prospered to the point that it must constantly find new platforms from which to broadcast its messages, new channels of perception to invade. Inevitably, this has prompted calls to curtail and control the marketing machine by, for instance, declaring certain places (like schools) off-limits to commercial propagandists. But still, embedded in this struggle is the idea that the reason we are drowning in marketing is that people buy its messages and enjoy its distraction—that advertising fills a need.

A more sinister scenario—the one posited by those APA members who protested outside the Golden Marble Awards—is that the marketing industry has only succeeded because it has manipulated, tricked, and mesmerized its subjects, particularly children, who are vulnerable and lacking in self-awareness. In this view, marketers have more in common with Big Tobacco than with car manufacturers, since people respond to their pitches not through any logical process, but through compulsion.

Did I witness anything at the Understanding Youth conference that bears out the latter view of how kid marketers operate? I'm still not sure. But there were instances that aroused some suspicion. I got a bit of a start, for instance, listening to Taylor Cousens, strategic planner with the U.S. kid-marketing powerhouse the Geppetto Group, who explained that the title of her talk—"The Six Pillars of Tween Advertising Wisdom"—was adapted from a book of military strategy written by T.E. Lawrence, better known as Lawrence of Arabia. Military strategy ... as in sneak attack ... as in conquest of the enemy.

"The name of the book was *The Seven Pillars of Wisdom*," explained Cousens. "It's really a classic book, but what made it so amazing was that it was also full of idealism and full of vision. When we started this company, we thought we would borrow from that title because that's the way we as a company think about the youth market. That, on the one hand, tweens require an enormous amount of military precision and strategy, but on the other hand, we always hope that we keep our vision and our ideals intact when we're dealing with this vulnerable target."

The focus of Cousens' talk was how the so-called tweens—kids variably pegged as between eight and twelve, or nine and thirteen, or eight and fourteen—react to the advertising images they encounter. Throughout this session I'm unable to decide whether this type of research is nefarious or neutral. It seems reasonable to suggest that advertisers have a legitimate interest in discovering what kind of images and themes attract or repel the kids with which they are trying to communicate. On the other hand, in the course of probing those kids' hearts and minds, one may discover all kinds of psychic sore spots (like that fear of appearing a "dork" who doesn't have the product of the moment), the mapping of which appears to leave kids open to manipulation.

Cousens' presentation feeds this sense of ambivalence as she wavers between a hard-nosed, businesslike determination and a New Agey empathy. A former preschool and elementary teacher, Cousens is a personable and sympathetic presence. She exudes a palpable sense of caring as she stirringly, almost poetically, describes the plight of the tweens, launched on a trying journey "from the light side of the fun and freedom of childhood to the dark side of adolescence, which is marked by cynicism and sarcasm. From innocence and feeling in control to being largely out of control, both physically and emotionally. From an environment where they know what the expectations are to a place they are mostly unfamiliar with, which is largely enemy terrain." Nothing evil here so far. Indeed, this portrayal of tweens as exiles from the enchanted land of childhood, warily approaching the shores of a dangerous new place, could surely be a tool of understanding, a therapeutic device, in the right hands. Parents and teachers might do well to place their tween charges' mystifying mood swings and personality contortions in this narrative context. Understanding kids is surely the first step in helping them navigate their way through the treacherous trek towards adulthood.

But here, of course, that is not the point. There's a practical, pecuniary end to all this soft-focus psychoanalytic exploration. The companies who pay for the research the Geppetto Group produces are interested in charting the joys and anxieties of their target market, not to ease their distress, but to sell them products more effectively. To this end, Cousens offers several general rules for advertising to pre-teens. She counsels her audience to avoid the ironic, cynical, or "edgy" appeals that often work with teens, but which will likely fall flat with slightly younger kids. Remember, she says, the tweens are kids who "come from being king of the hill, where the other kids all look up to them ... [to being] the smallest, the puniest, [who] don't really know anything anymore." More to the point, continues Cousens, they are moving from a situation where their childish foibles have been tolerated and even indulged by the adult world, to one where "they are constantly feeling that they are being evaluated, ranked, and prejudged. 'Did I say the right thing in that situation?' 'Are my friends going to get mad at me if I act in a certain way?' They feel under constant pressure to prove themselves, over and over again." This makes the hapless tween crave straightforward, simple humour in advertising, since it is likely to make them feel smart, current, and in sync with the world when they arrive at the realization that "I get it." Conversely, the feeling of inadequacy or insecurity that this group of kids typically experiences when ads go over their heads is likely to be transferred directly onto the product—it's the advertising (and, by extension, the item that's being advertised) which they'll say is stupid, not the kid who's watching it. In a similar vein, Cousens insists that tweens are eager to see ads that reflect teenage life in a glowing light, with all the uncertainties, turmoil, and angst airbrushed out. They need reassurance that life will get better, not worse, as they get set to enter the next phase of their existence.

These sorts of conclusions, at least on the surface, appear a much less Mephistophelian use of psychological trawling than that referred to by those disgruntled APA members. Isn't it reasonable for advertisers to want to avoid messages that alienate their potential customers? It may even be good for the kids, sparing them the aggravation of being hit with still more broadcast messages that vex and confuse them.

Alarm bells go off for me once again, however, when Cousens mentions her company's understanding of how products become a vital "need" for tween-agers, who use them to help formulate their new sense of identity. "Children say 'I need that, I need that,'" she elaborates, "but, in fact, children don't really need products. It's tweens who need them because it's those accoutrements and accessories that help the tweens communicate who they are, not only to other people, but to themselves. Those CDs, the clothing, the brands that they wear, and the things they have in their backpack help them to understand 'where do I fit in?'"

This line of thinking, it strikes me, comes close to confirming the fears of those crusaders in the APA: if advertisers can advance the conditions where consumer goods become indispensable to the formation of youthful identity, then who knows what damage can arise? What is the fallout when advertisers reinforce the idea that having certain status items is a necessary precondition for growing up? What happens, for instance, to kids who cannot afford those increasingly essential totems of belonging and self-worth? Is there a link between those attacks that make the newspapers periodically—where kids have been killed for a logo-emblazoned jacket or a pair of sneakers—and the advertising industry's creation of fetishes around brand names and logos? Has solidifying the link between consumer goods and self-image resulted, as psychologist Allen Kanner suggested, in refocusing the vision of many kids away from good works and noble callings and towards lives dedicated to merely making the money that will allow them to buy those things that confirm their sense of self?

How you answer those questions will likely depend on your cultural or ideological frame of reference, whether you think consumerism is enriching or degrading, and to what degree you believe that human behaviour is a product of social conditioning, family environment, or individual choice. There are some wildly divergent views about what marketing is doing to kids and how it really operates. Where the industry's critics portray the youthful targets of marketing as empty receptacles that take on the characteristics of the messages that fill them, Pavlovian puppies made to jump by the jolts and starts of the marketing machine, those in the biz protest that the power relations they must deal with are quite different. Max Valliquette, voicing a viewpoint that seemed to be the conventional wisdom at the Understanding Youth conference, insists that kids today are a new breed—bright, self-aware, well-informed as a result of their fluency with the Internet, materially indulged to the point where they are difficult to impress and almost impossible to boondoggle—all of which rolls up into that convenient cliché about "media-savvy" kids. It's these young consumers who are in the driver's seat, says Valliquette, and advertisers and marketers must come to them on bended knee, pure of heart and wary of causing offence.

"I believe that your average mainstream young person," he says, "is savvy—not skeptical, but savvy, very savvy, about marketing. That comes from a number of sources: having grown up on marketing; having a great facility with the Internet, obviously; having a great understanding of commercials, of the art of persuasion, of branding … They are learning about it in formal ways at a far earlier age. In Grade 4 or 5 [kids are] learning about marketing by writing an essay on 'the brand called Me,' as [management guru] Tom Peters puts it." Valliquette also brings the issue back to that new-style thirteen year old who's been taught to nuke dinner for his busy family—a kid who, having acquired new responsibilities in the trenches of domestic duty, heads off into the real world as a hard-headed consumer. "I think one reason why this group is so empowered, or why they find empowerment of one form or other to be so important, is because it's very difficult to not take control of spending or make demands as a consumer when you've let yourself into the house since you were twelve or made dinner for your family since you were fourteen, and you've been asked to make some fairly serious decisions about sex, drugs, and alcohol from a fairly early age. So of course people in this group wield power, because they've got it and they know it."

Some of the front-line stories surfacing at Understanding Youth—where marketing execs complained incessantly about how much they were sweating, running at full speed to convince the demanding young consumer of the early twenty-first century that their commercials are the funniest, their technology the best, their styles the furthest ahead of the curve—lend limited support to this idea that millennial kids are a much tougher sell than their predecessors. Several commentators warned that the lives of middle-class kids are already so saturated with consumer goods that they can afford to resist all but the most appealing pitches. A plastic whistle in a cereal box will elicit little but jeers from today's kids. That's why cereal manufacturers like General Mills, competing in an industry where gains in market share have generally only been won through deep price discounts, started giving away CD-ROMs with a value several times that of the cereal itself. If you want to impress the current blasé generation with a promotion, you've got to think big and expensive. Try giving away NBA tickets in another city, with hotel room and airfare thrown in, or a chance to meet a rock star, or a shot at a summer gig as a television VJ if you really want to generate some buzz. Is this kids being manipulated, or is this advertisers desperately pleading with the picky generation to give their wares a look-in?

Still, despite what the current market dynamics (i.e., a surfeit of stuff breeding choosy kids, at least amongst the ranks of the pampered middle class) might suggest, the marketing industry will have a tough struggle to eradicate the default answer to the question— posed by Aretha Franklin a few years back—"Who's zoomin' who?" There is a long line of popular histories of the advertising biz which have it that it's the Madison Avenue sharpies (and their e-world heirs) who are doing unto others, and the rest of us who are being done. The foundation stone underlying all of these works is the idea that the magi of marketing have cast some kind of hypnotic spell over us, which explains why the shopping malls and living rooms of North America appear to be filled with extras from *Night of the Living Dead*, zombified people who habitually make decisions that are against their better judgment and their own interests. Though most of these works deal with the targeting of adults—depending upon which way the demographic axis has been tilting, the favoured prey has been the 1950s housewife, the 1960s young male swinger, or the progressive college student of the 1990s—in recent years kids have stepped into the foreground. Given how the new baby boom of the past twenty years has boosted the social status of children, the marketing pros have been zeroing in on the schoolyard and, increasingly, the playpen.

CHAPTER 2

A Cornucopia of Conspiracies

One of the first and most influential of the post-Second World War indictments of the advertising industry was Vance Packard's 1957 classic *The Hidden Persuaders*, which sold over a million copies (a rarity for non-fiction in that era) and stirred widespread outrage against the manipulative techniques that were apparently becoming standard practice in the advertising industry of the 1950s.[1] According to Packard, the greatest sin of advertisers before then was overstating the attributes of the product, often to the point of being fraudulent. But the business took a radical turn with the ascendancy of the so-called "depth boys," proponents of a new quasi-science known as motivation research (MR in adspeak), who imported insights and techniques inspired by psychiatry and the social sciences (Freudian psychoanalysis in particular, but also sociology, anthropology, and communications theory) into the adman's universe. This new breed tended not to overstate their products' qualities. In fact, MR practitioners believed it was pointless to pitch a product on the basis of its intrinsic merits, particularly in an era when standardized production techniques made many competing goods virtually indistinguishable from one another. Instead, they preached that advertising should speak to deep-seated psychological needs: promising that the product would quell secret anxieties and guilt feelings; satisfy oral fixations; boost the buyer's sense of self-worth, power, and status; provide outlets for aggression; and so forth.

Packard credits two men with leading the charge to this new philosophy of advertising: Dr. Ernest Dichter, the Viennese-born director of the Institute for Motivational Research, and Louis Cheskin, director of the Color Research Institute, a former psychology major who had done graduate work in the field of psychoanalysis. Both of these men claimed they had been promoting the "depth" approach to advertising since the 1930s, although it wasn't until the late 1940s and 1950s that MR began to gain widespread attention when many ad agencies realized that traditional campaigns based purely on appeals to logic weren't delivering the desired results.

Previously, market researchers based their campaigns on simple "nose-counting" research, in which, Packard explains, "statistic-minded interviewers would determine the percentage of married women, ages twenty-one to thirty-five, in Omaha, Nebraska, who said they wanted, and would buy, a three-legged stove if it cost no more than $249." But discrepancies between the survey results and cash-register receipts caused advertising execs to question their assumptions that people were reporting their preferences truthfully—or that they even knew what those preferences were. A ketchup maker introduced a new bottle based on survey results but had to reintroduce the old one when the new container bombed in the marketplace. A brewery's survey revealed that customers preferred its light beer three to one over its regular beer, even though the company found it had to brew nine times more regular beer to meet the market demand. Emblematic of how disastrous it could be to assume that customers are rational animals, Packard writes, was the Chrysler Corporation's decision in 1952 to follow its survey results and the sober deductions of its engineers by introducing a smaller car in response to consumers' reported desire for a vehicle that would be easier to park and wouldn't add to highway congestion. "The public no longer wants a big fat car—the public wants a slim car," said a Chrysler exec. Actually, they didn't. When Chrysler gave them the slim car, the company's market share plummeted from 26 percent to 13 percent, prompting Chrysler to reintroduce that irrational "big fat car," which would continue to serve as an enduring symbol of the decade's social ethos.

In fact, the depth boys delighted in demonstrating that consumers' declarations about their own preferences were one of the least reliable predictors of marketplace behaviour. Cheskin's Color Research Institute, for instance, conducted one experiment in which a group of women could wait for a lecture in "a Swedish modern room ... a functional modern chamber with gentle tones," or in "a traditional room filled with period furniture, oriental rugs, and expensive looking wallpaper." Although almost all the women gravitated to the more comfortable modern room (only moving into the ornate room after the first one had been filled), when asked about their preferences afterwards, 84 percent said the ornate room was their favourite.

With the old advertising paradigm demonstrably in tatters, MR specialists commanded increasingly lucrative contracts to perform their kooky experiments aimed at reaching beneath the conscious mind and into a "deeper" stratum of consciousness (thus the term "depth approach"), where the individual was only vaguely aware of the feelings, sensations, and attitudes that motivated behaviour, or deeper still, to a level where buried emotions and impulses lay beyond the reach of self-scrutiny. The surveyor's clipboard was replaced by the slightly sinister behavioural lab. Experts sat behind one-way mirrors charting the pupil dilation, eye movements, and body language of children watching TV commercials. When adults were brought in for surveys, the questions were often mere distractions to put them at ease while their instinctive responses to other stimuli were studied. Group sessions aimed to induce a "reverie" in which "pleasures, joys, enthusiasms, agonies, nightmares" could rise to the surface. Hypnosis and Rorschach ink-blot tests became tools of the advertising trade. Packard describes one particularly weird experiment involving what was known as a Szondi test, in which heavy whiskey drinkers (who accounted for the majority of whiskey sales and were therefore a desired target) were asked to respond to a series of portraits of people who, unknown to the subjects, had been diagnosed as suffering from various psychiatric disorders (i.e., depression, psychosis, paranoia). The test was conducted both before and after the subjects had consumed a few drinks, with the goal of determining what state of personality the whiskey drinkers sought through their drinking and, therefore, what change in consciousness the distillers should promise in their ads. The underlying idea was that the drinkers would have a "rapport" with one of the personality types portrayed and that this was the personality they hoped to achieve by drinking.

This type of probing became so much a part of the postwar marketing industry, writes Packard, that "by 1955, for example, the McCann-Erikson advertising agency in New York had five psychologists manning a special motivation department." "Agencies that [did] not have resident head-shrinkers [were] hastening to employ independent firms, run by psychologists," according to *The Reporter*, a trade magazine cited by Packard.

In *The Hidden Persuaders*, Packard recognizes (as do some of the admen he quotes) the morally ambiguous nature of this work. Initiating a debate that continues to this day, Packard concedes, at least partially, the validity of the ad industry's defence that many of its attempts to uncover buried yearnings, fears, and desires were in the service of trying to give the consumer what he or she really wanted, to serve the true needs and desires of which even the consumer might not be aware. But Packard cites many cases in which the depth approach to designing marketing campaigns served nothing but the company's bottom line; cases where customers were drawn by psycho-manipulation to make decisions that were clearly detrimental to them. The campaign to revive flagging cigarette sales in the 1950s is a stunning case in point. The tobacco industry had seen its expansion plans stalled by embedded guilt feelings, particularly among women, arising from the earlier perception that smoking cigarettes was an immoral habit, and by the fallout from what Packard quaintly referred to as "the cancer scare of the early 50s"—a panic that created the "very genuine suspicion that cigarettes were coffin nails." On the advice of MR pioneer Pierre Martineau, the tobacco industry dropped its defensive-sounding ads, which protested that cigarettes were actually safe, and instead hired the firm Social Research, Inc., to study the underlying psychological associations that drew people to cigarette smoking. The company's report pinpointed about a dozen motivations for smoking, such as rewarding oneself after a difficult task, relieving work stress, and lessening the smoker's tension in new social situations. Social Research also believed the fact that smokers saw "smoking as proving their vigour, potency," was something that could serve as "a psychological satisfaction sufficient to overcome health fears, to withstand moral censure, ridicule, or even the paradoxical weakness of 'enslavement to habit.'"

That task—overcoming the consumer's inner voice of conscience (the conditioned and/or reasoned response that buying a particular product or too much of it may be unhealthy, unwise, or morally suspect)—became a daily struggle for admen in the United States of the 1950s, where the broader goal was to propagate the craze of conspicuous consumption to a nation of people who "were still basically puritans at heart." Thus, motivational researchers set out to find the psychological triggers that would help them peddle sweets to people who associated sugar with weight gain, instant cake mixes and labour-saving appliances to people with a strong work ethic, alcohol to people who had been taught to value sobriety. For Packard, the gravest problem with the advertising industry's attempt to remake America's social ethic (transforming Americans from puritans to hedonists) was not that people were being lured into unhealthy lifestyles, but that the cult of consumerism was making promises that couldn't possibly be fulfilled. Paradoxically, as the standard of living continued to rise, the happiness and sense of contentment promised in advertising seemed more and more elusive.

Indeed, Madison Avenue wouldn't have wanted to make the public happy, even if that was within its power. For the adman, it seems, happiness equals complacency, and complacency holds the promise of economic doom. Packard writes that while the growth in the post-Second World War economy gave Americans five times more discretionary income in 1955 than they had enjoyed in 1940, "one big and intimidating obstacle confronting the stimulators was the fact that most Americans already possessed perfectly usable stoves, cars, TV sets, clothes, etc." Without the impulsive spending of those discretionary funds, warehouses would overflow and the economy would grind to a halt. The solution was for advertising to equate old products with feelings of inadequacy or inferiority, such that "by the mid-fifties," as Packard relates, "merchandisers of many different products were being urged by psychological counsellors to become 'merchants of discontent.'" Packard's prescient portrayal of the pitfalls of rampant consumerism still has an eerie ring of truth in the early twenty-first century, when homes are bigger and cars more plentiful than ever, but when a multitude of indicators—from episodes of road rage to the brisk trade in antidepressants—suggests that these material advances have not brought happiness.

Beyond this criticism of the ad industry's "systematic creation of dissatisfaction," Packard's other big gripe was the potential for these covert psychological campaigns to change the national character. Americans had prided themselves on being clear-headed individualists, not the "bundles of daydreams, misty hidden yearnings, guilt complexes [and] irrational emotional blockages" imagined by the wizards of the advertising establishment. And to appeal to them as such, Packard believed, represented "regress rather than progress for man in his long struggle to become a rational and self-guiding being."

This was an especial concern when advertising turned its attention to children, since parents increasingly believed that their ability to guide their kids' moral and psychological growth was being subverted by the professional persuaders, and that advertising was undermining parental authority and weakening family ties. Packard recounts the ruckus that erupted in 1955 when Dr. Frances Horwich, who played the principal on the TV program *Ding Dong School*, "used the same studied tempo" to draw preschoolers' attention to the pretty colour of the particular brand of vitamin pills she was pushing, and to how easy they were to swallow. Those spots stirred outrage on the practical grounds that small children could easily decide to experiment with other pretty pills in the medicine cabinet, and also because of the more abstract concern that the doctor had abused her position as an authority figure for children.

Packard's examples of early attempts to win the enduring brand loyalty of young children seem strangely current close to half a century later. He cites a company called Project Education Material, for instance, which boasted to potential collaborators through a trade magazine ad that "eager minds can be moulded to want your products." Fifty years on, the language used to describe the advantages of marketing through schools is similar in tone, although more detailed and specific. In the 1990s, for instance, the former president of Channel One was quoted on the benefits that classroom discipline provides for advertisers who sponsor in-class programming. "The advertiser gets a group of kids," said Joel Babbit, "who cannot go to the bathroom, who cannot change the station, who cannot listen to their mother yell in the background, who cannot be playing Nintendo, who cannot have their headsets on."[2] And so the debate over the morality of marketing to captive kids rages on, a half century after it began.

The panic over what advertisements may or may not be doing to the human mind and character has recurred with almost predictable frequency. The outrage aroused by Packard's exposé of modern advertising techniques seemed to wane with time, but was revived by the media sensation that accompanied the release of Wilson Bryan Key's book *Subliminal Seduction* in 1973.[3] Key's argument was grounded in a similar fear that individual will and conscious intelligence were being subverted by an ad industry adept at dropping hidden messages into the subconscious like mines into a harbour. His specific focus, however, was a series of interrelated techniques noted only tangentially by Packard: the use of so-called subliminal images in movies and print ads. The concept of subliminals is by now an established fixture and common source of amusement in North American culture, resurfacing, for instance, in the 2000 U.S. presidential campaign with the allegation that the Bush team had planted the word "rats" in TV ads attacking Democrats, and providing the inspiration for Kevin Nealon's Subliminal Man comedy sketches on the TV program *Saturday Night Live*. Key first popularized this esoteric concept with his (at the time) novel insistence that ad makers were airbrushing emotionally charged words and erotic images into the backgrounds of print ads and dropping isolated frames into film sequences so as to convey messages that escaped conscious scrutiny but activated potent associations within the subconscious.

One example cited at length in *Subliminal Seduction* is an ad for Gilbey's gin, which appeared on the inside back cover of *Time* magazine on July 5, 1971. While at first glance the ad seems merely to depict a frosty beverage with ice in a perspiring glass, Key sees the word "sex" (one of a handful of emotionally charged words he claims have been hidden in a wide range of advertising backgrounds) embedded several times in the ice cubes and discerns figures dispersed throughout the ad, which he interprets as representing participants at an orgy. While Key maintains that subliminal suggestions and images are normally not detected by the conscious mind, he adds that in print ads such as these they can become visible when the observer is deeply relaxed, in much the same way that hidden images will jump out of optical illusions when the viewer's eyes are unfocused.

Key asserts that subliminal images in film, on the other hand, are impossible to see consciously unless the sequence is viewed frame by frame. As an example of subliminal messages in moving pictures, Key cites an eight-second sequence in a sixty-second commercial for Labatt's beer. When the film is slowed down, he writes, the bodies of the actors are aligned in such a way that, for a brief fragment of time, they appear to be engaged in a particular sex act. The author quotes one actor in the commercial who, when shown stills from the spot, said he suddenly understood why that eight-second sequence took a whole day to film. Though none of this is detectable at a conscious level, Key insists that the viewer subconsciously picks up these isolated words and images (intended to create an emotional charge—either positive or negative, it doesn't matter which) and can follow the complicated narratives (with complex implied character relationships and sequences of events) that have allegedly been encoded into a single print image or a few inches of film.

Wacky as all of this may sound, Key sought academic credibility by linking the theory behind subliminal imagery to the work of Dr. Otto Poetzle, a colleague of Sigmund Freud, who contributed to Freud's work on dream theory. Poetzle believed, to summarize roughly, that only a small fraction of the images picked up by the human eye are consciously acknowledged, with the rest stored in the unconscious where they become fodder for dreams. Poetzle also believed, according to Key, that "a conscious association can, in effect, trigger a subliminal precept buried deeply in the unconscious weeks, months, or possibly years after the subliminal precept occurs," thereby motivating behaviour in a way similar to post-hypnotic suggestion. It is this potential for subliminally received images, particularly emotionally charged ones, to trigger compulsive behaviour that Key believes is of obvious interest to the advertising industry.

A professor of communication, Key offered practically nothing in the way of clinical or statistical proof that Poetzle's theory about subliminal images is correct, or, if it is, that images perceived only by the subconscious can effectively compel consumers to buy particular products. Instead, he relied on anecdotal reports and the perceptions of impromptu assemblies of college students that functioned like large, ad hoc focus groups: reacting to that allegedly subliminally spiked Gilby's gin ad, for example, 62 percent of a sizable test group apparently reported that the ad suggested sexuality to them, though Key states that none of the subjects had been prompted to look for hidden images.

Although this kind of revelation provides only the most tenuous proof that subliminal ads might actually work, that almost seems beside the point. Sure, it's easy to write Key off as some kind of obsessive, conspiracy-minded wing nut who saw deliberately planted images of sex and death literally everywhere. Or to dismiss his theory as the twisted relic of an era (the 1970s) when society was fixated on sex and psychedelia and was slipping into a morass of New Age mushy-mindedness. But one still has to reckon with Key's assertion that the ad agencies themselves believed in subliminal suggestion and invested heavily in subliminal technology. He reports that machines aimed at planting subliminal images in the minds of cinema-goers were brought to market and used fairly widely.

That story, says Key, begins with American market researcher James Vicary, who in 1957 invented a machine known as the tachistoscope (which wasn't patented until 1962) that was essentially "a film projector with a high-speed shutter which flashes messages every five seconds at 1/3000 of a second." By the 1970s this machine was considered obsolete by an ad industry that had gravitated towards the "rheostat," a device Key says could project messages underneath the images picked up off the screen by the conscious mind, using light of such low intensity as to be perceptible only at a subconscious level.

Whether all this is solid or silly science is, again, practically beside the point. For if Key was correct in reporting that many large companies owned tachistoscopes and rheostats, that in itself is a powerful statement about the advertising industry's attitude towards the ad-consuming public, suggesting a willingness to subvert the public's free will by whatever means might serve that end.

Although most critics of the marketing industry do not endorse the claims Key made about the impact of subliminal advertising, there are other aspects of his argument—which do not rely on one's ability to peer deeply into airbrushed ice cubes—that resonate more with current-day analyses of advertising's appeal. A new crop of advocates for restraining children's marketing believe (as we'll see in Chapter 3) that kids are being manipulated by advertising images which play on their (sometimes hidden) fears and hopes, and which often exploit the disconnects between those two psychological poles of what children hope for and what they fear might happen. Key saw the adult men and women of the early 1970s being snared in a similar trap.

By analyzing recurrent symbols in magazines such as *Playboy* and *Cosmopolitan*, the great publishing success stories of the day, Key arrived at a sometimes chilling, sometimes comic explanation of how those magazines played on their readers' inner conflicts and complexities in order to promote brand loyalty. The trick was to be able to calibrate the tension between two contradictory sets of images, each one speaking to a different aspect of the reader's personality.

The *Playboy* reader of the early 1970s, for instance, was on the surface "a self-assured young man who is a giant among his peers. He is pursued relentlessly by exotic, beautiful, sex-crazed—though subservient—young women. He drives a high-powered sports car, dresses in the latest fashion, and dines only in the best of restaurants … This is the *Playboy* image, designed with loving—money-loving—care, and projected into the susceptible minds of 21.8 million readers monthly." But Key believed that *Playboy* spoke to its readers on two levels, affirming this idealized, fictional self-image created for the reader, while acknowledging the complex "emotional needs" and deep-seated insecurities that lay beneath the facade. Key makes a credible case[4] that the models in the magazine (particularly on the covers and in ads for the publication itself) are often in poses that suggest, not sexual conquest, but, rather, maternal nurturing. There are several examples, for instance, where they are holding objects (like a bundle of magazines) in precisely the same position that a mother would use to nurse a baby. Thrown into these scenes, invariably, are objects that Key takes to represent the father figure or the reader's repressed fear of castration (he suggests, for instance, that the famed Playboy logo itself resembles a pair of scissors). Yet these threatening symbols are incorporated into the scenes in ways that suggest they have been neutralized or held at bay. All of which communicates to the reader, in Key's interpretation of things, that he can safely place himself within these scenarios. The magazine addresses the reader in the persona of a little boy who has been given permission, within the magazine's pages, to experience maternal love without having to worry about the frightening forces that would separate him from his mother. "The entire basic concept of Playboy," concludes Key, "was built upon North American, upper-middle-class, young men's unresolved Oedipal conflicts."

The Cosmopolitan magazine of the early 1970s was similarly an expensive, meticulously produced publication that drew together editorial, advertising, and illustrative material in an integrated package designed to speak coherently to a very specific demographic group. Again, Key saw the magazine making a pitch at both conscious and subconscious levels. Like Playboy, it created a fantasy persona for its readers, manufacturing an idealized female self-image that jived with the aspirations of its core readership. The phantom "I" that emerges from the magazine's pages, says Key, is a single working woman in her thirties who is economically comfortable (the Cosmo fantasy character earned $10,000 a year, about twice as much as the average reader—a step up, but not so much as to make it impossible for the reader to identify with her), with an independent mind, a busy social schedule, and abundant romantic opportunities. But Key found in Cosmo (no surprise here) an undercurrent of images that spoke to countervailing, repressed fears of loneliness and child-lessness, and a rage, given outlet, in Key's view, by the appearance of symbolically castrated males (images of men are generally cut off at the waist). Key saw the use of such negative or frightening images in both Cosmo and Playboy as part of a kind of psychological good-cop/bad-cop routine: the secret terrors of the reader were being presented on the page so as to bolster the publication's promise of a safe haven from some looming threat. Readers were being told they should remain loyal to the publication (that is, buy it) because they could indulge their fantasies within its pages, safely, with the object of their fears and anxieties held in check.

All of this may (if you believe the claims made in Key's book) help to sell magazine subscriptions and push products, but at what price? Like Packard, Key objected to the use of subconscious ma-nipulation because of its potential to diminish citizens' capacity to make informed, rational choices, and because it was designed to foster a rampant consumerism in which people were programmed to buy outrageous quantities of products they didn't need and which wouldn't make them happier in any case. But Key saw an additional threat in the unintended psychological consequences that may arise when people are bombarded by messages they can't consciously detect. When one implants neurotic compulsions in order to sell products, do people become inexplicably neurotic or compulsive in their daily behaviour? When one uses fear or anxiety as a marketing tool, is there a chance that this will appear in the course of daily life in the guise of irrational panic?

Close to thirty years after Key weighed in on the subject, author Kalle Lasn declared that the answer is "yes"—that precisely this sort of psychological fallout is the chief legacy of an ever-expanding, in-escapable advertising industry. "From the moment your radio alarm sounds in the morning to the wee hours of late night TV," Lasn wrote in his high-octane 1999 manifesto Culture Jam, "microjolts of commercial pollution flood into your brain at the rate of about 3,000 marketing messages per day ... Ten years ago we didn't think twice about the chemicals in our food or the toxins generated by industry; we thought they were 'well within acceptable limits.' We were dead wrong about that, and today we may be repeating the same mistake about 'mental pollution'—nonchalantly absorbing massive daily doses of it without a second thought."[5]

Clearly a crusader rather than a fastidious detective, Lasn picks up on the central thesis of both Packard and Key—that advertising has been spiked with primal emotional charges to give product identities staying power in the subconscious—and then takes a leap of faith to predict the ultimate consequences of bombarding humanity with these fragments of discontinuous emotion. Observing that rates of suicide, depression, and multipolar disorder have risen globally since the 1940s, he wonders whether "the curse of plenitude, the image explosion, the data overload, the hum of the media that, like Denny's, are always open—are driving us crazy?" In a similar vein, Lasn posits that "growing up in an erotically charged media environment alters the very foundations of our personalities … I think the constant flow of commercially scripted pseudosex, rape and pornography makes us more voyeuristic, insatiable and aggressive—even though I can't prove it with hard facts." And God knows what kind of mayhem is being sown in the psyches of MTV viewers. "When you watch MTV," remarks Lasn, "you are in fight or flight mode the whole time. Random violence and meaningless sex drop in out of the blue and without context."

Out of Lasn's thick file of circumstantial cases, which link the advertiser's desire to grab the viewer by the id (through violent, sexual, and fearsome imagery) with the current compendium of mental malaises, some examples have more of a ring of truth than others. He seems to have common sense on his side when he links advertising to distortion of body image, which he in turn pegs as the wellspring from which flow the curses of anorexia, bulimia, steroid abuse, and a more nebulous inability to look beyond the superficial. This section assumes a special resonance when juxtaposed with Vance Packard's description of how gleeful cosmetics executives first pushed annual sales past the billion-dollar mark with a strategy specifically promoting customers' unhappiness with their looks. It's not too much of a stretch to think that the chickens may now have come home to roost. "Fact: Nine out of ten North American women feel bad about some aspect of their bodies," writes Lasn, "and men are not far behind. A 1992 survey of eleven to fifteen year old Canadian girls revealed that

50 percent thought they should be thinner. They didn't wish they were thinner, they thought they should be thinner, as if being thin were a kind of cultural law."

Lasn's *Culture Jam* is one part of a small wave of incendiary tracts published in the late 1990s that sparked a resurgent interest in the shadowy ways of the advertising industry and their effects in the real world. Another giant in this genre is Naomi Klein's mega-selling book *No Logo*, an indictment of the rise of "brand" culture. Both authors, in their attempt to bring the fuzzy sensations and ephemeral urges evoked by advertising into the light of day, appear to have picked up the gauntlet thrown down by Marshall McLuhan in his introduction to *Subliminal Seduction*, where he advised critics of manipulative marketing to "study the modes of the media, in order to hoick all assumptions out of the subliminal, non-verbal realm for scrutiny and for prediction and control of human purposes."

Lasn has been doing just that for a number of years, primarily through his *Adbusters* magazine, the stock-in-trade of which are parodies of popular ad campaigns that are intended to subvert the ad industry's implied, codified messages by replacing the seductive innuendo of the originals with more pointed and thoroughly off-putting allusions to the product's real-life impact. *Adbusters* monkey-wrenched the imagery used by Calvin Klein's Obsession perfume, for instance, by borrowing the same typeface to spell out "Obsession for women," a phrase that, as it does in the original, frames the image of an ultra-thin woman's arched back. The twist in the *Adbusters* version is that following the rounded lines of the woman's back to the extreme left of the page leads us to see that her head (out of the frame) is positioned over a toilet bowl—an obvious comment on how the cosmetics industry pushes body images that encourage eating disorders. Similarly, *Adbusters* piggybacked on the appeal of Camel cigarette's Joe Camel character (a cartoon creature that was later withdrawn after criticism it was designed to attract the interest of children) by featuring a look-alike named Joe Chemo, lying hairless and despondent in a hospital bed.

Although Naomi Klein's rigorously researched case studies are a counterpoint to Lasn's no-evidence-required style of argumentation, both Lasn's *Culture Jam* and Klein's *No Logo* share one common purpose: to deflate the commercial propaganda that dominates our mental environment, first by bringing its hidden messages into the open, and then by trying to redefine how those messages connect with the circumstances of real life. How much of their potency those messages derive from subliminal and other sorts of psychological or symbolic triggers is a question both Lasn and Klein sidestep. Lasn, however, leaves the door open to the possibility that Madison Avenue is still conducting devious experiments down in the sub-basement of human consciousness when he states coyly that "our emotions, personalities and core values are under siege from media and cultural forces too complex to decode." (This habit of stating as fact opinions and suppositions that Lasn says are impossible to prove or "too complex to decode" has had the disturbing effect, in more recent times, of leading Lasn into the dangerous territory of the paranoid conspiracy theorist. Shocked readers—some of them long-time readers of *Adbusters*, most of them sympathetic to the goals of the anti-consumer movement—were outraged when Lasn penned a piece on U.S.–Israeli relations that appeared to support the notion of an international Jewish conspiracy, an idea that has historically been used to justify anti-Semitic violence.)[6]

Similar in intent to *Culture Jam*, but quite different in approach, is Naomi Klein's *No Logo*.[7] While Lasn can be seen as clearly following in the footsteps of Packard and Key, always on the lookout for some devious hocus-pocus aimed at the nether regions of human consciousness, Klein's analysis is more social and historical. Her main focus is on marketers' stunning ability to move with the times, to respond to criticism in a way that makes the industry stronger, and to co-opt new trends and ideas and social attitudes (even the attitude held by anti-establishment rebel types that advertising is bad—a viewpoint that has found its way into a certain brand of irony-laden, self-mocking advertising that is designed to make it acceptable for skeptics to fall for commercial messages).

The fact that the advertising machine has withstood the intellectual and cultural convulsions of the past half century, and is today functioning better than ever, is, Klein implies, testament to an almost supernatural resilience. A succession of revolutionary tremors has shaken the soil on which the great North American advertising machine was built. That stifling 1950s consumer culture described by Packard, in which the acquisition ethic was intertwined with an overwhelming urge to social conformity (composed in equal parts of the desire to "keep up with the Joneses" and the necessity of toiling in grey flannel anonymity), was challenged and then vanquished by a 1960s counterculture that emphasized individual self-expression and inner-directedness. The standard-issue, post-World War II housewife, trolling the department store aisles for totems of the good life, was all but driven to extinction by the rise of feminism. And the idea of endless abundance—consumerism without consequence, a new car whether you need it or not—has been deconstructed and debunked by an environmental movement that has effectively equated our addiction to material goods with slow planetary suicide. Still, the ad boys have accommodated all of this, consolidating their influence within our culture to the extent that it's now practically impossible to find a two year old in North America who doesn't jump up out of his stroller with Pavlovian delight at the sight of the Golden Arches.

Klein's *No Logo* is largely an examination of the fallout from one specific instance of accommodation and co-optation by the advertising industry: the determination by many ad execs in the early 1990s that they'd be better off joining, rather than trying to beat, the so-called identity politics movement, which was then becoming influential on college campuses. The overly condensed definition of identity politics reads something like this: at its core was the idea that people who have been oppressed (women, gays and lesbians, people of colour, the poor) should have a greater role and more visibility as decision makers, spokespeople, and role models in our society. Identity politics sparked an immediate backlash, with vitriolic denunciations of "political correctness" filling radio talk shows and consuming the thoughts of conservative commentators, in the process making the careers of nouveau Neanderthals such as Rush Limbaugh.

Advertisers, however, took a different approach. Recalls Klein, who counted herself among the advocates of identity politics, "Many of our demands for better representation were quickly accommodated by marketers, media makers and pop-culture producers alike—though perhaps not for the reasons we had hoped …

We found out that our sworn enemies in the 'mainstream'—to us a giant monolithic blob outside of our known university-affiliated en-claves—didn't fear and loathe us but actually thought we were sort of interesting … If diversity is what we wanted, the brands seemed to be saying, then diversity is exactly what we would get. And with that, the marketers and media makers swooped down, airbrushes in hand, to touch up the colours and images in our culture."

This sudden conversion, according to Klein, was not based on any impulse to political solidarity, but on the cold calculation that the "defining idea" of Gen Xers was "Diversity," "as opposed to 'Individuality' for boomers and 'Duty' for their parents." And so, sensing that this new crop of youngsters was a far better target than its over-leveraged elders, the corporate go-getters unleashed throughout the 1990s "an orgy of red ribbons, Malcolm X baseball hats and Silence = Death T-shirts," as upstart brands such as Benet-ton, Diesel jeans, and the Body Shop competed for the allegiance of a new generation with ad campaigns that portrayed them more as agents of gay-positive, pro-feminist, and minority-friendly change than as peddlers of clothes and cosmetics.

Ironically, this drive to create new brand identities for the PC crowd came close on the heels of expert warnings that brand-based marketing was dead. Brand loyalty had long been a central concept in American marketing, and many familiar brands introduced as far back as the 1880s (Uncle Ben's rice and Aunt Jemima pancakes, for instance) had been designed to offset the sense of social loss that occurred when packaged goods replaced the old-time shopkeeper, who used to scoop staples like oats and flour from bins for his customers. (Brand names, in other words, were surrogate person-alities created for an increasingly depersonalized world.) Yet many Wall Street types suggested that the branding strategy had run its course after Philip Morris's 1992 decision to discount its Marlboro cigarettes (one of the best-known brands in the world) in order to compete with cheaper, generic smokes.[8] Klein says those pessimistic analysts only got it half right; while older consumers were indeed becoming "brand blind" in the early 1990s, content to shop in big-box outlets for cheaper no-name goods, the emerging generation was more than willing to pay a premium for products that came with a built-in social status, that told them who they were. Thus, the decision to wrap the new brands in the goals of identity politics, with its vision of dignity and a meaningful role for people of all backgrounds.

Yet Klein notes that the trend for corporations to see themselves increasingly as "meaning brokers," whose primary job is to create and sell product image, led to a breathtaking paradox. Since those companies were interested in little besides packaging and marketing campaigns, they routinely outsourced production of the actual goods to anonymous companies that operated sweatshop factories in the Third World. As a result, some of the brands that got rich promoting themselves as ambassadors of progressive politics were, in reality, key players in the continued impoverishment of Third World workers, mostly women. Maybe companies that promoted diversity in their ads did help create a healthier climate for people seeking emancipation in the developed world, but across the rest of the globe, the material effect was just the reverse. "Though girls may rule in North America," notes Klein with some irony, "they are still sweating in Asia and Latin America, making T-shirts with the 'Girls Rule' slogan on them and Nike running shoes that will finally let girls into the game."

CHAPTER 3

Taking It to the Streets (Or the classroom, or the daycare, or the movie theatre ...)

Fifty years of journalistic exposés and rants like the ones we've just sampled have led a significant chunk of the population to conclude that marketing is essentially a con—a sophisticated means of recruiting new patsies to buy whatever false promises have been piled onto the buffet table. That proposition has given rise to a vocal and rather flamboyant social movement in recent times. Both Naomi Klein's No Logo and Kalle Lasn's Adbusters enterprise derive inspiration from and feed back into the Culture Jammers movement, which seeks to break the spell cast over the land by mass advertising. Fuelling this quest is the conviction that advertising is harmful, not just for its intrinsic qualities, but also because of its pivotal role in sustaining (and diverting attention from) a much wider system of injustices, which can include, depending on your political preoccupations, the world trading system's reliance on sweatshop labour and the pillaging of Third World resources (business arrangements often enforced at the point of a gun); the peddling of junk foods and dangerous pharmaceuticals; the degradation of the physical environment with garbage, air pollution, and other by-products of consumerism; the smothering of more genuine, non-commercial forms of cultural expression; the list goes on ...

Operating parallel to the Culture Jammers is a fast-growing movement focusing more specifically on marketing's impact on kids. The band of protesters that picketed outside the Golden Marble Awards, for instance, formally gelled as the Stop the Commercial Exploitation of Children (SCEC) coalition (which in 2004 was renamed Campaign for a Commercial Free Childhood), boasting about two dozen member organizations including parent groups, health care professionals, educators, and advocacy groups. Like the Culture Jammers and anti-globalization activists, this group believes the marketing industry is implicated in a broad constellation of ills that have hurt children and compromised the safe haven of childhood. Junk food addiction and rising rates of obesity, the modern scourge of anorexia, incidents of schoolyard violence, vulnerability to sexual exploitation, and an apparently growing divide between kids and their families are all maladies that these advocates believe have gained a greater grip thanks to the power and pervasiveness of the marketing industry. Tackling these problems, so their reasoning goes, first requires dismantling the propaganda machine that keeps kids and their parents psychologically enslaved and prevents them from becoming part of the solution.

Certain distinguishing features separate the anti–kid-marketing forces from, for instance, the anti-globalization activists who want to rip down Nike's marketing facade in order to expose its labour practices. For one, the child advocates seem more focused on the psychology of marketing, more eager to revisit the "how" question that consumed earlier commentators like Packard and Key: that is, what psychological mechanisms are at work when kids are bombarded with ads? (This isn't surprising, perhaps, given that child psychologists have taken a lead role in organizing against the youth-marketing industry.) Groups like SCEC also see an urgent need to protect those they perceive as most vulnerable to the marketers' messages: kids. As marketers have sought out new frontiers, their targets have become progressively younger, to the point where the traditional caution "Let the buyer beware" seems ridiculous. Innocent children are, by definition, unable to be wary. Their limited life experience has not yet taught them to be skeptical.

How young are the youngest targets of the marketing industry? According to Dr. Susan Linn and Dr. Alvin Poussaint, associate director and director, respectively, of the media center at Boston's Judge Baker Children's Center, the introduction of those cute little Teletubbies in the late 1990s represented the first full-blown effort to market to the under-two set. Writing in The American Prospect magazine, the pair cite assertions made by the U.S. Public Broadcasting Service (PBS) that Teletubbies is intended for "children as young as one."[1] Alarmed that this may be the first of many attempts to market to pre-verbal tots, Linn and Poussaint are skeptical of the network's claims that Teletubbies serves an educational function for children in this age group by helping them develop their language skills and become comfortable with technology, and by stimulating their imaginations and facilitating motor development. Such claims, made on behalf of one year olds, would be difficult to verify, they write, given that a pre-verbal child is not able to tell a researcher what meaning she extracts from a TV program. (For this reason, television researchers at Yale University normally use children no younger than thirty months in their studies.)

Though it may seem misguided (given what appears on commercial TV) to focus on public TV—and on a seemingly innocuous program like Teletubbies, at that—Dr. Linn's previous life as a children's entertainer has led her to believe that even "educational" fare can be warped by the intrusion of commercial pressures. Her thirty years of entertaining children, she recalls by phone from Boston, included stints performing a live ventriloquist show, producing videos "on difficult issues for kids" for the same production company that made Mr. Rogers' Neighborhood, and doing puppet therapy for sick kids at Boston's Children's Hospital. It was during her electronic period that she first became aware of a new tendency for corporate sponsors to request more tangible quid pro quos. "There was often a fight about somehow plugging the product in my videos," she says, "which I always refused to do."

The article she co-wrote with Poussaint suggests that the U.S. public broadcaster has bowed to a similar kind of commercial pressure, leading the network to make claims about the *Teletubbies* program that might enhance its bottom line, but might not be based on good science. Although Linn and Poussaint accept that PBS may have research showing that parents believe the youngest members of their households enjoy the program, they caution against extrapolating that this proves the program's educational worth. They are also deeply troubled that PBS's claims about the educational value of *Teletubbies* appear to encourage parents to disregard the American Academy of Pediatrics' recommendation that children under two should not watch television—an edict designed to ensure that toddlers are not distracted from their real developmental needs and that they are given an early chance to avoid falling into the trap of excessive TV watching that often plagues older kids.

"What we know about how children under two learn and develop suggests that they should spend most of their time actively engaged in exploring the world using all of their senses," the authors elaborate. "Because we don't know what, if anything, very young children gain from watching television, and because it has been demonstrated that watching television can be habituating, it is irresponsible for PBS to encourage parents to expose their children to it at such an early age. Studies also show that excessive television viewing is correlated with poor school performance and childhood obesity."

Why would a public broadcaster with an admirable track record of providing high-quality educational programming for older kids decide to risk its reputation by pushing TV for kids who may be too young to be safely stationed in front of the tube? Linn and Poussaint blame the encroachment of commercial considerations into the sanctified sphere of public television. Starved of government funds and desperate for revenue, they argue, PBS was blinded by the promise of huge payments from the sale of licensed Teletubby products. The BBC—from which PBS bought the series—earned £23 million from the sale of Teletubby merchandise in 1997 alone, and although PBS's cut of American sales was not public knowledge, in toto the Teletubbies were expected to generate $2 billion in American toy sales in just one year.

With that kind of pecuniary incentive, PBS became a participant in a sales pitch that Linn and Poussaint portray as similar, in its psychological approach, to the cosmetics industry marketing that Vance Packard and Kalle Lasn so objected to: they became "merchants of discontent," manufacturing an ersatz "need" of which parents would otherwise be blissfully unaware. According to Linn and Poussaint, the programmers' highly contentious statements that *Teletubbies* would make pre-verbal children more comfortable in a world of rapid technological change (with the implication that simply being immersed in that world would not be enough) "are reminiscent of the advertising technique that suggests to potential buyers that they have a defect they can cure by buying a product. Each implies that children begin life with a deficit—a deficit that, in fact, doesn't exist. There is no evidence to suggest that children raised in a technological world are uncomfortable with technology." The authors also reject network officials' argument that one year olds are going to be exposed to television in any case, so it's better if they watch a program specifically designed for them. Linn and Poussaint reason that, since parents have been told (by the respected authorities at PBS, no less) that *Teletubbies* is beneficial for toddlers, these one year olds will likely be exposed to the program *in addition* to other TV that might be on when family members are watching. And because parents have been told that *Teletubbies* is a kind of television equivalent of broccoli, those toddlers will probably be encouraged to watch more intently.

Though it may seem churlish to slam the thoroughly cuddly Teletubbies—known for their otherworldly gentleness and innocent, friendly frolicking—Susan Linn believes the saturation marketing of Tinky Winky, Dipsy, Laa-Laa, and Po is just one deceptively adorable face of a thoroughly destructive trend, the ill effects of which show up daily in her clinical practice. Children are marketed to thousands of times daily. And the dangers seem to escalate as they get older.

"Most recently," elaborates the child psychologist and SCEC spokesperson in the course of our interview, "it's had to do with the World Wrestling Federation [now World Wrestling Entertainment] and the little boys in my practice doing wrestling moves all the time. I mean, these are four year olds. One little boy said to me that he didn't want to play with his brother because his brother always wanted to play wrestling, and he, the little boy, always ended up crying." Linn adds that it is so common for little kids to display this behaviour after watching wrestling on tv that the director of the Judge Baker Children's Center has had to send a letter to parents, asking them not to expose their children to this programming.

Indeed, the WWE is no stranger to controversy, but most of the negative attention has been related to its impact on older kids. A study conducted by Dr. Robert DuRant, a pediatrician at the Wake Forest University medical school, for instance, found that high-school students who habitually watch WWE wrestling are much more likely than non-WWE fans to be involved with violence on a date. The study reported that 18 percent of girls and 11 percent of boys who watched wrestling have had a physical fight on a date. DuRant's report also noted WWE fans' increased involvement in other risk-taking behaviour, such as the non-prescription use of Ritalin and carrying guns to school, although these correlations were not as strong as the one with date violence. While the researcher attributed these results to the disparaging commentary about women in WWE spectacles, and to narratives that portray women as sexual objects who get beaten up a lot, a WWE spokesperson told the Associated Press that the study was flawed because it didn't take into account factors like the family backgrounds of the teenagers surveyed. (One critical question raised by studies such as this is whether this is simply a *correlation* between viewing habits and dangerous behaviour, or whether the relationship is *causal*. For a more complete airing of both sides in this debate, see Chapters 8 and 9.) DuRant's research was released a month after a fourteen year old Florida boy was convicted of murder. The defence had argued that the boy's killing of a six year old girl was the unintended consequence of trying to replicate a WWE body slam.[2]

Linn is not surprised, however, that this practice of imitating WWE wrestlers has migrated down to the preschool set. Wrestling is broadcast in the Boston area at eight in the evening, she reports, and despite protests from the WWE that its product is aimed at an older audience, the marketing of wrestling action figures through toy stores and restaurant giveaways is a clear indication to her that little kids are quietly, but deliberately, being targeted as potential WWE stalwarts.

In fact, the peddling of older-market entertainment products to young children has become one of the flashpoints in the U.S. government's ongoing campaign to limit American kids' media diet of blood, guts, and gore. In a report released in the fall of 2000, the U.S. Federal Trade Commission (FTC) concluded that several segments of the entertainment industry (i.e., records, video games, and movies) were breaking their own codes and ignoring previous promises to the FTC by marketing adult-oriented products to children. Of forty-four R-rated movies studied, for instance, the FTC found that the marketing plans for 80 percent of those films included appeals to the under-seventeen audience (for instance, by promoting the films through high schools or in magazines read mainly by under-seventeens). The FTC also conducted research that indicated under-seventeens were frequently able to purchase tickets for R-rated movies.[3] This research was initiated on the orders of former U.S. president Bill Clinton in response to the shootings at Columbine High School in April 1999.[4]

The fact that large numbers of kids view material intended for adults is not just the result of resourceful youngsters finding ways around the controls, or lax parents helping their offspring subvert the vigilance of authorities. A New York Times report, citing documents submitted to the FTC, posited that film companies considered underage viewers such an important part of the audience for violent, R-rated movies that they have included children as young as nine in the focus groups used to determine how they will market films. According to the New York Times, the R-rated Judge Dredd, a movie "about urban anarchy and street war," was tested on a focus group that included over a hundred youths between thirteen and sixteen. An R-rated horror movie called Disturbing Behavior was test-marketed before more than four hundred youths aged twelve to twenty, with the fifteen to seventeen year old subgroup identifying a scene of "a blonde bashing her head into a mirror" as the high point of the picture. Meanwhile, fifty kids between nine and eleven were used in focus groups for the slasher movie I Know What You Did Last Summer. The Times story also noted Universal Studios' plan to increase awareness of the PG-13 film The Mummy among boys between ages four and fourteen by merchandising Mummy action figures through Toys "R" Us and K-Mart.[5]

It's not just images glorifying violence and aggression that have got anti–child-marketing activists steamed. Back in Boston, Linn says she's convinced that her daily work to promote healthy habits and sound relationships is undermined by the glitz of mass marketing. She's adamant that many problems she sees every day are caused—or at least exacerbated—by child marketing. Take relationships between parents and kids. Families she deals with often quarrel over what kids expect their parents to buy them, says Linn, which sometimes creates new problems in relationships that are already strained. Then there are the physical ailments like childhood obesity, a condition that's become endemic in the United States, bringing with it a range of related health threats, such as skyrocketing rates of diabetes and heart disease in youngsters.

What does the marketing industry have to do with this cluster of physical diseases? Several critics have linked their rise to the fast-food industry's development of an almost irresistible repertoire of marketing techniques. In his acclaimed book *Fast Food Nation*, Eric Schlosser recalls how McDonald's founder Ray Kroc sought to replicate the magic of Disneyland, partly by recruiting former Disney set designer Don Ament to design McDonaldland, and the Disney songwriting team of Richard and Robert Sherman to pen the hamburger chain's theme. The result, writes Schlosser, was that Kroc succeeded in "selling something intangible to children, along with their fries," a pleasant, enveloping fantasy that became more important than the food. Add to this magic the bonus of toy giveaways, and the picture emerges of a marketing juggernaut. During the 1997 Teenie Beanie Baby giveaway, for instance, McDonald's increased its Happy Meal sales almost tenfold. While the company normally sells 10 million Happy Meals in a week, that number rose to 100 million over ten days.[6]

The lure of this fantasyland environment, so the common criticism has it, makes it that much easier for parents to put aside their concerns about the nutritional value of the food, especially if they are constantly being badgered—as is the habit of many of the kids portrayed in the McDonald's ads—to treat the family to dinner under the Golden Arches. Drawn into the hamburger chains by the playgrounds and the free toys, it seems somehow incidental, and therefore less important, that children end up consuming large quantities of food that's heavy on the grease and calories, but light on nutrients.

These are the examples Linn cites to support her view of the marketing industry as a vehicle for pushing products—from junk food to junk TV—that aren't good for kids and that bring with them a variety of toxic side effects ranging from clogged arteries to clobbered siblings. She is particularly concerned about its impact on the groups that comprise the majority of her practice: African Americans (who are, statistically, bigger users of media than the general population, she says, and therefore more in the line of fire) and people from disadvantaged economic backgrounds (for whom advertising's promises of endless bounty, when measured against the economic limitations of real life, are sure to bring disappointment and inflame tensions between parents and kids).

Clear across the breadth of the United States, meanwhile, in a psychologist's office in Berkeley, California, Dr. Allen Kanner speaks to what he believes is the more general propensity of our surround-marketing society to dampen the human spirit, creating a condition of existential gloom that afflicts poor kids but can equally damage their counterparts who dwell high in the stratosphere of economic privilege. Kanner got a close-up view of the latter group while working at Stanford University and practising "nearby in an extremely affluent area—like, there were 14,000 millionaires in the county or something. So I saw quite a few rich kids in that stretch," he recalls. What struck him was that the surfeit of material possessions enjoyed by many of his young patients seemed to rob them of their enthusiasm and their reason to strive. "I saw the materialism—they had all the stuff and they were certainly into it—but they would still look at their parents and the amount of money their parents would make and they would get depressed about never being able to compete with their parents. This would come out after a while—like, "Why try? I'm never going to be the CEO of a big company like my dad in Silicon Valley." Having practised among both the disadvantaged and the very wealthy, Kanner has concluded that the materialism promoted by the great American marketing machine is an equal-opportunity disease, though its symptoms will vary according to class background and individual circumstances.

Kanner, you may recall, is the psychologist we met briefly in Chapter 1, where he talked about the rising number of kids in his practice who tell him their dream is to make piles of money rather than grow up to be astronauts or nurses or doctors. Warming up at the beginning of our long-distance tête-à-tête, the psychologist reprises that story, embellished with a few darkly amusing details that didn't make it into the earlier print report. "I remember one time a young adolescent told me he wanted to be a pharmacologist, which I had never heard before," he relates. "And I said, 'That's great, that's really interesting, why that?' And he said 'Well, I think you can make just as much money as a doctor, but you don't have to deal with sick people.'" Another indication that there was a cultural shift afoot was that the kids who came into his office, Kanner says, "started to reject my toys. I had some standard toys, and I had had them for a while. But they wanted, at the time, the latest—like a Transformer—and they wouldn't play with my stuff. It got to the point, because the toys were changing so frequently, that I just had the kids bring in their own toys."

Kanner remembers that these revelatory moments came during the late 1980s and early 1990s—about a decade after he began practising, and immediately after the marketing industry began to target a younger group of kids (kids below ten, for instance), whose personal spending power and leverage over family finances had previously been underestimated. That was the era, recounts Kanner, when experts like James U. McNeil started advising corporations to seek their customers' brand loyalty from the earliest possible age—and businesses responded by devising tracking programs that followed kids from the moment they left the hospital to the time they began thinking of buying their first car and on into adulthood.

It is also the era we've heard described in somewhat more positive terms (by commentators like Max Valliquette at the Understanding Youth conference) as a time of shifting sociological patterns, when new family, community, and economic dynamics transformed the Kid, genus *North Americanus*, from the status of economic innocent, who got to decide little more than what brand of soda pop to buy, to a semi-autonomous fiscal force within the hyper-speed two-income (or single-parent) family. In this version of reality, you'll remember, these changes equal something like emancipation, with the previously cloistered Kid rising to a role of self-directed self-assertion—reborn as after-school dinner nuker, family purchases consultant, a crucial agent of domestic economic planning. Within this narrative, the marketing industry portrays itself as merely reacting to fill a void. Its job is to make sure this new breed of Kid—finding himself in a changed world and functioning within a different kind of family—has the most and the best information to make informed decisions, to give him a sense of his own power, to help the smart and "savvy" junior consumer hone those smarts and that savvy even more.

Allen Kanner doesn't buy it. Social circumstances may have changed, he says, but marketers have used the new reality to exploit kids, not to help them navigate their way through it. He sees a pattern of compulsive behaviour in the fact that kids are spending ever-larger amounts of money, not evidence that they have been trained as more discriminating consumers. (He believes logic dictates that if marketers were competing just for kid's preferences—or to accommodate a transfer of fiscal decisions from within families to kids—there would be a levelling off of kids' spending at some point.)

Kanner believes that advertisers use a process of manipulation, rather than education, to get kids to reflexively, habitually head off to the shopping mall. In this respect, his view of the psychology of marketing is remarkably consistent with the model laid out by Packard in the 1950s. Like the peddlers of cars, cigarettes, and cosmetics in the period after the Second World War, today's marketers appeal to kids not on the basis of how good their products are, he says, but by tying brand image to the promise of satisfying some primal drive or quelling a deep-seated anxiety. "They raise this anxiety or desire, they make this promise, but they can't fulfill it," asserts Kanner. "[In kids' advertising] many of the kinds of needs or desires or anxieties they invoke are things you really can't control materially. They will play on the desire for friendship or for feeling competent."

One of the most troubling aspects of this process, for Kanner, is that members of his own profession are often hired to help locate those emotional reflex points and to design the imagery that lets advertisers activate them. Seeing this as a compromise of the psychologist's sworn duty to work to improve the health of children, he's been a prominent advocate of the idea that the American Psychological Association should demand greater disclosure of what work child psychologists do for advertisers and impose restrictions on what is permissible. The fact that he's unable to point to any specific devices in advertising for kids that have been contributed by psychologists, he says, is itself indicative of a problem: the proprietary nature of the research, and the resulting veil of secrecy companies maintain in the name of protecting their commercial, competitive interests, means that a psychologist consulting for a marketing firm is not subject to the same kind of peer scrutiny that a researcher in an academic or clinical setting would face.

"You know," the psychologist ponders, "the Geppetto Group and others like Saatchi and Saatchi, in their child department, have bragged that they hire psychologists and anthropologists, or they may talk about a certain campaign in which they used consultants. They say, 'Based on the following we came up with the following ad campaign,' but they don't say, 'A psychologist interviewed this many people, this many kids of this age in a focus group, and here is the design of the study'—they don't give that out."

Still, with his professional training, Kanner can make a few educated guesses about which commercials were likely to have drawn upon the know-how of his fellow psychologists. He's struck by the power of Nike's ad campaigns, for example. "Nike elevates athletics to some God-like ideal," he says. "You know, they stamp their brand on top of Michael Jordan and the God-like status they have created for him. So it doesn't have to do with any individual sport anymore, or a company, or an athletic accomplishment. It just has to do with this image of the athlete as a God-like figure and sport as transcendent. I can't say that a psychologist necessarily gave them that idea, but I can say that it's good psychology."

Those towering, almost archetypal images, their impact reinforced by the repetitive power of the multi-channel universe, are guided like smart bombs into precise sets of craniums through age-specific commercials and are probably far more effective than the shenanigans that some ad agency psychologists were apparently up to in the 60s and 70s. (Kanner's not sure that using subliminal images, for instance, actually works. And if it does, he says, its impact has surely been eclipsed by the increased sophistication of more mainstream advertising approaches.)

In other words, advertisers have gotten more sophisticated, and the images they produce are more compelling than ever before. Billions of dollars are spent making sure kids grow up immersed in a sea of well-produced, oft-repeated corporate propaganda. But does that mean the commercials, in themselves, are bad? Those Nike ads, for instance, seem pretty benign compared to other images that jump out of the TV screen these days, which may lead some to question "What's all the fuss about?" Kids have always had heroes (better Michael Jordan than Eminem, many parents will say), and often those heroes have sold things. That these images are overstated, made larger than life, is also nothing new, although the impressive technical effects that can be achieved today might make it easier to forget that your favourite sports hero is still a mortal. With all this in mind, the moral of the story starts to get a little cloudy for me … I'm starting to view this with the same ambivalence I felt when Taylor Cousens from the Gepetto Group made her pitch before the Understanding Youth crowd.

Cousens' description of the work of kid-centred marketing agencies seemed to portray a completely different beast than the one Drs. Kanner and Linn take aim at. Her presentation, as you'll recall from Chapter 1, suggested companies like hers spend a lot of time charting the life stages and preoccupations of kids so that their client companies can get in sync with the mindset of the kids they wish to communicate with. I raised this impression with Allen Kanner and asked him about some of the assumptions that might logically flow from it. Isn't it entirely reasonable and quite innocent that companies would want to know where kids are at so they can speak to them in their own language? And if marketing companies hire psychologists to do things like dissect the developmental stages that kids go through, is that necessarily wrong?

Psychologists, responds Kanner, are likely hired to find something deeper and more specific than merely what life stage a particular group of kids have arrived at. They are in the business of pinpointing motivation—identifying hidden yearnings, aspirations, and fears. For instance, many commercials now show toys being played with by kids somewhat older than the intended market. This indicates that it's not the developmental stage of the kids that's important to marketers, but children's compelling need to identify with somebody older than they are. Kanner sees this kind of mechanism at work in a more troubling context. The recent trend of marketing what may be seen as sexually provocative clothing to seven and eight year old girls "doesn't necessarily match what you might consider their natural developmental spaces," he says. "It looks sexualized, but it can't be titillating to them really." Rather, the likely reason that marketing strategy is successful, speculates Kanner, is because it meets some other psychological need: the need to belong, perhaps, or the need to identify with the image of an older sibling. Though he doesn't have any documentation to prove it, he suspects that psychologists have been pinpointing these psychological leverage points—telling companies that marketing the Britney Spears-type image will be a hit with preadolescent girls.

Beyond questions of how specific ad campaigns may have twisted the mandate of psychology as a healing profession, Kanner is convinced that any involvement in advertising leads psychologists onto dangerous ground because advertising, as an institution, has spread a certain sickness throughout society. This diagnosis is rooted in the idea that growing up bombarded by advertising—with its implicit message that buying material things will satisfy the deeper desires of the soul—has created a profound and destructive confusion about what people need out of life and how they can get it.

In a fascinating article, "The All-Consuming Self," included in a book of essays on "eco-psychology," Kanner and co-author Mary Gomes elaborate on some of the parallels between Americans' consumer ethic and the psychological condition known as narcissism.[7] That condition is characterized, they write, "by an inflated, grandiose, entitled, and masterful self-image, or 'false self,' that masks deep-seated but unacknowledged feelings of worthlessness and emptiness." Psychologists believe that this "false self" takes root within an individual "when a child attends to external demands and rewards in order to obtain parental approval and love. When these external pressures conflict with the child's own feelings, these feelings are ignored, until the child comes to believe that the parents' wishes are her or his own."

This inflated image of self becomes both a tyrant and a source of sanctuary for the narcissist. It allows the individual to experience a fleeting, superficial sort of happiness, to feel approved of and self-approving, since this hollow image of power, accomplishment, and success (which has vanquished a more realistic and equivocal understanding of self) reflects back to the individual the idea that he has become all those things that the parent expected him to be and is therefore worthy of love and respect. When this grandiose facade comes into conflict with reality, however, the result is often a storm of panic and despair. "Narcissistic individuals," write Kanner and Gomes, "constantly strive to meet the impossibly high standards of the false self, frequently feeling frustrated and depressed by their inability to do so, but also avoiding at all costs recognising how empty they truly feel."

The pair see a close parallel between the clinical condition of narcissism and the collective psychological traits of the modern consumer society. In the latter case, it is not a demanding parent that causes individuals to manufacture a new, overblown self-image for themselves, but rather the incessant badgering of the advertising industry. "American children come to internalize the messages they see in the media and society at large. They learn to substitute what they are told to want—mounds of material possessions—for what they truly want. By the time they reach adulthood, their authentic feelings are so well buried that they have only the vaguest sense that 'something' is missing. Having ignored their genuine needs for so long, they feel empty." Just as the narcissistic child believes that she will deserve affection only by being the best and most accomplished, so Kanner and Gomes see our society being indoctrinated with the idea—indeed, the central ethic of the consumer society— that one only becomes a worthy human being by acquiring the most costly and impressive homes, the fastest cars, the best clothes, the newest gizmos ...

In both cases, some unpleasant behavioural traits can arise from this process of ignoring one's real desires and merely seeking to satisfy social expectations. Narcissistic individuals are known for their lack of empathy and overbearing ways—traits that spring from their conviction that their superior qualities make them deserving of anything they desire, especially the adulation of others. Citing critics such as psychologist Philip Cushman and writer Christopher Lasch (author of the late 1970s classic *The Culture of Narcissism*), the authors note that a similar set of traits has been ascribed to American society as a whole (others will surely want to extend that judgment to the industrialized world in general). The idea that America is in the grip of a "consumer false self," with a bellicose attitude and voracious appetites that mirror the grand pretensions of the narcissist, goes a long way to explaining why "Americans feel entitled to an endless stream of new consumer goods and services," write Kanner and Gomes. "Material abundance is not only an assumed privilege and a right of the middle and upper classes but proof of the cultural and political superiority of the United States."

On a political level, they see this mindset exemplified by the first President George Bush's response to Third World delegates at the 1992 Earth Summit in Rio de Janeiro. When those delegates suggested that First World nations have a responsibility to curtail consumption in order to save the global environment, Bush the Elder's retort was that "the American way of life is not up for negotiation." That statement, the authors recall, was met with incredulity across much of the globe, along with a sense of bafflement as to why Americans would be so unwavering when the future of the planet was at stake and the inequities of global consumption were so obvious. Kanner and Gomes believe they can account for this response. Underlying his brash and egotistical self-assertion, they discern that the president was giving voice to the narcissist's "sense of emptiness"—the ache of despair that haunts an increasingly commercialized and technologized society that leaves people with little time or opportunity to enjoy the simple, deep pleasures of family, friends, or a walk in the woods. The right to boundless material consumption must be vigorously defended because, quite simply, that is all many citizens of "advanced" societies can rely upon to make them happy.

For its part in sustaining this system of self-delusion, Kanner and Gomes heap scorn upon the advertising industry. It is the peddler of "the Big Lie." No one consciously believes that "success in business, athletics or love ever depended on toothpaste." But being inundated with such messages thousands of times daily since childhood causes people to act in a way that suggests they've been convinced it's true. The result is a civilization that behaves in self-destructive ways that defy rational explanation. Newspapers report on a new class of people who pull in six-figure salaries but who spend so compulsively that they feel they are poor. Many people pull themselves out of a funk by going on spending sprees that leave them desperately in debt. This is a picture of consumerism as an addiction, triggered by irrational impulses, by the Pavlovian promises hidden in advertising. And given that kids are immersed in a sea of commercial messages even before they can speak, the prospect of future generations breaking free from this ersatz reality of false yearnings and empty promises starts to look, to the critics, more and more unlikely.

CHAPTER 4

The Counterattack: Marketing as a Tool for the Rational Kid

Fascinating as it may be to read Kanner and Gomes's portrait of a society made neurotic by advertising, the trouble with such a far-reaching and ambitious theory is that it may be impossible to break it down into component parts that are in any way provable. Sure, citizens of advanced industrial nations may, as a group, live lives that often feel empty, causing them to seek compensation with a spending bender at the local mall. Sure, Americans can be belligerent in defending their sacred right to consume. And sure, kids buy large quantities of mass-marketed products—from cheeseburgers to Britney albums and WWE toys—that may be, in many ways, injurious to their health. But does all of this spring from years of brainwashing at the hands of the advertising industry? Have we really been grabbed by the subconscious and hauled, oblivious, into this world of fake desires and false promises? Or are our compulsions more reasonably attributed to other influences we encounter in everyday life, and to the preferences formed by our real, lived experience?

The case for the latter point of view was advanced in two papers prepared by psychologists contracted by the European Union. The EU, which has been struggling with the question of how to regulate kid-focused advertising (an outright ban is one option under consideration), asked for research that would summarize the current understanding of the impact of advertising on kids. Since 1989 the EU has avoided taking a direct position on this matter by laying down only the most general guidelines in its Television without Frontiers (TVWF) directive (modified once before in 1997), which deals with a range of issues arising from the transnational nature of broadcasting in today's Europe. While the directive provided general statements of principle on how advertisers should relate to kids—for example, one clause in the directive asserts that advertising should not take advantage of the gullibility or inexperience of minors—the practical interpretation of those guidelines was left to the discretion of individual governments. Italy has declared that advertising is not to interrupt cartoons, while Luxembourg and Belgium prohibit advertising five minutes before and after children's programming. Sweden has been alone in banning children's ads outright, basing its policy on the government's acceptance of research purportedly showing that children under ten are unable to distinguish between ads and programs on TV, and that children under twelve are unable to define the purpose of advertising.

With the TVWF directive coming up for renewal (it was to be updated in 2002, but extensions to the process meant that new child advertising rules were promised for late in 2004 or beyond[1]), some countries favoured leaving the matter in the hands of individual governments, while others expressed support for strengthening pan-European regulations. To help its members move towards consensus, the EU sought to clarify the philosophical and scientific foundations upon which a new regime could be based.

This is not an abstract debate, but one with concrete significance for the businessperson, the taxpayer, and just about every European who owns a TV set. The prospect of moving towards Sweden's tough stand, for instance, entailed dramatic economic and cultural consequences that terrified some countries. Children's advertising is said to pump between 670 million and 1 billion euros (US$820 million to $1.2 billion) into the entertainment industry each year, helping to underwrite the cultural sovereignty policies of countries such as France, which limit the amount of children's programming that can be imported from the U.S. and Japan, and boosting the amount of homegrown children's product shown on national airwaves. There were also fears that restricting the children's advertising funds flowing to European broadcasters would simply transfer the advantage to U.S.-based satellite channels (such as MTV, Disney, and Nickelodeon) that beam their programming onto European soil and are not subject to the same restrictions as national broadcasters.[2]

In the view of University of Bonn psychologist Reinhold Bergler, these sacrifices were clearly not worth making, given what he believes is a complete lack of credible evidence that advertising has a real and negative impact on children. In his paper "The Effects of Commercial Advertising on Children," prepared for the EU, Dr. Bergler accuses advertising's critics of falsely extracting from the ubiquity of commercials the conclusion that they have a direct, causal impact on the behaviour, habits, and desires of young people.[3] Since "every advertisement is an exaggerated and emotionally charged brief burst of information," he writes, commercials elicit strong reactions of sympathy or antipathy from the viewer. This means that the political debate around advertising to kids has been conditioned by the public's "emotionally charged aversion to advertising" (that is, the fact that everyone can point to some ads they hate) and has led to a generalized assumption that, because they elicit these strong emotions, commercials have more power than they actually do.

In reality, writes Bergler, the power relations between advertiser and advertisee are just about the opposite of what those picket-sign-wielding alarmists in America believe to be the case. Drawing on surveys gauging the attitudes of youth in Germany, as well as some secondary research, he concludes that ads are mostly ineffective in changing the behaviour of kids, that the current generation has developed a high level of resistance to the commercial pitch, and that factors such as family life and children's physical and social environments have an impact on kids that's strong enough to outweigh any influence exerted by advertising.

Bergler's conclusions rest partly on his assertion that critics of advertising built their case on theories of human behaviour that have since been discredited. Their assumptions about how the human mind works, he states bluntly, are simply wrong. In what amounts to a fierce rebuke of all those commentators, from Packard and Key to the current-day American activists of SCEC, who fear the advertising industry's ability to pull the "want," "need," and "buy" levers inside kids' heads, Bergler declares that it is simply not possible to manipulate human behaviour via words and pictures on a TV screen. Where the critics first go wrong, charges Bergler, is in accepting the assumptions of an earlier school of behavioural psychologists (such as the American Edward Tolman and the Soviet Ivan Pavlov) that believed it is possible to apply a stimulus that will produce a desired response. Today, says Bergler, psychologists understand that human behaviour is too complex to be manipulated by other humans, whether they are in lab coats, business suits, or otherwise. "In scientific psychology," he writes, "the manipulation theory of human behaviour has failed." With more than a tad of condescension, he goes on to say that fears about advertisers somehow brainwashing or conditioning kids to buy their product are being propagated by "naïve" laypeople who are uninformed, unscientific, and out of step with the correct thinking of credible authorities like himself.

"The demand for bans on advertising," he writes, "is based on the naïve assumption—conviction—which is not scientifically tenable, that there are mono-causal links between advertising and the effect advertising has on behaviour. The central psychological assumption of all political discussion is that advertising aims at influencing and 'leading astray.' This naïve theory of everyday psychology on the effectiveness of advertising has nothing to do with current scientific knowledge."

Bergler uses European survey data to support the view that advertising, in essence, has no impact. If advertising programs kids to spend impulsively, he asks, then why do German children aged six to seventeen save 48 percent of the 12 billion Deutschmarks within their collective grasp rather than spending it wantonly? His subsequent citations imply that it has something to do with the fact that those kids are hardened skeptics who are able to "just say no" to advertisers. According to his stats, 57.1 percent of six year olds in Germany understand that advertising is meant to sell them something, a number that climbs to 88.6 percent for twelve to thirteen year olds. This appears to contradict the claim made by the industry's critics that kids are vulnerable because they are unaware of advertising's intentions. And while 62.7 percent of German six year olds rate the ads they see as "very good" (a measure Bergler refers to as "the sympathy and general acceptance value of advertising"), the figure drops to 22.8 percent for the twelve to thirteen year old group. The researcher is also impressed by the number of German kids who say they don't believe what the ads are telling them: they account for 33.6 percent of six year olds (just slightly above the percentage of their counterparts who reflexively believe everything ads tell them), with disbelievers rising to a peak of 41.3 percent of seven to nine year olds (but falling again in the higher age ranges).

If advertising isn't as potent an influence on kids as its detractors fear, what factors do shape kids' behaviour? Bergler believes the role of living, breathing humans in real-life situations has been underestimated. For starters, kids spend most of their time in the real world, rather than in the media world. Those surveys of German children, for instance, reveal that for every 680 minutes children spend playing, at school, reading, eating, or doing sports, music, or homework, they spend only 90 minutes watching TV programs and 11 minutes watching TV ads—meaning that non–television-related activity occupies 87.6 percent of their time. (American children have a much richer media diet than their German counterparts, consuming between four and five hours of television per day.)[4] Bergler supports the assumption that these figures, in the German context at least, indicate real-life factors have a greater influence than TV on the behaviour of kids by pointing to parallel studies analyzing the conditions that contribute to risk-taking behaviour among youth. Smoking, for example, has been found to be more prevalent amongst kids whose "framework conditions" include coming from families where there is conflict between parents and children (or between mother and father) and having "strong ties to a smoking and alcohol drinking clique with simultaneous deficits in the quality of the parent-child relationship." In other words, the quality of family relationships and the influence of friends are interrelated factors with a clear impact on young people's behaviour—TV, on the other hand, is not.

Bergler laments that parents are inclined to look outside the family and community for the reasons why Junior smokes, acts up, or eats too much junk food, in order to evade responsibility for the way their kids develop. He cites one study in which a group of mothers pinpointed "excessive media consumption, ozone, nuclear power, drugs, narcotics, genetically engineered crops, air pollution, chemical residues in food as well as accidents" as the major threats to their children, while mostly ignoring more immediate concerns such as smoking and alcohol consumption at home, poor hygiene, and lack of vaccination. He has stern words (the impact of which are blunted somewhat by the awkward translation) for those who would blame the media for their children's shortcomings: "The love of a 'no risks' society increasingly results in substituting scapegoats outside one's own sphere of influence for self-responsibility." This search for scapegoats is encouraged by research that he condemns as both misguided and incompetent. "Up to now," he writes, "the public and political discussion on 'children and advertising' is on the level of naïve everyday psychology, which puts human behaviour down to stimulus response mechanisms ... Additionally, with serious deficits in methods this theoretical procedure is bound to lead to wrong diagnoses."

Less judgmental in tone (and somewhat less equivocal in its statement of conclusions) is the work of Dr. Jeffrey Goldstein, a professor of mass communications at the University of Utrecht in the Netherlands, who penned a literature review on children and advertising for the EU.[5] Although Dr. Goldstein (who was formerly employed in the United States at Temple University in Philadelphia) opposes a ban on children's advertising, he refrains from issuing definitive judgments about which research is acceptable and which can simply be written off as the "naïve everyday psychology" of laypeople. While Bergler asserts that current scientific knowledge conclusively debunks the case against children's ads, Goldstein more diffidently states that "the scholarly research on children and advertising is not nearly as clear, reliable or relevant as is often supposed

… In the several hundred studies of children and advertising, it is difficult to find reliable results or useful guidelines for European policy."

Studies that examine the age at which children understand advertising, for instance, have produced widely divergent results, partly because individual researchers will use completely different definitions of what it means to "understand" an ad. While some studies maintain that two year olds can grasp the essence of advertising, others insist that kids don't clue in until they're eleven or twelve. (Goldstein suggests the point may be moot, though, since there is no clear evidence to support the claim made by anti–kid-marketing forces that children who can't distinguish an ad from a program are more vulnerable to being duped. On the contrary, he suggests that ads might only motivate kids to buy a product when those kids understand that the intention of a commercial is to sell something—when they grasp that going out and buying a product is what they are *supposed* to do.)

Although they arrive at essentially the same policy conclusions, parts of Goldstein's précis of the psychological literature on kids and ads contradicts key elements of Bergler's argument. While Bergler has no hesitation consigning to the laboratory wastebasket the idea that advertising can motivate human behaviour, Goldstein proposes just the opposite. "Advertising does affect us," he states. "If a message is repeated often enough, people will increasingly accept it." And common sense suggests this will have an impact on how humans conduct themselves in the world: "Of course the media influence behaviour," the professor opines. "No one would go to the cinema, listen to music, read a book, watch television or pay attention to commercials if they did not get something from it."

Yet Goldstein steps more closely into line with Bergler when he considers the *extent* to which advertising can shape our decisions. Since Western European children are subjected to thousands of advertising messages per year, he argues, kids could be expected to ask for thousands of products per year if the advertisements they watched were as powerful as the critics claim. But they don't. Like adults, children are selective in the requests they make. This might help explain the high failure rate of new products in the marketplace. Although most products are heavily advertised, 85 percent of the 85,000 new products introduced in the U.S. in the 1980s had become extinct by the end of 1990—a clear indication that advertising does not guarantee sales.

Whatever contribution advertising does make to the success of marketplace winners, Goldstein insists it is minuscule compared to the influences that spring from real life. In boldfaced, italicized type, he asserts that "every study of the subject finds that children are more influenced by parents and playmates than by the mass media." Goldstein reasons that the standard argument for banning commercials aimed at kids (the condensed version of which is that children, who are particularly vulnerable to media brainwashing, will become entranced by a new product and nag their parents to buy it for them, setting the stage for incessant child-parent conflict) ignores what happens when kids are not in front of the TV. Parents buy the argument that ads encourage "the nag factor," he says, because they rarely see their kids on the playground or amongst their peers, where the real sales job takes place.

"Youth fads, like in-line roller skates, POGS, and the earrings that adorn young men, began not with advertising but by word of mouth and imitation," writes Goldstein. "Children's fascination with the latest toy, video game, or musical group often precedes rather than follows widespread advertising."

This idea that on-the-ground culture can play a bigger role in boosting a product's popularity amongst kids than advertising has a certain ring of truth for me, especially in light of my experience at the Understanding Youth conference. If this idea was merely industry PR, designed to deflect criticism by convincing parents that ads aren't nearly as potent a mind-control weapon as critics say, then I doubt whether so much of the conference would have centred on "cool hunting" and other techniques to infiltrate youth social clusters. Some notable successes, so conference delegates were repeatedly reminded, have been built on the premise that the way to capture the youth market is not to lead kids into temptation, but to follow them into their element and commercialize what you see there.

Matthew Diamond, head honcho at Alloy Online (you may remember him from Chapter 1 as the architect of the "comprehensive convergence strategy," which includes sending kids commercial messages on their cellphones), explains how it's done. Cool hunting is a street thing. Its primary zone of engagement is at ground level, in myriad schools and communities across the United States where Alloy has identified fashion-conscious, trend-setting kids who are instructed to keep their eyes peeled for "cool and not-so-cool looks." This is the company's Cool Hunter Network—an informal web of operatives hooked up, CIA-style, to the head-office establishment. The cool hunters' job is to e-mail photos of recent sartorial innovations to Alloy's editors and marketing team, who in turn may post some of those submissions on the company's website to gauge reaction from a broader spectrum of kids. This process is not new. In *No Logo*, Naomi Klein notes that agencies such as Sputnik and Bureau de Style began cool hunting in the mid-1990s, mostly poaching style innovations from poor, black neighbourhoods and marketing them in white suburban shopping malls. (Tommy Hilfiger, on the other hand, went a step further, constructing a brilliantly self-contained feedback loop by promoting preppy white kids' clothes in black ghettos, then reintroducing them to suburban white kids on the basis of their newly acquired hip-hop appeal.)[6]

This reversal of emphasis—with companies less inclined to dictate to kids what they should be wearing or playing, and more inclined to hitch their boxcar to an already-moving train—is partly a testament to the erosion of the power of mass broadcast media and the rise of a decentralized, anti-centrifugal Internet culture. This transformed media environment has spawned a number of strategies that draw on the same general logic as cool hunting. The much-touted "viral campaign," for instance, is a means for companies to tap into the horizontal communication that links kids across wide swaths of geography and to capitalize on the power of person-to-person buzz, on the sense of excitement surrounding a particular look or sound, which—though it may sprout locally—can gather amazing force as it travels through cyberspace. Typically, the viral campaign involves motivating a cadre of enthusiasts to tell their friends and acquaintances about how good a particular product is, usually by e-mail.

Trying to harness grassroots communications power by stoking a local buzz can be a morally murky business. Does an adult who's been hired by a record company to post submissions to teen Internet chat groups, for instance, have an obligation to inform the other correspondents that she's been paid to say nice things about a particular band? Does a confederate who has been put on a company payroll to talk up a product at a bar or a dance hall have a similar obligation?[7]

These moral conundrums notwithstanding, the trend towards companies riding the momentum of pre-existing social waves, having a presence on the ground rather than a pulpit from which to preach, tends to support Goldstein's assertion that advertising has less intrinsic power than most people think; that it's much less of a persuader (and therefore less of a threat) than those of a more alarmist bent might have it. It's only logical to suggest that if mass-media advertising had such leverage over its targets' consumer habits, corporations wouldn't need to infiltrate the daily lives and personal communications networks of young hipsters.

Not that mass-media advertising—read: TV commercials—is insignificant. Towards the end of his paper, Goldstein reveals himself as a fan and champion of mass advertising, audaciously advancing the idea that ads are a powerful force for *good* in kids' lives and within the society they grow up in. Losing some of his veneer of scientific objectivity, Goldstein launches into a litany of the benefits of advertising to children, beginning with the most practical. "Advertising is a source of information about products," he says, explaining that "although children rely mainly on other children as their source of inspiration, adults rely upon advertising for ideas about appropriate gifts for children." Kids' advertising is also less violent than most television. Referring to three previous studies, Goldstein praises kid-directed ads as a source of "pro-social values" and positive qualities. Furthermore, Goldstein describes ads' power to give material goods a central place in the formation of kid's identities—one of the characteristics of kids' advertising that most alarms critics—as a positive thing. "Advertising," he writes, "gives meaning to goods and ultimately to ourselves ... In a world where one's identity is no longer determined solely by class or race, advertising helps us create and maintain a self-image and communicate who we are to others." So while some observers worry that brand consciousness (propagated through advertising) is making kids superficial, materialistic, and blind to more deeply rooted qualities that have traditionally defined the human character, Goldstein suggests that deriving a sense of identity from a brand of jeans is better than the alternative: that is, feeling rootless and alienated, falling into the identity void produced by a world where traditional markers of self have been erased. Better to be a GAP kid than a nobody.

Finally, Goldstein dispenses the standard logic that it's the responsibility of parents—not TV executives—to talk to their children about the advertising they watch. Yet he doesn't prescribe this with the sense of trepidation that usually accompanies this advice. The purpose of these little chats would not be to warn kids that they might be suckered by commercials, but to tell them that the advertiser is their friend. "The primary aim of such education is to provide a better understanding of how advertising fits into the society and the economy," he says. "This will enable consumers and others to see the role that advertising plays in the economy, in helping consumers to make informed choices, in supporting children's television programming, and in serving as a source of popular entertainment that enriches our lives."

†

Reading this, I can imagine the gagging sounds coming from Boston and Berkeley. Sure enough, both Susan Linn and Allen Kanner, the SCEC activists on opposite American coasts, express considerable disdain for this "public service" view of children's advertising. Kanner, for instance, feels that Goldstein's characterization of kid-focused commercials as "a source of information about products" is completely at odds with the content of most ads. Remember that old maxim that says advertising is about "selling the sizzle and not the steak"? Kanner believes that a scan of children-directed ads of the recent past proves this is still the industry's modus operandi. What do those Nike ads, the ones that portray Michael Jordan as a demigod, implying by extension that his brand of sneaker can be an agent of transcendental experience, actually have to do with the real-life qualities of the footwear? What tangible information do commercials for McDonald's or Burger King convey about the nutritional value—or even the taste—of the food that's served there? Can those children's ads that equate products with the attainment of coolness, popularity, or happiness be said to provide "information" to the viewer, or are they attempts to impart magical qualities to an otherwise ordinary object, to work some sort of alchemy that transforms the mundane into the mystical?

"When advertisers talk about making kids informed consumers," says Kanner, his voice suddenly becoming brittle when I mention the argument of the EU papers, "one of the main problems is that it portrays ads as having a cognitive function—providing information. But advertising works primarily at an emotional level. That's what marketing is all about: trying to find the most effective psychological manipulation possible, whatever the target group." Besides, he adds, any tangible information contained in children's ads "is usually one-sided and exaggerated."

That ads appeal to emotion over logic is one factor leading Dr. Susan Linn to believe that the Swedes have it right: there should be legislative restrictions on ads aimed at kids. Kids will not analyze advertising rationally. Rather, they will lock onto its emotional content, and there is no real antidote available to neutralize its impact. The most commonly prescribed alternative to bans or legislated limits on kids' advertising is the use of "media literacy" techniques, which urge parents to sit down with their kids and discuss the content of ads in order to bring the ad's purpose out into the open. However, although Linn believes this may foster an intellectual understanding of advertising, it's unlikely to give kids any immunity to the effects of a well-crafted, oft-repeated pitch.

"The research I've seen about media literacy," she says, "is that it may teach kids to be more skeptical, but there is no evidence that it affects purchases at all, or that the skepticism actually protects you. You can talk to any woman in the United States, practically, and it's almost certain she knows she is being manipulated by marketing. But everyone I know worries about how she looks and her weight and getting old and that kind of stuff. We all know we are being manipulated. Does that mean we can resist the messages advertisers are constantly bombarding us with?"

In the case of kids and teenagers, says Dr. Linn, behaviour is motivated by powerful impulses that are essential to the process of growing up, but which are also easily commandeered to support the aims of self-interested third parties. For example, kids instinctively need to express independence from their parents as they strive to cultivate the autonomy and self-directedness they'll require as adults. "Kids are in the process, from the moment they are born, of separating from their parents, especially when they get to be teens and pre-teens," Linn explains. "They are developmentally set up to disregard their parents, at least on the surface." Marketers play into this, setting themselves up as the kid's champion in the face of parental repression, and appealing to this powerful instinct with ad campaigns that help kids thumb their noses at parental authority.

The cultural critic Mark Crispin Miller, who teaches communications at New York University, notes how successfully the forces of marketing have appropriated the teenage urge to rebellion. To make it useful to them, however, the ad guys have had to strip youth culture of any political or intellectual baggage. The media critic believes that while once teen rebellion may have been *about* something — in the 1960s, for instance, much of the youth movement was about opposing the Vietnam War or the materialism that suffused North American society — today that energy has been tapped by corporate forces as just one more way to move product.

"It's part of the official rock video worldview," says Crispin Miller, "part of the official advertising worldview that your parents are creeps, teachers are nerds and idiots, authority figures are laughable, nobody can really understand kids except the corporate sponsor. That huge authority [i.e., big companies that advertise] has, interestingly enough, emerged as the sort of tacit superhero of consumer culture ... They are very busily selling the illusion that they are there to liberate the youth, to let them be free, to let them be themselves, to let them think different, and so on. But it's really just an enormous sales job."[8]

This is not a new story. History is littered with tragic tales of young men, barely old enough to shave, enthusiastically donning soldiers' uniforms as a way of finding adventure and a sense of purpose despite the anguished opposition of their parents. So perhaps it shouldn't be surprising that the marketers of today have cottoned onto the fact that kids are looking for a ticket out of their parents' world, and this makes them easy marks for a sales pitch.

On the other hand, researchers like Bergler dispute any suggestion that advertising activates the kind of subconscious triggers (e.g., the need to become independent of one's parents) that the critics say it does. Bergler's is a unidimensional world in which logic is the sole determinant of reality, and people—even young children—act logically. By his reckoning, the fact that the American anti–child-marketing crusaders don't have the clinical research to back up their hypothesis that marketing is warping kids is proof that their statements must be untrue. By extension, Bergler writes off the entire repertoire of popular assumptions about the impact of advertising—introduced to a broad public by Packard and accepted, for the most part, as conventional wisdom since then—as unsustainable in the face of serious scientific scrutiny. The hysterics who want to ban kids' ad have only their wild theories, says Bergler. And he's got the numbers to show that they are wrong.

But pledging one's faithfulness to the scientific method is no guarantee of arriving at the truth, and the anti–child-marketing campaigners find plenty of logical holes in the arguments advanced by Bergler and Goldstein. Examining Bergler's statistical constructs in the light of real-world conditions, Kanner finds the German's assertion that ads do not motivate kids to spend both illogical and implausible. "Why would advertisers spend their money on something that isn't working?" he asks. "These people are not stupid. They monitor this stuff really heavily, you know. That's part of the market research. The economic data tells them whether sales are up or not." And the fact that spending by American kids has been rising since the 1980s, when marketers began their push to expand the youth market, suggests that advertisers have been effective not just in pinpointing the consumer preferences that will help them hold onto their share of a static overall marketplace, but also in stimulating kids' appetite for goods, thereby creating a bigger pie for competing companies to carve up. Is there a psychological component to this process? Circumstances suggest, for Kanner, that the answer is "yes." Why would the major child-marketing firms boast that they hire psychologists to map the terrain of children's minds if they didn't expect to locate the mechanisms by which they could compel kids to spend? Why would psychologists be hired to perfect advertising campaigns if ads were not effective tools for persuading kids to buy?

Sure, this is a situational, largely circumstantial argument. Kanner and his colleagues have not built their case on identifying a direct, causal mechanism that explains how advertising works, but rather have correlated certain conditions that affect society (and kids in particular) with what they know about how advertising functions and what its purported goals are. Kanner does not dispute that his side lacks the necessary research to prove its case. But he says a re-angling of the playing field is necessary before anti-child-marketing forces will be able to replace their compelling hypothesis with hard data. As it stands now, critics can only guess what the marketing firms' psychological research is telling them about how kids can be motivated to shell out their allowance. This is because (to revisit some familiar terrain) marketers classify their studies as "proprietary research"—trade secrets they are forced to keep close to their chests so that Joe down the street doesn't Google-search his way to instant expertise and put the established firms out of business. Child-marketing firms are not about to tell the competition (or their sworn adversaries, like Kanner and Linn) what their high-priced market research reveals.

To retrace our steps, the big philosophical beef critics like Kanner have with the work of commentators like Bergler and Goldstein—who see advertising to kids as essentially benign—is that advertisers would not spend lots of money on advertising campaigns if they didn't appear to work. It is possible to dispute the EU-sponsored research on a micro-level, as well. Do the figures presented by Bergler, for instance, really prove what he says they do? In making the case that kids are largely immune to the impact of advertising, the University of Bonn researcher cited several clusters of figures dealing with their skepticism, understanding, and declining approval of advertising (as they get older). Bergler found reassurance, for instance, in the fact that a majority of six year olds (57.1 percent) understand that advertising intends to sell them something—with that number rising to 88.6 in the twelve to thirteen year old group. Skepticism also increases with age. While 62.7 percent of six year olds rate advertising as "very good," that figure falls to 22.8 percent for twelve to thirteen years olds. Bergler also trumpets the strong critical faculties that help children ferret out lies and distortions in advertising. He supports this view with statistics showing that 33.6 percent of six years olds don't believe what advertising tells them, with incredulity peaking at 41.3 percent for seven to nine year olds.

But these numbers can tell an entirely different story if you look at them from another perspective. Yes, 33.6 percent of six year olds say "I don't believe it" when asked about advertising; but an almost equal number (33.2 percent) respond to the same question with a blanket "I believe it," suggesting that a full third of German kids of this age approach advertising with total, wide-eyed naïveté. Another of Bergler's figures—the one which shows that close to two-thirds of six year olds (62.7 percent) have a high level of sympathy for and acceptance of advertising—can be interpreted as proof that children of this young age are very receptive to marketing messages. Even apparently impressive stats in support of Bergler's argument can be seen to contain contradictory messages. For instance, a large number of twelve to thirteen year olds (88.6 percent) know what the purpose of advertising is, but looking at the flipside of the equation, one can calculate that an alarmingly high minority of kids on the verge of entering the complex and turbulent teenage years (almost 12 percent) are clueless about the purpose of advertising. These are kids who will soon have to navigate the far more challenging issues of sex and drugs, yet they don't possess the rudimentary knowledge (knowledge that's fundamental to survival in our hard-sell society) that advertisers want them to buy something.

Indeed, statistics about majority preferences and attitudes may be next to useless for understanding what kind of grasp advertising has on kids' imaginations, for this is an age of niche marketing, defined by the industry's capacity to narrowcast its messages directly into the craniums of specific groups of kids. It is those marginal numbers—the 5 percent here or 7 percent there who don't fit the mold—that may be the most significant indictors of the marketers' power. Putting a Ford in every garage is no longer the goal of business; it's now a question of identifying that slim segment of the population who are likely to buy your particular product. Politicians, for instance, don't aim their rhetoric at some mythical "majority." They use sophisticated demographic modelling to identify the key issues for specific constituencies they can court, and then try to cobble together a winning coalition from those component parts. Casinos do not expect that the bulk of the population will be drawn to their roulette tables—but as long as a compulsive few are, and as long as they bring lots of cash, the casino owners will generate a very nice income, thanks very much. It's much the same with youth, says Susan Linn. The marketers are looking for kids with just the right chip in their circuit boards, that certain predisposition that makes them receptive to a particular pitch.

"All children are vulnerable [to marketing]," says Linn. "But how they are vulnerable depends on their personality and their life circumstances. If you are a little impulsive, for instance, then being marketed irresponsible sex, or tons of violence, is a problem for you. If you are a girl and you are concerned because your body doesn't conform to the image it's supposed to, you are vulnerable that way. If you tend to be materialistic, you are vulnerable in that way. Marketing exploits people's particular vulnerabilities; that's what it's all about. They are very frank about that in the marketing literature."

"All kids are vulnerable." With this simple phrase, Dr. Linn nails down a key aspect of the worldview that is advanced, implicitly, each time anti–child-marketing forces make a statement on a particular marketing campaign or sub-issue. Their underlying supposition is that the marketing machine of today is so massive, so pervasive, able to propagate its message across such a wide spectrum, with unfathomable strength and sophistication, that it's just about impossible to resist. That goes double if you're a kid, born into a world where commercial messages have become kind of like oxygen or electricity: an invisible but essential component of daily existence, a force so fundamental to the way things are that you're likely never to think about it. But besides its ubiquity in our current society, marketing is massively powerful because it is able to connect with the individual, to mind-meld with the target, to understand who you are and what you need. If you're a kid, no matter where you've come from and where you're going, chances are somebody has a focus group result in a file cabinet that describes your precise Achilles heel and tells Corporation X how to exploit it. They are good at what they do and they know your weaknesses. Resistance is futile.

The effect of all this is that youth are indoctrinated with a new ideology that replaces timeless values—say, the sense of community or of personal duty—with a consumerist, acquisitive ethic that views personal character as a suit of clothes that can be changed according to the dictates of fashion. We can refer to this, in shorthand, as the "hell in a handbasket" theory. You may want to scribble that down for future reference.

CHAPTER 5

The Kids Are Alright ... Maybe

Welcome back to the Understanding Youth conference, where a session entitled "It Rocks, It Sucks, I Don't Care ... " is unfolding beneath the glass chandeliers of the Toronto Hilton. The delegates had been promised that towards the end of the morning "three actual young people" would grace this conference, and here they are, sitting serenely at a long table in front of three hundred marketing types. There are two girls (aged sixteen and eighteen) and one guy (he's nineteen), all of them immaculately coiffed and surprisingly self-assured considering that they have been hauled up here to serve as specimens of the current youth culture, kind of like the exotic birds or medical oddities that accompanied the travelling lecturers who filled the vaudeville halls of the late nineteenth century.

Also at the front of the room, wielding a cordless mike and speaking with the same kind of choppy cadence and upward-drifting sentence endings one would expect of the participants, is twenty-three year old Nitasha Kapoor, "chief ideator"[1] at Youthography, who shepherds the assembled panel through a series of exercises designed to ferret out their true, honest-to-God opinions. While doing this, Kapoor also provides a running commentary for the audience, explaining the finer points of the process. The purpose of today's session is simple: to determine what communications media kids like these turn to when they want to be entertained or informed. Nitasha puts the question to the panel in the form of a four-part, situational query: what are your first and second choices when you want to (a) find out the time of a movie, (b) buy a cellphone, (c) be amused when you are bored at home at nine o'clock at night, and (d) listen to some music. Nitasha explains to the audience that the concreteness of those questions is one factor that engages kids, making this process seem relevant to their own experience. "What you want to avoid," she elaborates, "is the shrugging shoulders or blank stares. You want to be going for the 'It sucks, I hate this, this is the worst thing I've ever seen,' or 'This rocks, this is amazing, this is the best thing I've ever used, I love this product,' and why."

The results of today's session are hardly earth-shaking. Nitasha Kapoor's on-the-spot synthesis of responses suggests that the current generation relies heavily on the Internet, but will leap between old media and new when they feel one particular information source isn't giving them the goods. Despite the rather predictable conclusion (remember, the aim of this exercise was simply to illustrate how this kind of work is done), Kapoor expresses considerable enthusiasm for the underlying structural messages about the way in which kids plug into the process and what that apparently says about their overall cultural frame of reference.

The way she's formatted the session, for instance, is highly significant. Kapoor gives the participants the questions and allows them to huddle together and come back with prepared answers. She says that this means they can "say something on their own ... create a statement in their own words." Remember, today's marketers are hot on the idea that millennial youth see themselves as in control, as being the force that drives the machine. Allowing the kids their own creative space feeds into this idea, with the end result being the sense that "they actually own the research. They actually own the topics."

Sure enough, the participants injected plenty of personal flourishes into their responses, one of them by reading a piece of impromptu rap doggerel that goes:

So you want to target youth, you say?
Well, we've got advice for you, today.
TV and Internet is where it's at.
If you've got questions, we'll give you a chat.

The three high-schoolers also took every opportunity they could to strike the requisite pose of teenage rebelliousness. When they introduced themselves, one of them hectored the assembled crowd, warning audience members that they had better listen to what teens themselves have to say if they want teens' business. Another took a shot at a local chain of electronics stores, advising the powers that be to replace the current staff with people who know something about the products they sell.

Okay, so this—to use Nitasha Kapoor's term—is "ownership." They know they are the bosses and, within the tight confines of the exercise, can make their own demands. They may not be demanding much—preferring to lobby for Joe Know-nothing to be sacked from the local electronics big box rather than calling for a halt to global warming or a freeing of political prisoners in the country where their stereos are assembled—but hey, the point is they've got that "I'm in charge" attitude and they're not afraid to let it show. Or to use another term that's migrated from the lexicon of sociology to the world of marketing, they feel "empowered."

This concept was driven home to me a few days after the conference when, in the middle of our wide-ranging, post-conference debriefing, Max Valliquette raised his colleague Kapoor's focus session as a shining example of how kids themselves are setting the agenda, with big corporations feeling compelled to follow. "She [Kapoor] was able to stand up there and say 'Here's why you suck, here's why you rock, and here's what I need you to do' ... and we are able to do that and people will actually listen," he marvelled. This new power dynamic has arisen, Valliquette believes, because there is "a generation that's demanding things, demanding relationships, even with things like their brands."

What's weird about this kind of talk—with its implication that the marketers' focus group is some profoundly democratic forum, and that a statement of consumer preferences somehow reveals an evolutionary step towards a more autonomous, self-actualized human being—is that it employs high-minded language to describe a process that is purely, mundanely commercial. Buying cellphones, searching the movie listings ... these are not the kinds of activities that change the course of history. Yet marketers read tremendous social significance into the way kids approach these ordinary tasks. In different places, at different times, the energy and passion that are released by teenagers trying to find their place in the world might have been channelled into some higher cause—or perhaps the spilling of blood in a military crusade or gang war. But here in post-industrial, middle-class North America, so the marketing establishment is saying, asserting your right to consume as you choose has become cause enough in itself. This is an era where pop tunes have become anthems; corporate logos, flags to rally around; the shopping mall, a ritual battleground where adolescents can prove themselves to be adults.

How far we have come. Watching that focus group session reminded me of a reference in Marshall McLuhan's 1947 essay "American Advertising." McLuhan cites an American army officer, corresponding from Italy for the journal *Printer's Ink*, who "note[s] with misgiving that Italians could tell you the names of cabinet ministers but not the names of commodities preferred by Italian celebrities. Furthermore, the wall space of Italian cities was given over to political rather than commercial slogans." These were taken by the army/ad man as signs of the country's cultural and material underdevelopment. The officer's dire prediction, McLuhan recalls, was that "there was small hope that Italians could ever achieve any sort of domestic prosperity or calm until they began to worry about the rival claims of cornflakes or cigarettes rather than the capacities of public men. In fact, he went so far as to say that democratic freedom very largely consists in ignoring politics and worrying about the means of defeating underarm odour, scaly scalp, hairy legs, dull complexion, unruly hair, borderline anaemia, athlete's foot ..." Well, you get the point.[2] This colourful little passage suggests that the marketing world has long been contemplating how people, when they look into the world for a set of concerns to help define who they are and what is important to them, can be made to think of the products corporations produce, rather than to cast their gaze towards politics, art, or some other more abstract intellectual sphere.

Fast-forward half a century, to the conference centre in a North American hotel, and it's easy to conclude that the marketing establishment has successfully accomplished this task. The experts talk of a new generation that's assertive, self-possessed, and self-aware, but they measure these qualities solely by how kids behave at the shopping mall. It's as if every other aspect of life has been excised from their world. Determinedly upbeat focus group leaders celebrate the fact that today's kids will speak their minds with cocky self-assurance, but the only questions they address revolve around what products they are prepared to buy. That Understanding Youth focus group provides a luminous illustration of the way the imperatives of the marketplace have been grafted onto that timeless teenage urge to self-assertion: kids telling marketers how they can sell them products better is now considered an expression of teen rebellion.

Of course, you could argue that what transpires at a kid-marketer's conference is hardly representative of a generation's broader experience. The point here is to sell things, so it hardly defies expectations that those three kids on display at Understanding Youth would be quizzed about the products they use, rather than their thoughts on how to end world hunger or whether the current government is doing a good job.

The marketing machine is also notorious for trying to turn any phenomenon that captures public attention to its own commercial advantage. This may create the impression, for some, that anything young people get up to is either designed by business interests or has come under their control. For their part, the corporations seem to want to associate themselves with almost anything that captures the media spotlight. During the turn-of-the-millennium wave of anti-globalization protests that brought tens of thousands of young people to economic summits in Seattle, Quebec City, and Genoa, for instance, the Gap introduced a short-lived campaign of radical chic window displays featuring anarchist flags and slogans like "Freedom" and "We the People" applied in fake black spray paint.[3] The use of these symbols to sell a line of jeans is hardly proof that anti-globalization protests are a creation of the marketing machine. Rather, it's just one more example of how corporations will always try to hitch a lift with any social movement that has momentum. The starkest irony is no obstacle to this. (That Gap campaign was not unique in its attempts to use political images to advance a commercial end. Apple Computers, for example, has run ads that superimpose its "Think Different" slogan onto images of Cesar Chavez, Malcolm X, and young militants waving red flags. Since September 11, however, embracing the revolutionary impulse seems a much riskier strategy, so clothiers like the Gap opted to make a different kind of political statement by reintroducing the more traditional military look.)[4]

To some critics, the corporate world's ability to hijack images and identities of all sorts—to affix its commercial messages to any surface—has given it the power to refashion kids' experience of life. Psychologist Allen Kanner's critique, for instance, goes far beyond the statement (presciently expressed by McLuhan and his army officer/ad guy) that public interest in politics has been overridden by an obsession with products. For Kanner, consumerism has supplanted more than just politics. It has become the *spiritual* focus of life for much of the millennial generation—bigger than nature, bigger than human relationships, an all-consuming addiction that has voided many other aspects of the human experience. Forget this talk of empowerment and self-assertion. In Kanner's view of things, kids have little opportunity to glimpse a wider world of ideas and possibilities because their vision no longer extends beyond the shopping mall. They are trapped in an ersatz sphere of meaningless trinkets and manufactured images.

The notion that marketing has made kids' experience of life more one-dimensional, less complete, than it might otherwise be, also pops up in the PBS documentary "Merchants of Cool."[5] The filmmakers, Rachel Dretzin and Barak Goodman, explore this idea by examining how kid-oriented media companies conduct market research. Businesses that depend on the goodwill of youth—like MTV—tend to do a lot of research into the habits, likes, and dislikes of their audience and/or customers. Dretzin and Goodman believe, however, that the way MTV collects and uses this information is rigged. Rather than producing a true, nuanced image of its teenaged subjects, the research hones in on particular aspects of personality with a direct connection to spending habits. The aim is to create a composite character for the screen that teenagers will believe in enough to want to emulate. This is not research in the service of understanding, the filmmakers conclude; it is research as a tool for constructing a "feedback loop" in which an image that kids help to create, one that contains enough of their own reality to capture their attention, is sold back to them as entertainment product.

And what image is MTV peddling to its audience? After following MTV researchers on a field trip into the bedroom of a teenage boy (MTV likes to work on the kids' own turf), Dretzin and Goodman conclude that the raw material will be used to help refine a composite character they refer to as "The Mook." Variations on The Mook appear in shows across the MTV schedule and on other channels within the MTV Networks empire. The Mook is loud, obnoxious, and often obscene, "a creation designed to capitalize on the testosterone-driven madness of adolescence." The Mook's female counterpart is "The Midriff," who the filmmakers see as "a collection of all the old sexual clichés, but repackaged as a new kind of female empowerment ... If he is arrested in adolescence, she is prematurely adult. If he doesn't care what people think of him, she is consumed by appearances." Both of these stereotypical characters have an element of truth to them, but for the most part they are cardboard cut-outs. Their sole purpose, it seems, is to create a specific kind of identification—a feeling of being in like-minded company—that will activate the "spend" reflex.

This is a view that lines up fairly closely with the "hell in a handbasket" outlook promoted by the activists of SCEC and similar groups. Underlying that interpretation of how MTV's research is manipulated is the conviction that the wizards who produce the network's programming are able to control kids—though it's a subtle kind of control, like that of the judo master, which depends on your understanding and redirecting the energy of your opponent. Critics of kid media inevitably see this control as serving some poisonous purpose. Disgruntled liberals believe that the media machine is turning kids into reflexive consumers, soulless buying machines trained to keep the wheels of commerce turning at the expense of our environment and to the exclusion of more meaningful pursuits like addressing the roots of social injustice and conflict. The raging right wing, meanwhile, sees media outlets like MTV as peddlers of debauchery and sin, exalting a rock-video lifestyle based on casual sex, drug use, and rejection of authority.

But what if, as kid-marketing professionals sometimes protest, the manufacturers of media product do not exercise that much control over kids? What if the distinct characteristics of one particular generation's outlook do not arise primarily from the sea of media images they are swimming in, but from some other set of social conditions? Some commentators place a greater emphasis on the profound social and economic shifts of the last half century as an explanation for why kids have turned out different from their parents. Their prognosis is often decidedly more optimistic. While critics of mass media see the emerging generation as suffering the ill effects (obesity, superficial social values, lack of moral direction, obsessive materialism, propensity to violence ...) of growing up in a holographic, media-saturated world, their more utopian counterparts propose that kids in general have not lost their moral centre. It's just that the centre has shifted as a new reality has emerged, and their moral code has been updated. Not surprisingly, this view is often amplified by marketing gurus, who find that such positive representations of where kids are headed can be a useful shield for their own work, providing a blanket of sunlight that helps deflect questions about how the more unsavoury aspects of their business harm the young.

Even when it is aired in the context of a marketing conference, this idea that generational codes of being can evolve independently from the schemes and desires of the marketing industry has a ring of truth to me. At Understanding Youth, Mark Childs, a vice-president with Kellogg's, the breakfast food company, began his spiel on how marketing practices have changed throughout the rock video era by running a short film of great moments in recent pop history, *Welcome to Now*. It was a typically bombastic spectacle of techno-excess, with the sound cranked loud enough that the floor shook, and the giant screen at the front of the room convulsing to a quick-cut pastiche of the images that defined, for millions of North Americans, the precise historical and mythological moment they experienced that fleeting thrill of being young. The video starts with the by-now vintage moves of Madonna and Prince—the first super-stars of the MTV era—and works its way into the God-forsaken territory of Limp Bizkit and Eminem. Interestingly, the anthem that is chosen to represent the generational slice coming up behind those sullen rappers is "Be As" by the band Prozzäk. In case you haven't heard it (I hadn't), it's got a frothy teenybop kind of melody and a chorus that goes:

Be as white as you want to
Be as black as you want to
Be as brown as you want to
Don't let anybody stop you

Be as straight as you want to
Be as gay as you want to
You can wait if you want to
We all need something to hold on to

followed by some verses about kids at school trying to define their own identities and a few more choruses about being as loud, as small, as thin, as fat, and as short as you want.

After the video collage is done, Mark Childs singles out that Prozzäk song as emblematic of an emerging teen mentality that marketers have to be mindful of, a mentality he suggests was gestated and nurtured in other social settings, such as in schools and within the peer groups of the kids themselves. "Kids are really being encouraged to be who they are," remarks Childs. "We're seeing that a lot more in the schools, a lot more externally in the media ... The Prozzäk song probably puts it like the needle point on the target. Kids are being encouraged to be proud of who they are ... and I actually think that's going to have a role with the peers and the friendship groups, which are actually going to start to play a role that traditionally the family has played, in terms of supporting kids, acting like a support network."

For this particular audience—with their steno pads and Palm Pilots open, ready to receive the essential kernel of wisdom that will help them sell candy or soda pop more effectively—the point of Childs' philosophizing is likely that the new generation's acceptance of diversity, its veneration of individuality, can somehow be put to a pragmatic commercial purpose. For the rest of us, however, this portrait of a generation that's more inclined to use personal differences as the basis for creating a new form of family, rather than as the basis for exclusion or persecution, is—if it's true—big news, something on the order of the discovery of a cure for cancer. In a world riven by enduring tribal hatreds and ferocious nationalism made all the more powerful by the high-tech machinery of death, the emergence of a new kind of kid who accepts people who are different has to be seen as an encouraging prospect.

The idealist in me would like to believe that Childs has it right—that today's kids are more empathetic than they were in the past, and that this apparent ability to see the common humanity beneath surface differences is real, a harbinger of some new golden era of peace and understanding. As I look around me, that proposition seems to make some subjective sense. My own two kids attend school with children from a multitude of different religious, racial, and family backgrounds, and it seems, from what I've been able to observe, that these differences are mostly a non-issue for the kids at the school. (Then again, the playground is a notoriously impenetrable world for adults, so that rosy assessment may contain some wishful thinking.) But if those surface impressions, corroborated by the images of a harmoniously pluralistic cartoon kidsworld that now jump out of the electric box on Saturday mornings, do not deceive, then perhaps one can dare to believe that the current generation has moved beyond the racism, xenophobia, and general maliciousness that were rampant three or four decades ago—and that were the very definition of normal a century ago—and that, someday soon, this may have an impact on the wider world.

This outlandish idea, that kids are now being raised as more tolerant and peaceful creatures than in the past, stands up reasonably well when considered in light of some popular commentaries on the evolution of twentieth-century social attitudes. Current claims that video games and movies are turning kids into violence machines, for instance, inevitably assume that our society has deviated from some prior tradition of peacefulness and civility. Yet a backwards glance over the past hundred years shows that's not the case. I'm struck by Vance Packard's offhand remark, in The Hidden Persuaders, that "In earlier more innocent days, when the pressure was not on to build future consumers, the boys' magazines and their counterparts concentrated on training the young for the frontiers of production, including warfare."[6] Though Packard presents that contrast in order to decry what consumerism and the marketing machine had, by the 1950s, done to the young—making them connoisseurs of various brands of cola and cigarettes rather than toughening them up for the difficult tasks of life—perhaps the more frightening revelation contained in the statement is that, historically, the dominant purpose of children's play, and of the mythologies that children were fed through boys' magazines and the like, was to prepare them for the drudgery of the assembly line or a death in battle. (Even now, that remains the status quo in some countries outside the normal range of vision of the Western media. In countries like Sudan and the remote regions of Colombia, for instance, children in their early teens are commonly put into uniforms and given guns. Though in some cases they are coerced into becoming soldiers, in other cases it is the promise of excitement and prestige that draws them to the vocation of killing.)[7]

Those who argue that today's onslaught of media images has corrupted the young rarely measure the current reality against what our traditional acceptance of officially sanctioned, state-sponsored violence wrought in the past. While today's social critics agonize over what role the communications media may have played in incidents such as the Columbine and Jonesboro school massacres, our not-too-distant history contains examples of violence on a scale that dwarfs those tragic episodes. Less than a century ago, for instance, virtually an entire generation of young men in the British Commonwealth marched happily into the trenches of Europe to take their part in the mass slaughter known as the Great War. Thanks to the wonders of mechanized warfare, hundreds of young men would die at once in assaults on enemy lines. Survivors returned to civilian life burdened with the memories of comrades reduced to pulp and body parts in the soaking, disease-ridden trenches from which they waged war. And in a much clearer sense than is the case with massacres at Columbine or Jonesboro, cultural images were crucial to sustaining the bloodletting and inspiring the shooters. As Peter Buitenhuis shows in his incisive book *The Great War of Words*, what persuaded these young men to play their part in this hellish drama was a rousing propaganda effort, directed by government, but relying on the talents of the leading cultural figures of the day—artists who had a stature and influence similar to that of our present-day film, television, and recording stars.[8]

In the early twentieth century it was the masters of the printed word who were the superstars, and the writers secretly assembled by British propaganda minister C.F.G. Masterman were the aristocracy of their art form: Rudyard Kipling, H.G. Wells, Arthur Conan Doyle, Edith Wharton, G.K. Chesterton, and others. They approached their task of luring young men to battle with a Victorian sense of decorum and discretion. While today's media is accused of inciting violence by providing lurid spectacles that feed an animal bloodlust, these literary propagandists built their case for war using precisely the opposite techniques. They appealed to a sense of idealism and noble self-sacrifice, and they presented a sanitized portrait of the actual conduct of war. Another essential, propulsive ingredient added to this mix was an appeal to racial and national enmity. The enemy was portrayed as a barbaric, subhuman race, with the home team the sole hope for the survival of civilization.

"British authors," writes Buitenhuis, "soon created a propaganda myth which prevailed, in spite of all evidence to the contrary, until the end of the war. The Allies, they wrote, particularly Britain, had no responsibility for starting the war, which was a product of German militarism and lust for conquest. The Germans, Huns of ancient memory, left behind them in invaded territories a trail of ruins, blood and terror, murder and rapine. The French, on the other hand, the most urbane and civilized people in the history of the world, were defending their ancient homeland from enslavement. The plucky British army was filled with loyal and cheerful soldiers, enduring their rounds of trench duty without complaint."[9]

Most of the young men of the day—products of a much more insular world than our own—bought the story. They didn't suspect that the leading authors of their time were fictionalizing events by, among other things, inaccurately portraying Germany's invasion of Belgium at the start of the war as an orgy of murder and atrocity. Although there was considerable evidence, including a signed statement by six prominent American journalists on the scene, that widespread atrocities were not committed in Belgium by the Germans, the British government relied on a mood of national fervour and the flourishes of its fiction writers to persuade the public otherwise. "Very soon," writes Buitenhuis, "the invasion of Belgium became in the popular mind a chronicle of murder, rapine, pillage, arson, and wanton destruction ... In poster and report and appeal, Belgium is the raped and mutilated maiden, left to die."

Of course, the "demonization" of an enemy—the portrayal of a people as less than human, certainly less than civilized—is standard practice during wartime. It's a device that's essential to sustaining the hatred that fuels a war. But have subsequent generations developed some immunity to this appeal to hate their enemy? Have multiculturalism, the multi-channel universe, and cheap international travel created new generations of more cosmopolitan kids who are less vulnerable to the jingoistic disparagement of whole peoples?

In her book *The Hearts of Men*, American commentator Barbara Ehrenreich contemplates the Cold War counterpart to C.F.G. Masterman's campaign to airbrush the humanity out of Britain's First World War enemies.[9] Ehrenreich mines more downscale material to support her case—for instance, a Mickey Spillane gumshoe novel, whose hero, the hardbitten Mike Hammer, justifies having "killed more people tonight than I have fingers on my hands" on the grounds that "they were Communists. They were red sons-of-bitches who should have died long ago." Not people. Communists. In Ehrenreich's view, John Wayne movies and James Bond films served the purpose of defining America's enemies in the Soviet Union and countries under its influence as opponents who were never to be pitied and always to be feared. They were "formidable foes" whose deviousness was matched by their austere toughness, a muscularity of mind and body that posed an alarming counterpoint to an increasingly soft and complacent America. "Communism," writes Ehrenreich, "demanded ideological vigilance, crew cuts, and a talent for rigid self-control."

The eventual crumbling of that image of menace, Ehrenreich believes, came about partly because "we met the Communists in person. A total of 2.8 million Americans fought in Vietnam and perhaps a hundred million more watched the war on television … The enemy turned out to be women, the thinnest of youths, old men and children." Events like the My Lai massacre, where Vietnamese peasants (men, women, and children) were butchered and burned by a platoon of U.S. soldiers, served not only to discredit American foreign policy, but also to deflate the myth that the Cold War was a struggle against a towering enemy.

Television, whose reporters brought home much more of the reality of war than the First World War's newspaper scribes, whose access was carefully controlled and whose copy was heavily censored, may have had an impact, but Ehrenreich sees the new reluctance to take up arms stemming from a fundamental change of psychology wrought by the rise of consumer culture. She cites the work of David Riesman, who as far back as 1950 had drawn attention to the remaking of the American male as an "other directed" person. "In the past," writes Ehrenreich, summarizing the central hypothesis of Riesman's landmark treatise The Lonely Crowd, "industrial society had spawned 'inner directed' people, who followed a course set early in life by stern parental authorities. Once his internal 'psychic gyroscope' was set, the inner directed man was relatively immune to the cavilings or nudgings of peers. He tamed frontiers, built up cartels or madly pursued white whales—whatever his inner script dictated."

But this took a radical turn in the era of material abundance and mass marketing after the Second World War, as the quintessential 1950s "Organization Man" found himself toiling in complex bureaucratic environments and taking his behavioural cues from the celebrities and assorted authorities he watched on TV. For the white-collar, middle-class American male of this era, maintaining a place in this new world of comfort became increasingly dependent on his having the ability to divine the social dynamics of community and workplace, to read the feelings and attitudes of co-workers and friends. Thus the "other directed" male was born, with Ehrenreich using this label as a less-confrontational way of saying that American men were being feminized, since this trait of focusing on external demands lined up pretty well with women's traditional roles in Western culture as wives and mothers.

It was, however, just a first step. Ehrenreich goes on to connect the tightening embrace of consumer culture with an escalating erosion of the distinctions between the sexes—with the rise of the "androgynous" culture of the hippie movement in the 1960s, for instance, and the trend of the next decade, described by Charles Reich in his book *The Greening of America*, for American men to turn away from stoicism and embrace a certain sensual, epicurean approach to life. (Emblematic of this for Reich was the fact that the more varied flavour of wine gradually replaced the traditional antiseptic martini as the standard libation of the business lunch.)[10]

At every stage, the softening effects of living amid the abundant pleasures of consumerism have caused a great gnashing of teeth. Vance Packard's lament (which we encountered earlier) that advertising was turning Americans into "bundles of daydreams, misty hidden yearnings, guilt complexes [and] irrational emotional blockages," rather than autonomous, self-controlled individuals, shows that there was considerable anxiety about the remoulding of the national character even back in the 1950s. As the postwar economy was ramping up nicely, the creeping suspicion arose that the atmosphere of conformity created by a new economic reality was breeding men of hollow, insubstantial niceness—affable, easygoing guys with no moral centre or personal convictions. That was half a century ago, and the consumer society has not crumbled since then. Today there's a new generation of kids (or perhaps more accurately, a privileged section of a generation) who have not only been born into a world where the shopping mall is the focal point of life, but who are also the products of parents (and possibly grandparents) who themselves have known only this world dominated by the ethos of consumerism. They have no direct connection, therefore, to the pre-boom world where "character" was said to be bred by hardship and deprivation. Is it any wonder, then, that commentators from across the social and political spectrum continue to characterize the current generation as lacking in spine and inner strength? Right-wing preachers bluster about how an ungodly world is undermining kids' ability to live a life of virtue. Liberal social reformers, meanwhile, blame blanket marketing for making a generation of kids overweight, prone to violence, and unable to control their impulses.

In the face of this near-universal chorus of woe, Ehrenreich's suggestion that consumer culture has done the world a favour by making young men less warlike (or, at least, by making them less vulnerable to that Pavlovian reflex of heading off to a recruitment office the moment a brass band marches down their street) seems counterintuitive. Of course, many people will interpret this apparent immunity to the traditional demonization of one's national enemies as merely a lack of resolve, an inability to face up to duty and make a personal sacrifice for a cause. Commentators like Ehrenreich, on the other hand, see the historical moment when many young Americans felt empathy for the Vietnam War's distant victims as a positive omen on the road to an uncertain future.

Ehrenreich's more general contention that the consumer society—and the technological advances that have accompanied it—has changed the human psyche in positive ways seems to have resonated with a number of commentators since then. Some of them offer restrained, qualified readings of why we should be optimistic about where the current crop of kids is headed. Others are wild-eyed evangelists for the generation that's poised to, someday soon, take over the world.

Clearly in the latter category is Douglas Rushkoff, author of *Playing the Future: What We Can Learn from Digital Kids*.[11] For Rushkoff, the turn-of-the-millennium generation is living evidence that the rise of the other-directed mentality has been advancing at warp speed, aided by the personal computer and its telematic adjuncts. Following through on Reisman's mid-century observation that the close quarters of the modern, bureaucratic office space were gently nudging the American male away from his inner-directed stoicism, Rushkoff asserts that the microchip is now leading to a full-scale revolution, pushing humanity towards an evolutionary leap that spells the dissolution of individual identity as we know it.

"By devising mediated networks and an electronic communications infrastructure," he writes, "we human beings are ... constructing and participating as components in a new, highly networked
life-form." This is sure to sound sinister to many, the foreshadowing
of a Borg-like future in which human beings are reduced to bits of
data on a hard drive, existing only to be manipulated by some larger
intelligence. Rushkoff, however, doesn't see it that way. The main
characteristics he associates with this "highly networked life-form"
of the electronic era are the abilities to negotiate differences and to
deal with uncertainty and complexity.

Kids have apparently got a head start on both these tasks. Most
of *Playing the Future* is devoted to explaining how a gigantic range of
current youth-culture artifacts, some of them dreaded, reviled, or
ridiculed by adults—"house" music, Japanese anime, role-playing
games like Magic or Dungeons and Dragons, *Teletubbies, Beavis and Butt-
head*, Jackie Chan, snowboarding, e-mail, body piercing, Goth culture—serve as instruments to help young people adapt to a world
where the tidal waves of information that flow through daily life
reassemble themselves into random, non-linear patterns that pretty
much define chaos. Apart from an afterthought about how the hor-
rors of Bosnia might be proving him wrong, there are few suggestions in this determinedly utopian book that kids' responses to
a technologically remodelled world can be anything but positive.
Rather than viewing youth culture with fear and trepidation, advises Rushkoff, adults should be prepared to absorb its valuable lessons and to seek guidance from a generation that is "less in danger
of becoming obsolete" than its elders.

Rushkoff finds encouragement even in areas where health professionals express great concern. This is based on his belief that adults
often mistake kids' innovation for dysfunction. For example, Rushkoff audaciously reinterprets higher incidences of attention deficit
disorder (ADD)—which is commonly used as a marker of how
excessive use of television and other electronic media is damaging
kids—as evidence of a superior, more rational approach to living
in an information-surfeit society. In response to those critics who
would have it that TV's rapid-paced editing has eroded kids' ability
to concentrate, Rushkoff counters that "the ability to piece together

meaning from a discontinuous set of images is the act of a higher intellect, not a lower one. Moreover, the child with the ability to pull himself out of an argument while it is in progress, re-evaluate its content and relevance, and then either recommit or move on, is a child with the ability to surf the modern mediaspace." If these kids appear antsy, then so be it. The impatience that kids bring to media consumption, asserts Rushkoff, is in practical terms a positive trait. It shows that they are less vulnerable to being propagandized than their more docile parents, the "well-behaved viewers" who Rush-koff derides for being easily led, step by step, through linear arguments that have been constructed in such a way that they compel the viewer to swallow them whole.

Rushkoff doesn't even bother trying to offer empirical proof for his hypotheses, and in shucking that burden he leaves himself free to offer outrageous, anti-conventional ideas based on a series of random and abstract associations. For example, he claims snowboarding (and its urban counterpart, skateboarding) illustrates how a younger generation is adapting to a world of discontinuity by embracing that world's apparent chaos rather than denying it. How does Rushkoff know this to be true? Because snowboarding operates on the same kinds of principles as the cutting-edge mathematics that revolves around fractal equations. Rushkoff explains that while traditional mathematics allows human beings to map out reality in ways that are linear and direct ("like charting the forces acting on a wheel or a space shuttle"), fractals promise greater understanding of systems that are dynamic, discontinuous, and chaotic (the topography of a mountain, for instance, or the way the weather works). Here we are asked to make a synaptic leap with Rushkoff, who explains that the difference between traditional mathematics and fractal math is like the difference between traditional downhill skiing and the gonzo art of the snowboarder. While the old-style ladies and gentlemen of the slopes make symmetrical, predictable patterns on smooth and well-groomed surfaces, the scruffy snowboarder "seeks out the most dangerous nooks and crannies ... Snowboarding is about finding breaks in otherwise smooth terrain, and thrashing them for everything they are worth."

So now it's crystal clear, isn't it? A kid on a snowboard heading down a rough hill at breakneck speed is intuitively giving a middle-finger salute to traditional Western mathematics and our assumptions about the laws of physics. If you still doubt the connection, consider Rushkoff's revelation that a fractal equation translates, in visual form, to the kind of pulsing, organic design that was popular at raves in the early 1990s. And that's got to mean something.

Not all of Rushkoff's arguments require the reader to take such dramatic leaps of faith. Analyzing the steadily increasing popularity of complex fantasy role-playing (FRP) games—a movement descended from the infamous Dungeons and Dragons craze that allowed math-club geeks to master imaginary civilizations—Rushkoff finds enough signposts in the recent history of North America to construct a credible explanation of their importance in the lives of large numbers of kids. The youth-culture guru views these and other post-hippie, post-punk cultural expressions (like Goth music and dress, and the cult appeal of Hong Kong martial arts films) as a double-sided response to the realities of growing up in a world dominated by technology—a force that has plunged previous generations into deep malaise, given its power to discredit pre-existing intellectual paradigms and obliterate more sentimental cultural mythologies. Rushkoff believes FRP games are an attempt to strike a balance between the need to satisfy the demands that technology makes of humans born into the wired world, and the need to replace part of what the technological onslaught has destroyed. On one hand, these games require the mathematical acumen, concentration, and steel-trap mind of an accomplished computer programmer. They can therefore be seen as a kind of vocational training, preparing kids to take on a role in the techno-economy in much the same way that Packard saw traditional games preparing the young for a life (and perhaps death) in the factory or the army. On the other hand, FRP games are played out on a "magical landscape of goblins, wizards, brutes, dragons and damsels" drawn from "Arthurian and Tolkienesque mythology," which refer back to a pre-technological world where enchantment and mystery had not yet become obsolete. In that respect, such games promise a potent antidote to the mechanistic outlook of today's world, where machines—and the logic they represent—dominate human beings and the natural world that spawned them. In essence, these games attempt to reassert the idea of life governed by spirit, not mechanics.

Rushkoff also notes that FRP games can function as a form of personal therapy for the players. Most of these games require that the players manipulate characters who have definite, yet sometimes subtle, personality traits. The characters can have awe-inspiring strengths (which often involve magical powers), but they are also afflicted with weaknesses and blind spots. Often a player cannot increase the characters' valuable attributes without a corresponding increase in their personal deficits. When a game (which can sometimes last for days) is in progress, the players must act within character. And this, says Rushkoff, allows kids to use the game to try on new personalities, to see the world through other eyes, and to gain insight into the human condition as it's lived by people (and other types of creatures) who inhabit a diversely populated world. The games also facilitate moral education, Rushkoff contends, by giving players the opportunity to observe how different actions and moral outlooks affect events and conditions in the artificial world of the game.

Rushkoff's appraisal is that participating in these role-playing sagas is just one way kids have chosen to engage with a world of greater flux and uncertainty, and it's a decidedly different route than previous generations have chosen. While the postwar baby boomers accommodated a much more volatile social reality by taking solace in conspiracy theories and sometimes-authoritarian New Age religions (approaches that cast the individual in a more passive role, says Rushkoff), their offspring have gravitated to cultural forms (like FRP) that enable them to navigate their way through the uncertainty, to learn as they go along. The whole point is to acquire the tools to deal with the world they now inhabit, a world of multiple identities and the constant surprises that come from ever-more-frequent leaps in our technological capacities. Of the game Magic, a card game developed in 1993 by mathematician Richard Garfield, which has since become a mainstream cultural artifact, Rushkoff writes: "It combines an ancient spiritual aesthetic, a highly mathematical combat sequence, a free market collecting/trading strategy, and a broad-based, non-prejudicial social scheme." It therefore provides just about everything you need to get by in the chaos of the early twenty-first century: a means of escape from the monolithic mentality of the technological establishment; the mental/intellectual tools to survive within that technologically dominated society; a metaphor that gives some understanding of the current global economic system; and a social paradigm that accommodates people of different cultures, backgrounds, and outlooks who co-exist on the same landscape.

Magic, as it turns out, is something I have a passing familiarity with, although that's not at all a result of my own curiosity. As I write this, a group of my sons' friends are playing a game of Magic at a rather disconcerting decibel level in an adjacent room. Most of them are aged ten and eleven, so they don't play for as long a stretch or with the kind of Jungian sensibility that Rushkoff ascribes to older, more seasoned players. Like Rushkoff, I'm impressed by several aspects of the game, such as its complexity and its demands for concentration and mathematical skills. My son Ben tried to explain it to me a few weeks ago, but I was lost. Despite his almost patronizingly patient tone and his willingness to repeat himself as much as necessary, my overtaxed, forty-something grey matter was simply unable to calculate how that labyrinthine collection of qualities and powers would play out in a game. He dealt me a hand of cards and proceeded to whup my collection of beasts and wizards, though I don't have the slightest inkling how he did it.

But in spite of admiring the tenacity and mental nimbleness these games require, I'm still put off by the central role of the "battles" in Magic contests and by the gruesome imagery on many of the cards. When Rushkoff speaks approvingly of the "broad-based, non-prejudicial social scheme" of the game, the implication is that the object of encounters in this fantasy cosmos is to make friends, to prosper by working together. In reality, the point is to understand your opponents so you can annihilate them (much as it is in the ornate yet bloodthirsty world of Tolkien, which is accepted as classic literature). I cringed the other day when a friend of my son advised, "What you've got to do is kill all those stupid wood elves." When I talked to my son about how disquieting I find the violent undertones of this game, he seemed surprised I didn't understand that none of it is real. "Dad," he responded, spitting the words out slowly so I'd understand, "it's a very educational game. You have to think through your strategy. And the violence is just something we ignore." Though that made rational sense to me, I still haven't accommodated this reasoning at a gut level. Having been introduced to Magic cards with names like Faceless Butcher, Chainer, Dementia Master, and Pestilence (which, to be fair, are the exceptions—many of the cards play on rather pastoral themes), I marvel at the power of the purveyors of youth-culture artifacts to freak out fresh crops of parents who, a few years earlier, thought they had cornered the market on freaking out their own parents.

†

As admiring of the current generation as Douglas Rushkoff—but for entirely different reasons—is David Brooks, conservative author of the acclaimed study of Clinton-era boomers, *Bobos in Paradise*, and more recently his homage to suburbia, *On Paradise Drive*. In between these books, Brooks wrote about turn-of-the-millennium college kids for the *Atlantic Monthly*.[12] Though he and Rushkoff both adopt a respectful, appreciative tone, in substance they are worlds apart. Partly this is a matter of focus. Many experts in the field talk about how post-1960s generations tend to divide themselves into distinct "tribes," and these two commentators have clearly chosen two very different tribal groups to lead them to the truth. So while Rushkoff sees the in-your-face ambassadors of fringe culture (snowboarders and Goths, for example) as emblematic of a generation's collective ability to leapfrog beyond conventional wisdom, Brooks believes the vast majority of today's youngsters are simply too busy to bother with body piercing, boarding, or fantastical journeys … and are of far too practical a frame of mind to be interested in any case.

While Rushkoff portrays a generation that has embraced and come to understand chaos and flux, Brooks found a group of kids whose outlook on life has been conditioned by a sense of structure and certainty unknown to previous generations. The wider world may be a place of turmoil, but the personal worlds of the emerging generation are models of order and predictability, governed by a compulsive self-discipline that's been instilled over the years by legions of determined daycare workers, soccer coaches, and fastidious parents. Some of the college students Brooks talked to remain so tightly scheduled, what with all their studying, volunteer commitments, and organized sports, that conversations with friends have to be pencilled into their daytimers. And while conventional wisdom once had it that the first task of college students is to break free from the yoke of parental authority, this generation, in Brooks's account, seems to be defying the laws of nature by continuing to strive to meet their parents' expectations and to uphold the parental worldview. Brooks does concede that the sample group he has chosen to put under the microscope (students at Princeton University, an elite group, which the writer refers to as "the next ruling class") is hardly representative of an entire culture. Yet he also insists that there have been some sweeping, crosscutting forces at work that make the basic outline of his theory applicable throughout society.

The genesis of what Brooks calls "the organization kid" can be traced back to the revolution in child-rearing practices that took place in the early 1980s, right around the time the current crop of university undergraduates was being born. At that point the defining idea of permissive postwar parenting—that children are born innocent and good, and that they should be given the space to realize their own innate potential, free from the corrupting influence of adult control—was rapidly falling out of vogue. What replaced it was a biological paradigm (as opposed to a spiritual or a psychological one) largely concerned with how the brains and associated wiring of young humans develop and grow, and what can be done to help the process along. In essence, this is a model that sees kids as programmable, perfectible. Its central message is that, with the right kind of stimuli and a range of enriching experiences, parents can set their kids up for a lifetime of fulfillment and boundless achievement.

Most of the people born after that philosophical shift in the early 1980s have likely experienced a number of its consequences at various stages of their lives. The process generally begins not long after baby comes back from the hospital, with parents being encouraged to unlock their wee one's inner genius by piping Mozart into the crib, and to make use of new lines of educational toys that have sprung up to jumpstart junior's understanding of language and spatial relationships.

Brooks sees the vast changes that have been made to the U.S. educational system (along with similar changes enacted in Canada) as a response to the entry into grade school of that first wave of hyper-programmed kids. The mid-1980s ushered in what Brooks refers to as "the big backpack era," the hallmarks of which have been the assignment of increasingly onerous levels of homework and the dismantling of the child-centred educational reforms of the 1960s and 70s in favour of a new emphasis on order, authority, a rigorous curriculum, and formalized testing. Within this regimen, kids are expected to sit still and cram their brains. When they can't, the pharmaceutical solution (the dispensing of large quantities of Ritalin, since eclipsed by the arrival of antidepressants like Prozac) seems to be the preferred means of making them get with the program. After school, meanwhile, just hanging out has been supplanted by a range of organized activities that cost lots of money and often take place on well-manicured fields. Parents' engagement with their kids' vocational training and leisure activities tends to continue through the teenage years (which, according to other commentators, is not necessarily a good thing).[13] Partly, says Brooks, this is because parents remain concerned about safety issues. It can also be understood, even though Brooks doesn't mention this, as a reaction by parents to memories of their own adolescent excess back in the decadent 60s and 70s.

This journey through the life cycle of the post-countercultural kid leads Brooks to describe the youngster of the early twenty-first century as "the most honed and supervised generation in human history. If they are group oriented, deferential to authority, and achievement-obsessed, it is because we achievement-besotted adults have trained them to be."

Generally, Brooks is not unhappy with the results. He describes the young people he's met as personable, polite, industrious, and optimistic. Growing up in the wake of the civil rights movement and the rise of feminism, they seem to have rejected much of the racism, sexism, and restrictive social categorization that was embedded in previous generations. They generally shun debauchery and embrace the spirit of voluntarism. They respect and like their parents and professors.

Yet one disquieting feature of this group portrait is the sense that today's kids are overwhelmingly passive. Those commentators of the 1950s who raised the alarm that mass society was robbing Americans of their independence, dampening the fires of their personal convictions, would be positively spooked to see what's become of the generation born in the waning years of the twentieth century. Far from continuing the American tradition of the "rugged individualist," they more resemble the breed of Japanese technocrat that powered that country's economic ascent after the Second World War. Motivated by the promise of escalating prosperity and a certain esprit de corps, they've put their shoulders to the wheel, but apparently also put aside many of the questions of conscience that preoccupied their forebears. This generation can process massive amounts of information but seems unwilling to question its elders' convictions. Protest, for example, was a rare occurrence on the campuses that Brooks visited, a fact that he and others see as natural for a generation that has never experienced the military draft or a devastating economic downturn, two primary forces that have driven young people in the past to question those who were running the show.[14] Mostly, though, he believes this reluctance to rock the boat is explained by the more mundane reality that today's students are too busy to involve themselves with issues outside their immediate sphere. Brooks quotes one journalism student who, irony of ironies, doesn't have time to read newspapers.

There are strong echoes of Brooks's argument in the work of Neil Howe and William Strauss, authors of *Millennials Rising*, an unrelentingly optimistic book that also celebrates the apparently conservative, civic-minded values of today's youth.[15] Unlike Brooks, who discerns a lack of moral fervour in today's youth,[16] the duo can find no Achilles heel to diminish their enthusiasm for this generation-on-the-move. These aren't just good, well-intentioned kids, write Howe and Strauss (who seem completely unafraid of drifting into hyperbole), "but a new force of history, a generational colossus far more consequential than most of today's parents and teachers (and indeed, most kids) dare imagine." They see in this demographic "tsunami" many of the same specific traits noted by Brooks: they are optimistic, oriented towards group activities, highly accepting of their parents' values systems and behavioural edicts, only minimally conscious of race, and generally intolerant of rule-breakers. But while Brooks accounts for these qualities by focusing mainly on that sudden shift in child-rearing strategies, Strauss and Howe look to more far-reaching historical forces to explain the current generation's sudden detour onto the straight and narrow. Here the authors extrapolate from a theme they developed in their previous books, *Generations* and *The Fourth Turning*. In those works they proposed that social/cultural epochs are created by predictable cyclical reactions. One generation with a specific ethical outlook yields to a new generation, whose replacement worldview attempts to compensate for its predecessors' perceived shortcomings or excesses.

Howe and Strauss have apparently worked out the details of their theory to the point that they are able to predict the tenor of an approaching era by observing the behaviour of the generation that's headed into decline. "We found," Howe explained to an interviewer in 1991, following the publication of *Generations*, "that every generation belongs to one of four life-cycle types that seems to repeat in the same order over time. The appearance of young war heros is almost always followed by the appearance of a young generation that appears indecisive and conformist to others. The appearance in history of passionate young moralists is always followed by a generation which appears wild and uneducated to elders."[17] In its most recent manifestations, Howe's template seems to describe the toppling of the Second World War GI by the 1950s Organization Man, and the 1960s flower child by the disaffected drifter of Generation X.

Their conviction that any new generation will veer away from the course set out by its elders, rather than following the established trajectory, is the basis of Howe and Strauss's explanation why many millennials appear to have forsaken the prevailing post-60s culture of sex, drugs, and rock and roll—which they believe is a positive trend. "There's a revolution under way among today's kids—a good news revolution," write Howe and Strauss, with all the fervour of revivalist preachers begging for a chorus of hallelujahs. "This generation is going to rebel by behaving not worse, but better. Their life mission will not be to tear down old institutions that don't work, but to build up new ones that do. Look closely at youth indicators and you'll see that Millennial attitudes and behaviours represent a sharp break from Generation X, and are running exactly counter to trends launched by the Boomers." To wit, levels of violence in schools are down, and kids are telling pollsters that they dislike selfishness and have confidence in themselves (although poll responses, arguably, might better demonstrate how kids want themselves to be perceived, rather than how they actually behave). Even their taste in movies has changed. Howe and Strauss maintain that one of the big surprises for the Gen Xers and boomers who write movie scripts and run Hollywood studios is that the emerging generation has overwhelmingly rejected gross-out comedies and R-rated cinema, preferring to spend their seven or eight bucks on uplifting, moralistic movies like *Pearl Harbor* and *Harry Potter* (not that the teen audience did *Pearl Harbor* much good at the box office).[18]

Howe and Strauss represent the most glowing, most extreme variant of a school of thought that states kids today are in much better shape than their parents were at their ages. As a group, they are less violent, more sociable, harder working, and more accepting of diversity. They have cast off the cynicism of generations that came before them. Howe and Strauss see the horror that was Columbine, for instance, as a hangover from the dark musings of Generation X, an anachronistic aberration that signifies what the millennials have cast off rather than what they are. For this is a generation with a sense of purpose and optimism—the generation that will solve the world's problems.

The problem with such rosy appraisals—from the perspective of anti–kid-marketing/media campaigners—is that even if only some of the enthusiasm is warranted, such optimism tends to undermine the idea that a saturation-marketing environment has destroyed kids' experience of life. Some of the commentary summarized in this chapter (that of David Brooks, Neil Howe, and William Strauss) suggests that social factors such as child-rearing practices, social norms, the demands of the economy, or even cyclical intergenerational struggles are so important (and recently have been so positive) that they make the impact of marketing and media almost irrelevant. For others (that is, Douglas Rushkoff) communications media have played a formative and positive role in pushing kids towards a new evolutionary phase that's fitting for the times. We've also sampled thoughts from a handful of commentators, writing earlier in the twentieth century, who saw the rise of marketing-driven, materialistic, consumer culture as ambiguous in its effects. Barbara Ehrenreich, for example, corrals a wide range of punditry that suggested living in the commercialized, ad-centric culture that so disturbed Packard may make people more sympathetic to others, less reflexively militaristic, more accepting and open in their outlook.

In short, this small and random sampling of opinion tells us that there has never been consensus on where a particular generation of kids is headed and what this might mean for the wider arc of history. One person's signpost on the road to utopia is another's omen of imminent collapse. This instructs us, at the very least, to beware of commentators whose view of the current youth zeitgeist is unambiguous and overly self-confident. We might also want to remain skeptical of those who pin the particular attributes of a generation on one specific element of the environment that surrounds them (all right, let's not be coy: you know that in this context we are referring to the marketing machine and its adjuncts in the mass media).

The zeal with which arguments about kids' role in society are presented also raises questions about what should be considered foreground and what background in this complex set of debates. People who write about the state of kids invariably insist that the centre of their work is a concern for the wellbeing of the young and vulnerable. Certainly there are real and pernicious threats to the welfare of children, and these must surely remain a prime concern for a civilized society. But popular assessments of the state of the young inevitably require consideration of some broader processes of social transformation—for example, the introduction of new technologies, the implementation of new economic arrangements, the evolution of social attitudes—processes that affect children and adults equally, and that children have had little role in creating.

So perhaps, in order to understand these competing theories about what social change is doing to kids, we need to move kids slightly out of the foreground and scrutinize more carefully *who* is promoting these theories, what their underlying assumptions are, and what kind of symbolic statement their view of youth culture makes about the state of society in general. That's what we'll attempt to do in the next chapter.

CHAPTER 6
Children of Change

Peter Silsbee is contemplating the troublesome chasm between those two competing views of the current generation and its place in the world—between the one that says today's kids are destined for glory, and the other, which portrays them as damned to a life without values and human feeling, trapped in a commercialized culture where temptations abound and the meter is always running. The author of a string of children's books in the 1980s, Silsbee took refuge in the world of market research when his literary career came into conflict with his desire to keep paying the rent. A decade or so later, he finds himself surveying the kid cultural scene from his lofty perch as director of the youth division of Harris Interactive, a prestigious American polling firm whose most high-profile work has included the Kidpulse and Youthpulse online surveys for Nickelodeon and MTV. In his view, neither the glowingly optimistic nor the bleakly desperate version of the state of today's kids really describes the way young people experience life nor sheds much light on how the adult world can help lighten their load as they continue on the tumultuous journey to adulthood. Both of those narratives, Silsbee believes, are based on adult overreaction, and both of them fail to deal with the specific circumstances that have shaped the world kids find themselves living in.

The more negative portrait of youth—the one that says kids are all being warped by Eminem and video games and are clearly on the road to ruin—is the default position of the adult world. It's at least as old as James Dean's brooding, nihilist thrill-seeker in *Rebel Without a Cause* or Marlon Brando's leather-jacketed hood in *The Wild One*. This perspective (which inevitably sees the younger generation as hurtling towards the abyss) is so entrenched that when contradictory statistics came out showing declines in the rates of teen violence, drug use, and pregnancy in the 1990s, the good news was easily undermined by a few well-placed news stories that played on adults' established, archetypal fears. Silsbee believes that, as a culture, we're primed to expect bad news about kids.

"If marijuana use ticks up by one or two percentage points, which is often within the margin of error for these types of surveys, we instantly get these headlines about increased marijuana use," says Silsbee, sitting in his Manhattan office, where he's devoted a big chunk of one morning to reflecting on the larger themes that have emerged from his company's inquiries into the minutia of life as a kid. "And then the media feels they have to talk about the moral fibre of this generation—they are compelled to." Not that the motives of the news media and their readers aren't often noble ones. The reason that the public's ears perk up whenever a government agency releases numbers on how likely young people are to smoke, take drugs, contract a sexually transmitted disease, or experience violence, Silsbee believes, is simply that people care about what happens to kids.

"I understand why people use kids as a kind of flashpoint for discussion," he says. "We can't seem to agree on much in terms of where the United States is going as a society, but we do understand that kids are some kind of special population, and that the choices we make as adults will have an impact on them and that we should probably be pretty careful about those choices." But at the same time, this constant emphasis on the behavioural flaws of young people means that "what's communicated to kids is that we don't trust them, that we have this kind of hysterical perspective of them, that in some ways we are afraid of them."

In essence, Silsbee believes that young people have been designated as what some sociologists call a "hot minority," which means that they are thought of as "not rational, often immoral, and not able to think for themselves. Similarly," he relates, "women were often characterized as a 'hot minority' before they began to get some political clout—they couldn't be trusted to drive a car or a boat. And Black Americans have always been characterized that way." As was the case with the other groups, putting this tag on youth is unfair. "It's true that kids don't have quite the intellectual skills, quite the maturity—their brains haven't developed as fully as someone who is twenty-one or twenty-two—but most of them are pretty smart, and they sort of see the world for what it is, given where they are in their lives."

Recently, though, that standard image of a younger generation on the road to damnation has been, as we saw in the last chapter, subject to some re-evaluation. A few experts have spun around 180 degrees, pushing the idea that the post-Gen-X crowd is some kind of sainted generation, a breakthrough in the evolution of humanity. To Silsbee, however, this new stereotype is as unreal as that obsolescent image of the dim, untrustworthy slacker—an absurd overcompensation and an image applied so broadly that it has virtually no meaning. He recalls a National Public Radio broadcast he heard a while back, which had gathered together "some youth experts at an auditorium in a high school somewhere in the Midwest. I think it was Iowa. One of the experts was saying that this is the most optimistic generation of kids ever, and then he went on, in great heights of hyperbole, to say that this was going to be the new greatest generation. They were going to be greater than 'the Greatest Generation,' which is Tom Brokaw's characterization of the people who came of age during the Second World War." Silsbee rejects both aspects of that comparison, however, partly because the premise that generations have their own intrinsic qualities is unprovable, and partly because it serves to diss the other generations which haven't been anointed as the saviours of civilization.

"That phrase [The Greatest Generation] is something I thoroughly object to," he says. "It's as if the generation that came after or came before wouldn't have reacted in a similar fashion given that set of circumstances" (i.e., finding themselves in the middle of a world war). Still, while he professes to be "skeptical of this whole notion of a generation having a certain gestalt," Silsbee does allow that individual generations appear to have some distinct characteristics, which he believes are mostly outgrowths of the way kids relate to the technology that's contemporaneous with their own growing up. But to read these minor variants as the markers of some broader, more intrinsic characteristics, he believes, would be a mistake.

"I think we do a disservice," says Silsbee, "when we pull kids out of society and look at them as a special case, because kids are firmly encased in society. They are perhaps the most firmly encased population because they have very little political clout—they have only the political clout of their parents—and they have very little sense of the history of things that came before them." In other words, kids remain fluid and flexible, dedicated, for the most part, to the timeless struggle (faced by all those who went before them) of trying to cope with the day-to-day demands of a social environment over which they have little influence.

And with this pivotal piece of reasoning (that kids are one with their social environment, not something apart from it), Silsbee neatly turns the logic of most youth-culture commentators on its head. Most of the pundits I've heard or read attempt to explain how social reality has crafted a new kind of kid (which is a more commercially rewarding proposition, because if you can convince the adult world that kids are a different breed of being that speaks a different language, you can sell those adults a method for communicating with those kids, either as customers or as family members). Silsbee, however, has reversed that equation. He's more interested in how the behaviour and attitudes of youth shed light on how our society is put together. In a sense, he sees kids as the canaries in a coal mine. If there are things that disturb us about youth culture, it is a sign of something amiss in the world that adults have created for all of us to live in. We're all bound up in a complex kind of feedback loop—or maybe a house of mirrors—within which it's pointless to look at the lives of the young without being prepared to scrutinize where the rest of society is at.

Those who are skeptical of the kid-focused media/marketing complex will dismiss such an approach as the rationalization of a person who's protecting his profession. Critics of the industry concentrate on the traits of youth in order to shed light on the impact of a commercial establishment that's acquired more influence over each succeeding generation, captivating the minds of progressively younger kids. Silsbee is pointing the finger elsewhere, those critics might say, to deflect criticism from the companies for which Harris Interactive conducts polls. As a collector of information that will wind up in the hands of corporations like the one that runs Nickelodeon and MTV, he's far from a neutral observer.

Well, fair enough, Peter Silsbee does have a stake in the issue, but then again, so does just about everybody else whose opinions get quoted on this matter, from the right-wing think tanks who use angst about kids to drum up support for their political program of returning society to "traditional" values, to the liberal media critics and academics whose access to funding dollars and microphones similarly depends on their ability to keep a controversy boiling. In a strange way, Silsbee is more of a free agent than those players because his job description involves telling his clients what kids' lives are like, who they are, and how they think, rather than toeing an ideological line. That's one reason I'm not inclined to write off Silsbee's opinions simply on the basis of where his paycheque comes from. Another reason is that his conclusions are far enough out of sync with both sides in this debate that it's difficult to think of him as some industry flack or apologist. Silsbee's background also suggests that his motivations are not mercenary in origin, that he didn't come to the field in order to exploit kids.

Market research, in fact, was an accidental career choice. "I always planned to be a writer, but I had to make a buck," explains Silsbee, whose combination of rumpled, bearded bohemianism and business suit speak to the dual strands of his career. Actually, his literary ambitions stayed on track long enough for Silsbee to publish four children's books, two of which are pseudonymous tomes, "which I'm not very proud of and I don't really talk about," he says. The other two, however, were distinguished examples of a new movement in young adult fiction that dealt head-on with the tougher issues many kids face during adolescence. *The Big Way Out*, a story about a boy's attempts to deal with his father's mental illness and threatening behaviour, was published by Dell in 1987. Three years later, Bradbury Press (famous for being Judy Blume's first publisher) brought out Silsbee's *The Temptation of Kate*, in which the devil "fights for the soul of a young girl troubled by her parents' divorce and by a recent move from New York City to the country," according to a summary posted on the Internet by a California library.

Both books were part of a genre that Silsbee, borrowing a phrase from fellow Bradbury author Paula Fox, characterizes as "bitter-coated sugar pills." "Those books served a kind of therapeutic function," he says, "since they gave children a chance to understand that they were not alone in a particularly difficult situation. That was the 70s and the 80s [when this literary movement began] and there were vast social changes in America. Most tellingly, divorce rates were skyrocketing, and a lot of books tried to treat that theme of family breakups. They often laid out very difficult situations, but essentially, at the end, some kindly adult or perhaps someone in the therapeutic community would step in and kind of set things right. I think I was firmly on the side of the kids, who I saw as often trapped in circumstances beyond their control and having to fight their way out of it."

The author, however, found himself in a financial "difficult situation" of his own, the effects of which he offset by taking part-time work in market research. In the 1980s, a friend who worked for a research firm contracted Silsbee to transcribe tapes of focus group sessions, and he'd sit at his new computer (having just made the leap out of the typewriter age) and transpose kids' thoughts onto the printed page. "It was a way to fund myself while I wrote a book, and I sort of found it interesting," he recalls. "It actually gave me an idea for my third book, the one about Satan, where I used transcripts as a device to report on the goings-on of a committee meeting down in hell."

One thing led to another. Finding there was a big demand for writers who could breathe some life into dry research reports, he took a job with a company called Research and Forecasts. In 1993

Silsbee moved to the more influential Roper Starch outfit and by 1999 had worked his way up to vice-president. After that he moved over to become youth director at Harris Interactive. In some ways this was an alien world, one in which people were unprepared to ask the kind of probing, get-to-the-heart-of-the-matter questions that had been his stock-in-trade as an author. Travelling to various youth marketing conferences, Silsbee was dissatisfied with what he saw as business's unidimensional, stereotypical way of looking at kids, although he was also unimpressed by the counterview advanced by the opposition.

"What I began to discover was that people had blinders on," he says. "Many of them couldn't think beyond 'I've got a company that makes things for kids and I have to understand kids only to the extent that I can get them interested in my product.' And then, of course, you have the people on the other side—the hygienic forces, if you will—who are constantly measuring kids and trying to figure out what's wrong with them, why they are smoking, why they are eating ... I saw that kids were being pulled in two different directions and I thought, 'I've got to get a larger perspective on this.'"

So Silsbee began to read widely, trying to find a context that would make numbers from his surveys more meaningful. Not that this would be a great chore for a guy who seems too bookish to work in an adjunct of pop culture manufacturing. He reports, for instance, that he doesn't have cable TV at home, and one of his favourite pastimes is writing book reviews (to send to his friends) on his Palm Pilot while riding the subway to work from Brooklyn. In conversation he seems the farthest thing from a marketing guy, peppering his conversation with references to the likes of Max Weber, Jürgen Habermas, and Alan Wolfe—academics who inhabit an entirely different universe from the one where you will find the sales forces of Mattel or the WWE.

In print, as well, he makes you wonder what he's trying to do: push product or re-engineer the reader's view of the world. For example, in "The Marketer's Field Guide to the Past," which was published on the website of the Zyman Marketing Group, Silsbee examines why the allure of "brand new" products has given way to the appeal of all things "old." His examples range from George Lucas's counterintuitive success with the movie *American Graffiti* to Ronald Reagan's construction of a winning political platform based on resurrected, reconstructed memories of a more innocent past, and on to Martha Stewart's creation of a media empire based on the vision of an idealized, 1950s-style domesticity that never existed. Whether marketers find practical use for all this seems secondary; first and foremost, Silsbee's examination of the notion of nostalgia functions as social commentary. His point is to debunk the myths contained in those images, to make plain the fact that nostalgia is fiction. Through repetition, he says, the mythmakers have established in the public mind a kind of shorthand within which the 1950s have come to be associated with the values of community and social conformity, and the 1960s represent the quest for individuality and freedom. But in reality, Silsbee reminds us, "the polarized meanings of these decades have less to do with their actual history, and more to do with the clarity this binary opposition provides in describing a persistent and pervasive historical split-mindedness in American culture." After accomplishing what a media literacy teacher might hope to do—that is, to impart some understanding of how cultural myths are made—the attempt to give some point-form "implications" for marketing professionals seems tacked on, an afterthought, or perhaps a half-hearted nod to the necessity of paying the piper.

In total, Silsbee seems like a bit of a heretic, which is why he's getting substantial ink here. He seems disinclined to buy into orthodoxies. He's fairly direct about the fact, for instance, that he simply doesn't believe many of the assertions that are taken as gospel by marketing people. As an example, he cites the oft-repeated chorus about the current generation being masters of "multitasking." In essence, that's just a myth created to help sell multimedia ad campaigns.

"I don't mean to belittle people who say that technology changes the way that people see the world," explains Silsbee. "I think that's true. But we hear all the time about how this generation has the genetic ability to do all kinds of things at the same time, which I find, frankly, laughable. I think we are all able to multitask within our own technological construct. Let me give you an example. When my father and mother used to drive us around, there was never any food in the car. We'd go to McDonald's, and we'd get out and eat, but we were never driving around and eating. Then I began to drive a car, and I'd usually have a soda and drink that, and maybe eat some fries. And be playing with the radio. A few years later I got a cellphone. And pretty soon, here I was in my car, and I had this total environment, and I'd be hurtling down the thruway at 75 miles an hour, talking on the phone, with the radio on, drinking a soda … Wasn't I multitasking? And in the middle of all that activity, I was bored. I was actually able to drive this vehicle at this hair-raising speed, and somehow my body had became so acclimated to the challenges of that, that it seemed unremarkable to me.

"Young people are described now as multitasking because they may be online while at the same time they are watching TV, they have a magazine open, and they may have a CD on. But they are not somehow genetically different. It's not a new species being formed. It's just that there's this tremendous avalanche of new technological spaces that they inhabit with much more familiarity than we do, so we look at them as if they are different."

There was the same maverick sensibility—this willingness to ig-nore conventional wisdom and to reference more than the standard sources—reverberating through Silsbee's presentation in Toronto at the Understanding Youth confab, which is where I first became aware of his approach. Silsbee's presentation was called "Jane and Joe Tweenager Meet the New Time-Space Continuum," and it was essentially an attempt to map out the broader features of the terrain that today's kids live on, to put their lives in a broader social con-text. His assessment was partly drawn from the kind of nuts-and-bolts data collected by Harris Interactive in one of its typical sur-veys: How big is an average kid's bedroom? How many electronic gadgets does it contain? How do kids spend their time? How often do they see their parents? Yet Silsbee went beyond sketching out the spatial, temporal parameters of the North American kid's daily existence (that is, the upscale North American kid, which is who market surveys tend to focus on) to ask why and how things got like this. He found the answers encrypted in some historical land-marks not even hinted at by any of the other conference speakers, but which, in retrospect, seem obvious as towering influences in the lives of the "millennials." The end of the Cold War, the fall of the Berlin Wall, the unimpeded rush of a supercharged, self-aggrandizing form of Western capitalism to just about every peak and valley on Earth—this astounding sequence of events, which began to unfold in the late 1980s and early 1990s, clearly sets the context for the lives of a new generation born around that time. All of this amounts to a cataclysmic historical shift—one that's bound to have an effect on kids who have grown up in its wake.

And how has that historic shift made itself felt in the daily lives of kids? Essentially, says Silsbee, by creating a new interplay between time and space, and by creating new forms of time and space. No time or space is now off-limits to the imperatives of the marketplace. It has become cliché, for instance, to refer to businesses that operate "24/7." And this new reality has had a clear impact on families, obliterating the old and predictable markers of time—breakfasttime, lunchtime, naptime, dinnertime—and replacing them with "flextime" and "quality time"—concepts designed to persuade us that we can still squeeze more experience out of our time, even if it's in shorter supply.

But the compression of time has been offset by the opening of new spaces and the expansion of old ones as the global economic machine bursts its prior boundaries. Kid's bedrooms have become bigger and often contain an appliance that gives them access to a whole new pseudo-spatial domain: cyberspace. When they go to the mall, kids often gravitate to the mega-space of the flagship store, which is "primarily conceived of as an entertainment space designed to promulgate and defend a brand in the brand space," as Silsbee wrote in the print version of his "Jane and Joe Tweenager" presentation. "Jane and Joe judge these new spaces as much by the spectacles they provide as the goods they sell."[1]

Silsbee writes that although most young people are probably far too involved in the moment to really care about how this new time-space continuum came to exist, their parents may explain it by referring "to global competition, to world financial markets, even to the annihilation of space by time through new communications technologies starting with the jet airplane and ending with email.

They might use old phrases like global village or new words like NAFTA." Silsbee sees the whole process unfolding within the logic of what sociologist Max Weber called "the creative destruction of capitalism." Contained in Weber's phrase is the idea that the elements of our lives are like the buildings in a city—old buildings are torn down and new ones constructed in their place as the capitalist economy seeks new outlets for its energies, new terrain to conquer and re-conquer. With the crumbling of the Communist bloc in the early 1990s, the pace of this "creative destruction" quickened considerably, since there was no longer any viable competing ideology or economic system to restrain the movements of this newly globalized, re-energized capitalist economic machine. In highly industrialized nations, the result has been the kind of mutations of time and space that Silsbee highlights. The question that remains, of course, is whether the creation of those new spaces has been worth the loss of our precious time, whether the new buildings kids find themselves growing up in today are better or worse than the ones their parents used to inhabit. (Stay tuned for the answer, a few pages from now).

Coming out of the blue as it did, smack dab in the middle of what struck me as merely a series of variations on the entrenched truisms of the business, Silsbee's analysis was a bit of a shock. This is not the kind of talk one expects to hear at a marketing conference. For one thing, it broke with the mood of unblemished optimism that most other conference participants exuded. Before Silsbee ambled up to the podium, for example, I'd listened to a panel of three people compete to outdo each other with overheated descriptions of the current generation's march to glory. There was the standard stuff about how this is the most optimistic generation ever, how today's kids are more tolerant and would be better educated than their parents, etc., etc.[2] Although such optimism may not be entirely misplaced, in this particular context it came across as more than a trifle self-serving, intended to reassure the troops that their work is pure and noble and that they are promoting products which, rather than polluting kids' psychic environment, serve as useful tools in the hands of the "empowered" generation.

The tone of Silsbee's presentation was much more ambiguous.

True, he hit a few notes that resonated with this theme of youth as take-charge and highly adaptable—qualities that make them all the more likely to triumph over adversity. The print version of Silsbee's time-and-space spiel, for instance, refers to his youthful protagonists as "new masters of time and space," which suggests that even though their lives have been turned upside down, they are destined to overcome the obstacles. His conference presentation similarly noted the current generation's "search for personal mastery" and proposed that today's kids attempt to cope with the temporal/spatial fluidity of their environment by seeking "self-definition."

Still, Silsbee uses some pretty loaded, negative words to describe how the global economic machine has sucked time out of the average family's routine. In print, he muses: "Wishfully, Jane's Dad sometimes wonders if quitting time will ever get re-attached to a time-line so that he can leave the office." At the conference, delivering his fifteen-minute version of the theory of relativity, a PowerPoint slide glowing behind Silsbee lists various types of time, old and new. "Time Starved" and "Time Crunch" leap out. The word "Downtime" has a question mark after it. In the bottom corner of the graphic are the equations "Time = Enemy" and "Time = Weapon," which sum up Silsbee's view that, in the new reality, which runs on Internet time in the service of an economy organized around the principle of just-in-time production, we humans are constantly racing against the current of time lest our competitors beat us to the punch and put us out of business.

Silsbee is not the only person to notice this realigned relationship between time, space, and the things that fill it. In her book *Born to Buy*, Boston sociologist Juliet Schor laments the rise over the past couple of decades of "the cycle of work-and-spend, in which the compensation for longer hours was a rising material standard of living. People were accumulating stuff at an unprecedented rate. Demanding jobs and escalating debt in turn resulted in higher levels of stress and enormous pressure on family life. Some tried to buy their way out of the time squeeze by contracting out more household services, jetting off for stress-busting vacations, or finding a massage therapist, strategies that themselves require greater and greater household income."[3]

Schor sees kids as anything but bit players in this scenario. She remarks, for instance, that among people who have become "down shifters"—consciously forsaking more material wealth in exchange for quality of life—it is extremely rare to find people who have kids. She believes this is not just because raising children is more expensive than it once was, but also because kids have become the marketing industry's secret agents within households, programmed to cajole their parents into buying more and more expensive trinkets. Downshifting is the precise opposite of what advertising tells kids life should be like.

And the kids, Schor insists, are worse off for their role in this drama. An economist by training, Schor designed an experiment to compare kids' "involvement in consumer culture" with their mental health. She had three hundred kids in inner-city and suburban Boston fill out a thirty-minute survey describing, for example, their relationship with their parents, their experience of stomach aches and headaches (classified as psychosomatic illness), their media time and shopping habits, etc. Schor's subsequent number-crunching told her that "the children who are more involved in consumer culture are more depressed, more anxious, have lower self-esteem, and suffer from more psychosomatic complaints." Skeptics will question the ability of an essentially numeric exercise to lay bare a complex social reality, especially when it is based on the response of children whose specific histories are not known. Schor herself acknowledges that compiling agree/disagree responses to simple statements ("I feel like other kids have more stuff than me"; "I wish my parents gave me more money to spend"; "I like collecting things") in order to quantify a complex and amorphous quality like a child's "involvement in consumer culture" is an inherently problematic task (one that surely calls for value judgments and interpretation by the researchers). Still, she is convinced that the use of a "sophisticated statistical technique called structural equation modeling" allows her not just to observe a *correlation* between consumerism and poor mental health, but to be certain that the former is the *cause* of the latter.

Silsbee, naturally, is less direct about how he feels society's deepening involvement with big spaces and expensive things affects kids.

In conversation, I ask him (twice) if "Jane and Joe Tweenager Meet the New Time-Space Continuum" is, in the final analysis, a happy story or a sad one. The first time, he more or less ducks the question, preferring to concentrate on kids' techniques for dealing with social turmoil. Although social critics have always believed that "the world was becoming unravelled," he says, "my sense is that kids simply respond to the world as it is. Their response is to try to find the things that delight them, that are interesting, that speak to some sort of drive towards their growing up and maturing and being able to demonstrate that they are able to handle all sorts of different, new things." The whole process is ancient and archetypal, with kids of whatever generation growing up as inseparable parts of the society that surrounds them, but feeling compelled, by early adolescence, "to ask some very deep questions about why things are the way they are." Out of this process of searching, kids will hopefully find some vision of a bright future for themselves. "I think for us to determine whether these are happy or unhappy times may be a disservice to them," he opines. "If you ask them, mostly kids are optimistic. They probably always have been—it's just something in the nature of growing up. It would be a terrible thing if kids were not optimistic."

We get a little closer to dealing with the bleaker side of Silsbee's analysis with a second run at the question, which involves a little reframing. I ask him what real, practical trade-off is implied with all this talk about the expansion of different forms of space and the contraction of time. Since space is usually equated with possessions—in terms of owning real estate or controlling space that you can fill with the things you own—the creation of more space suggests that our society has become materially richer. But on the other hand, does the shrinking of time—a sphere that is usually filled by experiential things, like having relationships with other human beings—imply ...

"... that our internal lives have somehow become more impoverished?" offers Silsbee, finishing the question for me. "That's the conclusion a lot of people draw, and I'm not saying that in some ways I don't agree with them." The trend towards social fragmentation has been noted, for instance, by American sociologists such as

Robert Putnam (the author of *Bowling Alone*, which documents the decline of community organizations in the United States since the 1970s) and Alan Wolfe (who wrote about the way economic pressures have eroded "the gift of society"). Silsbee adds that, as a parent himself, he often worries about the way technological advances and the economic pressures they create propel family members onto different timelines and drive a wedge between kids and their parents. The polling data he reviews also sheds some light on the way economic pressures have realigned family relationships, sometimes by casting parents as the "monsters of over-preparation," who continually set new tasks for their children. He explains that for many kids, whose parents have been made uncertain about the future by the rapid pace of economic change, "there is more pressure on them, in terms of the amount of homework they are doing, the amount of activities their parents feel they have to engage in. All of this is to prepare them for what their parents know is going to be an extraordinarily competitive environment when they get out of school and finally start their lives ... The amount of time where kids can just be kids has been rolled back."

So is the story of Jane and Joe Tweenager an uplifting and inspirational tale or a tragedy? Silsbee returns, without prodding, to this pesky question a little later in the conversation, still trying to focus on the silver lining—i.e., the idea that kids are resilient and adaptable—but this time delivering his pep talk with a clearly diminished sense of conviction.

"I've been very careful to try not to characterize what's happening as either moral or immoral," he says. "But I think they [the current generation] are growing up in a meaner world. You know, kids are always up to the task. But whether or not this is where we want to be as a society, where we want to be as a world, I think that's an open question."

It's rare to hear kids' issues discussed in this way: as something bound up with the broader fate of society, intertwined with and inextricable from the realities adults face. Marketers often speak of youth as a separate social class, with a distinct culture that needs to be decoded before the briefcase brigades can infiltrate it and start peddling their products. Social crusaders tend to use the same kind of exclusionary language, speaking of youth as a special case whose innocence needs to be protected.

This is nothing new. Society as a whole has long embraced the idea of childhood as a refuge from the harsh realities that adults must endure, and when that notion of childhood is perceived as being under threat, the tendency is for social critics to focus more on the ways that childhood is distinct from adult culture—not on how it is connected to the wider world.

How long have we been thinking of childhood as a tranquil island unto itself? The media critic Neil Postman, in his book The Disappearance of Childhood, points to Gutenberg's invention of the printing press in the sixteenth century as the specific event that gave rise to our current understanding of childhood.[4] Before that, he writes, an eight year old was regarded in the same way as an adult of thirty—which indicates just how fluid, tenuous, and delicate the concept of childhood has been. Postman argues that although infancy is a biological condition, childhood is something defined by culture. Different societies will hold entirely different notions of when childhood begins and ends, or whether it even exists. The ancient Greeks, for example, had no clear word for a child, and their unsentimental view of youth is reflected in the fact that their society, although it did make provisions for educating the young, imposed no legal or moral prohibition against infanticide. By contrast, Roman society viewed the growing child as a fragile being who requires physical protection and who, psychologically, "need[s] to be sheltered from adult secrets, particularly sexual secrets" (a view we would recognize today).

Postman believed that the Roman conception of the child as too vulnerable to be exposed to certain aspects of adult reality (sex, death, drunkenness, suffering, vulgarity, etc.) developed as a consequence of the Roman culture of mass literacy. Essentially, a segregated childhood was made possible by a printed word that functioned as a device to keep certain types of knowledge out of reach of the young. Contentious subjects could be locked away within the pages of books, where they were accessible only to those who had spent several years learning to read. With the collapse of the Roman Empire and the banishment of its print culture, however, Europe of the Dark and Middle Ages reverted to "a 'natural' condition of human communication, dominated by talk and reinforced by song." It no longer possessed the symbolic tools (i.e., the letters of the alphabet) to protect the ears and minds of children from dangerous or hurtful knowledge. Suddenly, most of the enchanted kingdom of childhood vanished. Family members were now generally considered to have reached adulthood at seven: the age at which a young human can be expected to have mastered spoken communication.

In medieval Europe, the result of this loss of literacy was a society that saw no reason to put even the most sordid or grim spectacle out of bounds to the child. "Unrestrained by segregating institutions," wrote Postman, "the medieval child would have had access to almost all of the forms of behaviour common to the culture. The seven year old male was a man in every respect except for his capacity to make love and war." Evidence of this is found in the painting of the day. Postman quotes the historian J.H. Plumb, who wrote that "the coarse village festival depicted by [the painter] Brueghel, showing men and women besotted with drink, groping for each other with unbridled lust, have children eating and drinking with the adults." Postman also notes that, during this era, the lack of distinction between children and adults led to the widespread sexual exploitation of children.

Then came Gutenberg, whose printing press inadvertently led to the reinstatement and expansion of the Romans' vanquished ideas about the need to construct rigid borders around childhood. With the revival of a mass-literate culture (as opposed to a written culture shared only amongst a priesthood or some other small elite), the "secrets" of adult life were once again taken out of the public sphere and sealed in the pages of books. "A fully literate adult had access to all of the sacred and profane information in books, to the many forms of literature, to all the recorded secrets of human experience. Children, for the most part, did not," Postman writes. The advantage of this print-based separation of adults and children is that adult knowledge is revealed to children by degrees as they reach various plateaus in the process of decoding and interpreting the printed word. A ten year old might read *Old Yeller*; a sixteen year old, *Catcher in the Rye*. Ideally, the ability to process written information will correspond to the child's psychological readiness to receive more adult knowledge. So children are protected from knowing more than is good for them.

But the bad news, in Postman's view, is that "with television, the basis of this information hierarchy collapses." The essence of TV—the dominant communications medium of the post-Second World War era—is the pictures, and nobody needs to spend years in school to learn how to interpret television's visuals. The fact that TV is accessible to everyone "means that television does not need to make distinctions between the categories 'child' and 'adult,'" writes Postman, who backs up his point by citing statistics showing that millions of American children watch TV after 11 PM. The larger social ramifications of children being plugged into "the medium of total disclosure" are, in Postman's view, grim. He chooses 1950—the first year that televisions could be found in the majority of American homes—as the beginning of the end for childhood as it has been defined in the modern age. "The new media environment that is emerging provides everyone, simultaneously, with the same information," he explains. "Given the conditions I have described, electric media find it impossible to withhold any secrets. Without secrets, of course, there can be no such thing as childhood."

Postman's depiction of electronic communications eroding the boundaries that separate children from the coarse realities of adult life remains a prominent theme in more recent critiques of what mass media is doing to kids. The newer material, of course, speaks more directly to the technological advances, and the drift away from censorship, that distinguish our current media environment. *The Disappearance of Childhood*, published in 1982, obviously makes no mention of the Internet, and its references to TV programs such as *Laverne and Shirley*, *The Odd Couple*, and *Phil Donahue* as assaults on children's innocence seem decidedly naïve to people who dwell in today's media universe of cable and pay per view. Still, an echo of Postman's concern about the lack of effective filters in the electronic age is clearly evident in such recent exposés as the 2002 Fox Television special *The Corruption of the American Child*. In the opening minute of that shock-doc, host Bill O'Reilly—one of the best-known and most vitriolic of U.S. conservative ideologues—prefaces his outraged tour through the of realms of rap music, WWE wrestling, and Internet porn with the suggestion that today's children are citizens of "a media world where no limits exist."[5]

A number of O'Reilly's guests build on the theme that advances in electronic technologies have removed the barriers between children and the "secrets" of the adult world; that today's wired kids are being exposed to spectacles similar to those which Postman, the liberal commentator, imagined as influences in the lives of medieval children. Jan LaRue of the Family Research Council, a lobby of the U.S. religious right,[6] goes one step beyond this critique, claiming that not only are young children stumbling accidentally onto pornographic Internet sites, but they are being drawn there intentionally by porn peddlers who embed the names of popular toys into their website's meta-tags, so that a search for Pokémon or My Little Pony will produce a link to a porn site. The pornographers do this, LaRue says, to cultivate their future consumers in much the same way that tobacco companies have allegedly tried to hook impressionable teens on smoking in order to guarantee tomorrow's sales. Like Postman, LaRue sees the exposure to more sordid influences as an assault on the very concept of childhood, with the result that young kids are now trading in the sandbox for the psychiatrist's couch. "I have a friend who's a therapist who is treating an eight year old Internet porn addict," LaRue tells O'Reilly in an on-camera interview. As bizarre and unlikely as this tale may seem to many of us, LaRue insists that, far from being unique, the story foreshadows the widespread woe that will befall our entire culture. "We're looking at the next generation becoming sexual predators because of what's happening on the Internet," she predicts. "They have turned cyberspace into a sewer."

Despite the availability of filtering devices (the v-chip for television, and software like CyberPatrol for computers), it may indeed be that the open, unmediated character of electronic media is demolishing the walls that make the idea of childhood possible. You can arrive at that conclusion ... if you assume that those media are a dominant influence in the lives of kids, which may be true in families where parents face pressures to work longer hours. This is one variant of Silsbee's story of the mutating time-space continuum that is clearly a tragedy: as parents lose family time to workplace demands, kids are increasingly left to their own devices in the modern media-space, which often means watching television or surfing the Internet.

But if families are fortunate enough to have the means to retain some control over their time, the influence of media may be offset by other factors—parents, friends, teachers, to name a few. In those circumstances, the hallowed sanctuary of childhood has not been ripped apart; rather, the adult world has been attempting to fortify its barricades. This is the generation, after all, that Howe and Strauss characterize as the most regimented cohort in history. When Mom or Dad can't be in the bleachers for Junior's little league game, they make sure he's enrolled in some organized activity—or up to his eyeballs in homework.

In contrast to Postman's vision of the disappearance of childhood, what one large segment of the North American population seems to have experienced recently is a disappearance of adulthood. Perhaps partly in reaction to the picture that Postman saw emerging at the end of the 1970s—i.e., a society in which kids were left to fend for themselves in an undifferentiated, virtual landscape— many adults seem to have become so deeply involved in directing their kids' leisure activities that the whole family's recreation now revolves around some offshoot of kid culture. This is true even in relation to electronic media. While it's correct to say that a kid with free rein over the channel changer or unsupervised access to the Internet can familiarize himself with the most unsavoury corners of the adult world, the same electronic revolution that created this situation has also given birth to a range of media outlets expressly dedicated to keeping the safe haven of childhood intact. Cable outfits like the American Nickelodeon and Canada's YTV have become giants in their respective broadcasting environments by offering a slate of programs—like *Rugrats, Spongebob Squarepants,* or *Jimmy Neutron*—with an unfailingly sentimental point of view and a moral lesson that's impossible to miss. As a rule, those outfits salt their programming with just enough parent-directed references to hold the interest of the big person with control over the on/off switch, which indicates the networks expect that many parents will be in the room watching these programs with their kids. The U.S. radio network Radio Disney provides another example of how kids' entertainment has become the focal point for family life. An invaluable tool for keeping youngsters' moods buoyant during those torturously long commutes that are common in metropolitan areas in the United States, Radio Disney programs a savvy blend of bubblegum hits, product giveaways, and DJ banter aimed at kids, and just enough retro-pop to keep the adult at the wheel from migrating further down the radio dial. Kids' movies are also increasingly aimed at adults. One film studio exec recently remarked that, with the movie industry now based largely around blockbuster weekend releases, it is important that family films (think Shrek, Finding Nemo, or The Incredibles) have a direct appeal for mothers and fathers.[7]

There's a convincing case to be made, in fact, that all the kid-focused television programs, movies, electronic games, specialty products, extracurricular tutoring, and soccer leagues, which have surrounded young people growing up in the 1990s and beyond, form a kind of cultural cocoon that has allowed them to make the biological trip to adulthood without having to absorb the "real world" concerns they might otherwise have come into contact with. True, there are probably large numbers of kids who sneak into R-rated movies and make unsanctioned fact-finding tours on the Internet (with both types of expedition seemingly aided, abetted, and encouraged by the industry, as the critics suggest). But for a large segment of the youth population, the collective efforts of the adult world appear to have kept kids confined to the realm of childhood, secluded from the realities of grown-up life, for longer than they might have been in the past. Some commentators have suggested that this has led to an arrested emotional development for many kids coming of age in the millennial era. The authors of a Newsweek magazine article on overscheduled families, for instance, suggest that "students who've never learned to make their own choices can feel lost and confused once they get to college." They quote one college professor, who says she sees many students who have acquired a wide range of skills but are unable to express an opinion of their own because, having been chaperoned by adults and pushed so hard to achieve, they've had little time alone with their thoughts.[8]

Lately, this idea of young people being confined to a separate psychological solitude, sheltered from the messy realities their parents endure in daily life, has been on the minds of a number of people who make spectacles for the big and small screens. The 2001 cinematic hit *Spy Kids*, for instance, spins a tale of pandemonium from the simple premise that a brother and sister learn their parents used to work as international spies and then are drawn into that world. Appearing at first to be a typical, middle-class, minivan clan, with the parents facing the daily frustrations of the commute to their kids' school, and the father constantly complaining that his son spends too much time watching mindless television and playing electronic games, they begin their comic romp when the kids discover that their parents once had an identity outside the tightly circumscribed domestic routine of work, school, dinner, homework, and bedtime. Similarly, the cable-TV series *The Sopranos* has a recurrent fixation on its subjects' increasingly untenable separation of their orderly, kid-centred, upper-middle-class life from the family patriarch's work as a crime boss. The program routinely cuts from scenes of high-school recitals and cramming for college entrance exams to glimpses of the hideously violent world of drug dealers and loan sharks. In one episode, the tension between these two realities comes to some sort of resolution as the Soprano daughter uncovers the facts about her family's gangster pedigree by visiting an Internet site that documents the lives of famous American criminals.

Of course, few parents work as spies and mobsters, but that's not the point. Entertainment properties like *Spy Kids* and *The Sopranos* seem to be riffing on the fairly obvious disconnects between our conception of childhood and our expectations about how things work in the adult world. Which brings us back to Peter Silsbee's contention that it might be useful, for a change, to look at youth, not as a "special case," but as the product of, and an integral part of, society at large. Silsbee isn't suggesting that young children should be allowed to watch what plays on cable television at all hours of the day and night, or that barriers between childhood and adulthood should not exist. What he *is* saying is that, rather than examining kids' lives as something removed from the sphere of adult life—a composite product of the music they listen to, the movies they watch, the games they play—it might be more instructive to examine how the meta-conditions that shape the world we all live in filter down into the daily existence of the young.

One aspect of the broader social reality that has touched the lives of all members of families, young and old, is the consolidation of our global, hypercompetitive, 24/7 economic system. This, you'll remember, is what Silsbee sees as the primary agent creating the new time-space continuum, which has played such a prominent role in shaping the lives of the younger generation. Our supercharged global economic machine is at once a ubiquitous, unavoidable force, and also a largely invisible one. We don't reflexively look to broader, global economic trends to explain why kids' values are different from the ones their parents may wish to promote. Instead, moralists of both the left and right see the problem as an inner, personal one. They suggest the problems and perplexities that young people face can be eliminated by just wishing our way back to the 1950s (a time, supposedly, before Ecstasy, single-parent families, and jaded materialism, when the vision of ideal domesticity, planted in the heads of boomer parents by all those sappy sitcoms they watched as kids, was in full flower).

Paradoxically, though, for the past three decades the most high-profile proponents of a return to the past have been working in a seamless coalition with the forces most responsible for bringing about the radical economic reforms that some say have shaken the foundations of family life. In the United States, the so-called New Right, a movement that backed Ronald Reagan's rise to the presidency in 1980 and set the tone for much of the political and public policy debate since then, has been based on an unlikely and illogical alliance between social conservatives and economic libertarians, whose social outlooks and policy prescriptions have often been working at cross-purposes.

On the one hand, the social conservatives dream of a return to a "pre-Lapsarian time," as Silsbee puts it, "which is usually identified as the 1950s," when families stayed together, authority was obeyed, and there was a greater sense of community, social cohesion, and stability. Yet the other partner in this winning political amalgam has promoted a series of economic policies based on intensified competition, freer markets, and less government involvement in society, which have arguably created considerable social dislocation and undermined the viability of families.

This blend of social conservatism and laissez-faire economics has fairly deep roots in the United States. Silsbee cites Princeton historian Lisa McGirr's book *Suburban Warriors*, which documents the rise of a nascent New Right movement in southern California in the 1950s and 1960s. This movement, given expression by the John Birch Society and the Goldwater for President campaign, introduced the blend of old-time, Bible-belt moralism with a strong commitment to unrestricted free enterprise that would later prove its potency across the United States and even internationally. In large measure, McGirr sees the dislocating effects of laissez-faire economics reinforcing the commitment to an old-fashioned moral code. Unfettered free enterprise was creating so much change that the future began to look uncertain and ominous. Each week a familiar orange grove would become a new subdivision. Small communities ballooned into large population centres, taking their place within the sprawling, impersonal suburban behemoth that was evolving. To cope psychologically with this, McGirr believes, residents who were ideologically unwilling to embrace restrictions on free enterprise turned to fundamentalist religion and a nostalgic campaign for the restoration of small-town values. Though the physical/technological environment was changing by the minute, these conservative stalwarts believed social norms could be maintained simply through force of will.

Now that virtually unrestrained capitalism has become the dominant guiding principle of the entire world, what has it done to the institution of the family? Silsbee believes its greatest impact has been creation of the "time crunch," which has driven many parents and children into their own separate spheres.

"The sociologist Jürgen Habermas uses the phrase 'the colonization of the life world by systems logic,'" Silsbee says. "And what he's saying in terms of time is that the capitalist system, the system of the state, all of those things have thoroughly infiltrated our lives—and our lives have been sped up accordingly. When you think about world financial markets, for instance, and how trillions of dollars can be exchanged with a touch of a button on a keyboard, how global corporations can move their operations according to how good a deal they can get, that means that we're all working that much harder, racing against time and against our competitors. We're into that slide where the exigencies of global capitalism have even penetrated into the lives of kids … Despite all this, I think that we as Americans are so individualistic that we don't see the connections, or we choose not to. We believe that we are leading our own lives quite apart from any global economy, we're making it on our own, just trying to do what we have to do."

But there are many concrete ways in which the new economic reality is visibly creating additional stress for families. An emphasis on giving businesses the "flexibility" they need to take on competitors has shifted a huge burden onto the family unit: increased corporate mobility means that employees must often relocate at the whim of employers, and the cutthroat nature of competition requires that breadwinners work increasingly onerous and unpredictable hours. For a society that constantly champions the cause of "family values," the United States has a remarkable shortage of policies to help families cope with the rigours of life in this new economic reality. Residents of more interventionist, less free-market countries like Canada, Sweden, or France may be shocked to discover, for instance, that in many U.S. jurisdictions, companies can meet legislated requirements by granting maternity leaves of only six weeks. Even policies ostensibly intended to give struggling families a "hand up" have had detrimental impacts on children. A study of recent American welfare reforms requiring single mothers to re-enter the workforce, for instance, revealed that even though the income of the mothers tracked by the study rose to an annual average of $13,000 (higher than welfare payments, but still below the poverty line), their children did not benefit. The researchers concluded that children spent less time with their mothers and more time watching television, and that the mothers were prone to depression, did not improve their parenting skills, and continued to have difficulty paying the rent and buying food.[9]

In more middle-class surroundings, where the economic revolution has opened up those new spaces like the mega-store and the mega-bedroom, filled with the latest technological devices, the problem seems to be one of psychological separation rather than economic want. Peter Silsbee believes that Americans, in particular, have suffered the painful consequences of being torn between their reverence for technology and the idea of progress, and their competing desire that the generations be bound together in a stable family unit. "In America," he says, "we unquestioningly grab hold of the latest technology. When the radio came out, it was only six years before 80 percent of the whole United States had one. Similarly with the television and the automobile, the adoption rates were extraordinary. The Internet is just the latest example of how we embrace these things and sort out the details later. We've adopted a kind of hands-off policy when it comes to technology and our children because we think that to not give them access will somehow handicap them against their peers."

At the same time, the technology that parents see as enabling their kids to better forge their path through the world, also helps drive a wedge between parents and kids. The Internet creates more "horizontal relationships," disrupting "vertical" communication between family members in the home and replacing it with links between children and other influences in the wider world. This obviously means that parents have to deal with competing viewpoints when they try to pass on specific sets of values to their kids. Technology is also seen by some commentators as a motivation for the scheduling overkill to which many middle-class parents have subjected their offspring. Historian Stephanie Coontz, of Wintergreen College in Washington state, believes that the shift to a digital economy has created the same kind of anxieties for parents as existed in the 1820s, at the height of the Industrial Revolution, when occupations such as blacksmithing were headed towards extinction. The overriding question for most parents, she says, is "What do you do to protect your child and secure them a good future?"[10]

This idea that rapid technological change produces a generalized but unspecific sense of anxiety in society was championed by the celebrated cultural critic Marshall McLuhan. In his 1968 book

War and Peace in the Global Village, McLuhan expresses astonishment at how Western society—with its history of ceaseless technological change—consistently fails to recognize or appreciate how these advances will reshape the social environment.[11] When the elders in society finally do discover that technological leaps have created an entirely new world for the next generation to inhabit, "our consternation in facing this development is entirely of the 'didn't know it was loaded' variety," McLuhan writes. Although "the business world ... imagines it can introduce vast innovations without any ensuing consequences," all technological innovations—the wheel, the printing press, gunpowder, etc.—have altered the way in which people relate to their fellow humans and their own environment and have refashioned our perceptions of time and space. McLuhan believed that information technology, particularly the computer (which at the time of McLuhan's deliberations was merely a primitive prototype of the beasts that govern today's world), would have far greater impact because it could extend and mimic the basic human functions of thinking and feeling. "As much as the wheel is an extension of the human foot, the computer is an extension of our nervous system, which exists by virtue of feedback or circuitry ... [As such,] the new information environments ... have a much more profound relation to our human condition than the old 'natural' environment."

McLuhan's greatest concern was how the disruption wrought by technological change could stoke the human urge to violence. He saw the social realignments accompanying a change in technological regime as a threat to the self-image of those whose lives are changed, and he points out that "when our identity is in danger, we feel certain that we have a mandate for war. The old image must be recovered at any cost." Because it's unlikely that a culture spoiling for a fight will see that its enemy is out-of-control technology, it will seek some surrogate target. "As in the case of 'referred pain,'" writes McLuhan, "the symptom against which we lash out may likely be caused by something about which we know nothing."

It's clear from his writing that when McLuhan spoke about the impact of "media" on the world, he was not worried about the images and ideas that flow through a new medium of communication, but rather the real-world transformations that arise when a new technology is introduced. (Silsbee's remarks reveal a similar concern, dwelling on questions of how the consolidation of a global economic machine has reordered the daily domains of time and space, and how this has led to such phenomena as the family time crunch and the substitution of consumption for relationships.) McLuhan, in fact, was singularly uninterested in the content of communications media. He once remarked that content is "the juicy bit of meat carried by the burglar to distract the watchdog of the mind"—in other words, a red herring that provides a distraction from the real issue of how information technologies themselves mechanically alter the social landscape and realign human perceptions.

Nonetheless, McLuhan did attempt—a couple of decades before the so-called culture wars broke out in the United States—to explain why the content of media had become a lightning rod for society's free-floating angst. Partly, he says, it's got to do with the need to not be reminded of the chaos of the moment; to seek solace in nostalgic images.

"When a new technology strikes a society," McLuhan writes, "the most natural reaction is to clutch at the immediately preceding period for familiar and comforting images. This is the world of The Virginian and Bonanza and frontier entertainment. If 90 per cent of all the scientists who ever lived are now alive, we might say that Hollywood houses more redskins and cowpunchers than ever existed on the frontier." McLuhan went on to extrapolate that the space program of the 1960s—commonly perceived as a manifestation of "progress and advanced thinking"—was actually a nostalgic exercise designed to revive the extinguished excitement of frontier culture and the drive to colonize new worlds in order to neutralize a deep-seated sense of uncertainty in the present. "It [the space program] has no relevance to our time anymore than Bonanza does," he writes. "Projecting missiles into outer space is no different from the activities of Columbus and Magellan."

McLuhan's intuition that people look for guidance in times of flux by glancing into the "rear-view mirror" may provide a useful reference point to help explain some of the approaches taken by contemporary groups that are concerned about children's entertainment.

When I Googled the key words "media" and "children," a while back, my computer spat out a list of websites, towards the top of which was a site run by American Vision, a fundamentalist Christian outfit based in Powder Springs, Georgia. The mission of this organization, according to a statement on its homepage, is to work towards "the restoration of America's biblical foundation. Our goal is to help Christians think biblically. Right thinking precedes right action." As one means towards this end, the site featured a guide to "family-friendly viewing" (since taken down) assembled by Gary deMar, who appears to be the driving editorial force behind American Vision. Most of the films cited on Gary's Movie List were made in the 1930s, 40s, and 50s. There are a few titles from the 1960s (although the early 60s classic Dr. Strangelove is not one of them—it is cited as an example of modern movies that are spoiled by the inclusion of sexual situations). There are only a handful of entries from the 70s, 80s, and 90s.

Gary deMar is well aware that his choices skew heavily towards the black-and-white world of Frank Capra and Jimmy Stewart, a world that vanished long before today's kids were born—but he's not about to apologize for that. "Most of what comes out of Hollywood today is rubbish," he writes. This makes it far preferable to seek out films "produced at a time when the Legion of Decency and the Production Code of the Motion Picture Association of America saw to it that a moral context was always present. There was no need for a ratings system. In an era before special effects, blood and gore, and sexual innuendo, a movie was carried by character development and good story telling."[12]

DeMar may be correct in saying that special effects, cinematic bombast, and titillation have shifted the emphasis away from good storytelling and compelling characters, but what's worrying in his approach is the assumption that kids today can find answers to all their problems in the relics of a lost era. Sure, Frank Capra was a great filmmaker, and many of his messages are timeless. But his films were set in a world that's unrecognizable to contemporary kids, with few signposts to guide them through the particular minefields they face as they try to make a life on the cusp of the twenty-first century. Is it possible that this attempt to resurrect a world that lingers only on brittle rolls of celluloid may be more about consoling oldsters who pine for the lost days of their youth, rather than helping kids come to terms with the realities of their own lives?

Perhaps. Yet it seems almost inevitable that old people's generalized discomfort with the way society is changing will be expressed as a specific concern for the plight of youth, since they are most directly affected by such change. Whether kids will benefit from those trips down memory lane is another question. They need to adapt quickly to the emerging world where they must find work, friends, and a sense of place and purpose. For them, the past provides little refuge.

Anyhow, the point of all this discussion is to lead us to ask one fundamental question: How much of the furore over the mass-media/mass-marketing establishment's invasion of childhood is actually about the effects of mass-produced images on kids, and how much is what McLuhan called "referred pain," a disguised reaction to the broader effects of sweeping technological change and runaway economic "progress"?

Since the expanded role of media in kids' lives and the acceleration of turbocharged techno-capitalism are related occurrences, it's impossible to arrive at a definitive answer. But leaning to one side or the other will surely influence which public policy prescriptions a person is likely to support. If you accept the proposition that the real problem—underlying the kerfuffle about kids being brainwashed by media and the marketers who piggyback on their programs—is an out-of-control economy that drives families apart and substitutes commercial values for human ones, you may not believe that putting the youngsters on a steady diet of Shirley Temple and Jimmy Stewart films will accomplish much. Conversely, if you buy the line that corrupting media images are, in themselves, the problem with kids these days, it's a fair bet that you'll spend more time trying to keep your offspring away from Eminem and Marilyn Manson concerts than contemplating how the four-day workweek or expanded parental leave might mend the tears in the fabric of family life.

CHAPTER 7
Scripts and Soundtracks from Real Life

Who's to blame? When adults complain that kids today are too materialistic in their outlook, that they consume too much junk food, that they lose their naïveté and sense of innocence too early ... is all this the fault of an irresponsible media and unscrupulous marketers who take advantage of gullible, impressionable kids? Or are these maladies the products of deeper social processes in which we all play a role?

Some commentators critical of the media and marketing establishments do hint that the indoctrination of kids by Hollywood and Madison Avenue is only one part of a broader problem. Much of the negative commentary that I've read on mass media's effects on kids has come with the rider that parents are working too hard and so are unable to monitor their offspring's media consumption or to form close enough bonds to influence their tastes in cultural products. Even conservative warrior Bill O'Reilly, whose Fox special was vociferous in its conviction that rap, rock, and the Internet are the primary agents that keep minority youth in poverty and put eight year olds on the psychiatrist's couch, conceded that parental distraction made kids more vulnerable to mass-media "corruption."

The common assumption that parents are too busy to be accessible to their kids is given some statistical flesh in *Fool's Gold*, a report primarily concerned with what its authors say is the misguided drive to increase computer use in the classroom. Produced by a group of prominent child experts and advocates known as the Alliance for Childhood,[1] *Fool's Gold* cites one study that claims children in the late 1990s spent 40 percent less time with their parents than children did 30 years earlier. It also refers to a 1999 study by Pittsburgh's Fortino Group, which estimates that kids of the current generation will have a third fewer face-to-face encounters than members of the preceding generation because they will be spending more time using electronic media at school and alone in their rooms at home.

The "new media" of the computer revolution take some blame for this sense of isolation, but *Fool's Gold* focuses less on the hardware and software of the digital dawn and more on the underlying mentality that has accompanied their introduction. Although several prominent critics of the entertainment industry and opponents of marketing to children have joined the Alliance, what's interesting about the group's report is that it transcends its membership's individual, sectoral interests and takes an expansive view of the subject. The fundamental concern is how the underlying logic of our current economic and technical system is being transferred into the lives of children. The Alliance report focuses on one particular medium through which those values are communicated: not television or the Internet, not the advertising missives that bombard kids, but the school system and its ancillary technologies.

The release of *Fool's Gold* in 2000 coincided with a brewing public backlash against a North American educational system accused of being obsessed with achievement and oblivious to the risks involved in demanding more and more output from young children. It's interesting to note that the broader criticisms of this brand of results-oriented schooling are virtually identical to the complaints that are levelled against the marketers and media peddlers who take aim at kids: it is making kids superficial, materialistic, and vain; it is making kids grow up too fast; it is creating a generation that is sedentary and physically unhealthy. All of this raises the question:

which would be the more effective vehicle for promoting these syndromes? The commercial messages that critics charge assault kids' eyeballs three thousand times a day, or the school system that has physical custody of a child for eight hours each school day, with its messages often reinforced in the home?

The primary indictment laid down in the Alliance's *Fool's Gold* report is that, much as the educational system of the industrial revolution treated students as would-be extensions of the workplace machinery (a role in which punctuality and obedience were of much greater value than creative thinking), today's educational establishment is attempting to remake the children in its care in the image of the almighty computer, the defining icon of our age. Adopting the computer as the central metaphor for education doesn't only find practical expression in the push to plug more computers into the classroom (where they can be expected to take over the roles once filled by teachers, thereby giving students even more time at the keyboard and less time with a human mentor). It also provides the philosophical underpinning for such phenomena as the vast increases in homework, the rise of so-called academic kindergartens (within which games, music, and exercise have been replaced by rigorous math and reading drills, in the hopes of providing five year olds with the foundations for an illustrious college career),[2] and the more general expansion of math and science in school curricula at the expense of art, music, and other forms of creative expression.

All of these developments have been given intellectual legitimacy by the idea that the human mind is akin to the circuitry in a computer. The more information is crammed into its memory, and the more it is programmed with high-quality data, the better. The authors of *Fool's Gold* see this as the importation of an alien and inapplicable idea—a clear example of what Silsbee referred to as the "systems logic" of a technological economy "colonizing" the everyday lives of children.

"Attempts to engineer faster learning in childhood," the report's authors recall, "grew out of military research in the 1950s and 1960s that had nothing to do with children. The military sought to program computers to perform complex logical operations, in part by analyzing how humans process information." Although the initial purpose of this research was to enhance information technology for weapons systems, "a new discipline, now called cognitive science, sprang from those studies ... In time, its educational focus shifted to cognitive engineering—attempting to improve the efficiency and productivity of human learners. Its emphasis was frequently on developing generic 'problem solving skills', often divorced from any context of social needs or the personal goals of the learners."

The authors insist that this approach is at odds with the biological realities of how children learn and how their brains develop. "Complex intellectual tasks and social behaviours," they write, "proceed from a successful integration of a wide range of human skills, not just a narrow set of computational and logical operations." In fact, the maturation of an individual child's brain appears to mirror "the evolutionary history of humanity," with the lower centres, which control movement, developing first, followed by "basic brain structures governing emotion," and then the centres of the brain responsible for abstract thinking. During the grade school years, the mastery of motor and perceptual skills occurs only incrementally, while far greater strides are made in developing social and emotional skills. Since emotional and intellectual functions appear to be integrated in humans, with emotional input almost invariably informing the logical judgments that humans make, focusing on chores to develop logical, rational thinking (to the exclusion of more experiential forms of learning) is unlikely to produce balanced individuals, or even intelligent ones. The Alliance for Childhood insists that you can't separate a kid's intellect from the rest of his or her human capacities.

"Research findings across many scientific disciplines," the report reads, "suggest that later intellectual development is rooted in rich childhood experiences that combine healthy emotional relationships, physical engagement with the real world, and the exercise of imagination in self-generated play and the arts ... Treating young children like small scholars and overwhelming them with electronic stimuli that outstrip their sensory, emotional, and intellectual maturity may actually be a form of deprivation. It is reminiscent of failed experiments of the 1960s in which preschoolers were pushed to learn to read and write. By the middle of grade school, they had fallen behind less rushed children in both academic and social skills."

Part of the gathering backlash against this tendency to see children as empty vessels to be crammed with facts and equations is motivated by this concern that stuffing kids with data won't succeed in making them smarter or better equipped to cope with the emerging world or workplace. Britain's National Foundation for Educational Research, for example, surveyed research studies on homework conducted between 1988 and 2001 (mostly in the United States and the United Kingdom) and concluded that children who do excessive amounts of homework each night have a poorer academic performance than those who do just modest amounts of homework. "At the primary level, there is no conclusive evidence that homework boosts achievement," concluded chief researcher Caroline Sharp.[3] Critics of today's academic zealotry believe there are many reasons for this finding, such as the tendency for overwork to destroy children's zest for learning, and children's diminished ability to learn when tired.

Yet some of the criticism of the cram-and-drill style of education raises issues far beyond the question of whether or not it actually works. There are concerns, for instance, that the heavier academic workload has exacerbated existing social inequalities, since wealthy parents can adjust to increased amounts of homework by hiring tutors, while poorer parents who spend more time working will be hard pressed to oversee their children's evening homework efforts. There have also been complaints that excessive amounts of homework are quite simply inhumane—almost tantamount to child abuse. In the 1930s, New York, Chicago, and other cities banned or limited the amount of homework assigned, and the American Child Health Association considered it "child labour." Yet these restrictions were reversed in times of rising technological angst: first in the late 1950s, after the Soviets launched their Sputnik space capsule, and later after the influential 1983 government report *A Nation At Risk* addressed the role of education in getting the United States back on an equal footing with its economic competitors such as Japan.[4]

And what has this push for "achievement" in education done to students' values? "Secondary schools are breeding stressed-out, materialistic and ill-educated students" is the answer from London's weekly *Observer*, reporting on the findings of prominent American educator Denise Clark Pope. The author believes that teachers and parents, with their unrelenting emphasis on results, have given kids the message that achievement is more important than ethics.

"Instead of fostering traits such as honesty, integrity, co-operation and respect," says Pope, "schools are promoting deception, hostility and anxiety. The students told me they didn't want to act like this, but they felt they had no choice if they were going to get the grades they needed to get to the colleges, and later, to the jobs they wanted. The students admitted to feeling the need to manipulate the system and devise crafty strategies to get ahead. They felt compelled to betray their friends and deceive teachers, and they felt they had no choice but to compromise their integrity for future success."[5]

This general criticism — that young people today are overly materialistic; that they have placed their individual aspirations ahead of the wellbeing of their peers, the community, and their own higher values — is virtually identical to the analysis advanced by the media/marketing critics we heard from a couple of chapters back. The only major distinction is in the competing explanations of exactly who has warped kids in this way. Groups like Stop the Commercial Exploitation of Children lay the blame on MTV, Channel One, Nintendo, McDonald's, and all the other corporate mesmerists that bombard kids with commercial messages through their televisions, cellphones, the Internet, at school, at home, and in transit, at all hours of the day. By contrast, research like that done by Pope and the National Foundation for Educational Research suggests the modern scourges of materialism and self-centredness are embedded in the fabric of the educational institutions we normally assume are dedicated to social advancement and the personal growth of the child. There's also been plenty of reportage suggesting that these institutions have adopted their survival-of-the-fittest pedagogy largely at the behest of anxious parents, who have been obsessing about Junior's college entrance exams and the square footage of his future real estate holdings since before he was out of diapers.

So which do you think has the more powerful influence over the development of a young person's value system: (a) the inescapable, perpetually morphing, eternally in-your-face mass media, or (b) the institutions of school and family, which set an example for kids more through practice than spectacle? If your answer is (a), you're likely to put some stock in the idea—aired earlier in this volume—that the nefarious forces of marketing have filing cabinets filled with secret formulas for dazzling and entrancing kids so they'll buy the products that corporations are pitching. They've figured out the combination to those secret recesses in your kid's soul, and they're in there right now, proselytizing for the new religion of consumerism.

But if your answer is (b), you might see the balance of power differently, calculating, perhaps, that while the marketing industry has the power of persuasion, the everyday forces of family and school enjoy the powers of coercion. Parents and teachers can ensure that kids stay on the treadmill—taking the right courses, studying hard for exams, clawing past the competition ... all of this leading to enrollment at a good college and the spoils that brings in the job market—not just by promising material rewards and social acceptance, but also by threatening dire consequences (everything from being grounded or humiliated in front of peers to falling into poverty later in life) should the expectations of the adult world not be met.

If the student persists in the belief that this regimented road to the good life denies certain other key aspects of his or her being, the powers that be can always fall back on the chemical option. Consider how a dramatic increase in the prescription of psychiatric drugs to children has coincided with the tough new approach to education. In the United States, sales of a class of drugs known as analeptics, prescribed mostly to children to control attention deficit disorders, roughly doubled between 1995 and 2000, from just under $400 million to almost $800 million. (In Canada, the picture is much the same. Prescriptions for Ritalin, Dexedrine, and their generic equivalents rose by 55 percent [from 664,000 prescriptions to 1,030,000] between 1996 and 2000, accounting for an increase in sales from $21.7 million to $32.5 million.)[6] With suspicions mounting that some young children are being drugged, not to control a bona fide medical condition, but rather to ensure compliance with classroom routines that require too much sitting and rigorous academic drills at too young an age, several American states have introduced bills that prohibit schools from insisting parents put their children on the drugs (Minnesota's legislation states that only a doctor can direct parents to medicate a child).[7]

Child psychologist Dr. Peter Breggin, a leading critic of using Ritalin and related drugs to treat young children diagnosed with attention disorders, sees a link between the rising prescription rate and the intensifying demands of the school system. "We have this idea that our kids should be courteous, kind and obedient," he says, "whether or not they are ready to be all those things, and they should be getting A's in school even though they may not be scholars and they may hate school and grow up to do something that has nothing to do with school. So we're making these extreme demands for conformity, which we confuse with being an ideal child, and then we drug the child into conformity."[8]

If critics like Breggin are correct, then the use of drugs is just one of many enforcement mechanisms aimed at ensuring young people's compliance with a new, more determined, "pragmatic" philosophy of education, the primary goal of which is clearly materialistic. Remember, when reports like *A Nation at Risk* (calling for higher, more rigorously enforced academic standards) were released, the crisis that was predicted was not that lax schools would erode American kids' ability to grasp the wisdom of Shakespeare, Einstein, or Thoreau, but that losing ground to economic competitors would diminish an American standard of living that's measured in new cars, toasters, and wide-screen TVs.

Family life can also be an effective tool for propagating a materialistic outlook. Again, it's crucial to ask who's likely to wield most power in influencing a young person's value system: an advertising exec whose spots for soda have grabbed Junior's attention when he should be down at the family dinner table, or a parent whose working and spending habits send the practical message that collecting expensive trinkets is worth whatever sacrifice is required? Sure, marketing companies might hire psychologists to tell them how the Nike swoosh can be equated with a deep-seated desire for transcendence. But family members provide a living example in three dimensions. In the estimation of Harvard psychologist Dan Kindlon, the lesson that most parents in middle-class Western society convey to their children by their example is that materialism, competition, and self-interest are the highest of our culture's ideals—the only way to go.[9]

"We are driven," Kindlon writes in his book *Too Much of a Good Thing*. "And our kids feel driven—driven to get good grades, get into the right college, get a good job." Kindlon makes it clear that this is not a good thing for adults or their kids. In stark contrast to Howe and Strauss's optimistic portrait of a generation set on the path to glory by involved parents who have cultivated their offspring's talents and inner strengths as they would a garden of rare orchids, Kindlon's bleak assessment is that career-minded, overachieving parents often warp their children's social worldview. In his clinical practice, the psychologist has seen meddlesome, overanxious parents from privileged circumstances indoctrinate their kids with superficial values and shelter them from the tough lessons of life that build character and conscience. These kids may work hard in school and aim high in life, but their drive to achieve is habitual and joyless, motivated more by conditioning than by a heartfelt urge to self-expression. Their acceptance of the proposition that you can buy happiness and self-respect has made them prone to a series of psychological disorders, which Kindlon refers to as "the seven syndromes of indulgence." They range from self-centredness and excessive anxiety to eating disorders, lack of motivation, and smouldering internal anger.

Kindlon finds many specific explanations for this sorry web of maladies. Overall, parents today are too "self-identified" with their kids, he writes. They push their kids to get ahead because they view their children's successes as their own. They will connive to get their kids off the hook when they are in trouble, using bullying tactics and deceit without hesitation (clearly a mindset imported from the business world). They are so dependent upon their friendships with their children that they are reluctant to put that bond in jeopardy by chastising their kids when they've done wrong. It's revealing that within his list of poisonous influences, Kindlon mentions the messages of the mass media only parenthetically—and then more as a reflection of society's misplaced values than as an evil in itself. On the other hand, the psychologist sees a direct and powerful connection between youthful neuroses and parents' ability to mould their children in ways that make them accept a vacuously materialistic society.

"Our expectations for our children have changed," he writes "Our society supports external signs of achievement—high grades, big salaries, symbols of wealth and conspicuous consumption. The bumper sticker 'He who dies with the most toys wins' is ironic—to a point. Many of us snicker, but live our lives as if it's true." And the pressure parents put on kids to be winners, in a society more starkly and cruelly divided between winners and losers than ever before, ensures that this logic is replicated in the next generation. "Ours is a society of comparisons—who has the most luxurious office, who drives the best car, who has the nicest clothes, the biggest house. I was shopping in an exclusive clothing store recently. A huge sign proclaimed: 'Before they see your house, your car, or your wife's diamonds, they'll see your tie.' Our kids follow suit. They compare grades, their accomplishment on the athletic field, and ... the rank of college that accepts them."

In other words, it's a systemic problem. Although mass marketing may provide the most obvious illustration of our cultural acceptance (perhaps even veneration) of greed, envy, and cutthroat competition, those are values so deeply embedded in daily life that we rarely notice them. They are as common yet as unremarkable as the sky above the office towers. When middle-class parents insist that the schools be turned into boot camps to prepare their kids for the combat of tomorrow's borderless, hyper-technologized economy, they are promoting the values of materialism. When parents ferry their kids to school in gas-guzzling SUVs, racing against traffic, cellphone activated to conduct a little business on the way, they are expressing by their example a preference for commerce over community. The lessons from daily life are profound, and yet they rarely come to our attention. They're part of the background noise as we move from today into tomorrow.

The picture created by Kindlon and others suggests that there has been a resurgence of materialistic values recently (as the communal values of the 1960s social revolution recede deeper into history), and that this has had an impact on family life and society's attitudes towards child-rearing. Peter Silsbee's suggestion that the logic of globalization has penetrated our individual, private worlds provides a plausible explanation for how and why this occurred at this particular time. Yet it's odd to hear this kind of reasoning articulated by a guy who works for a polling firm that functions as a part of corporate America, selling data about kids' opinions and preferences to toy makers and television networks. Could it be that Silsbee, the polling company executive in the suit, is not all that far out of line, philosophically, with the people protesting against marketing aimed at kids? Is it possible that Silsbee's analysis of the new time-space continuum takes the anti–child-marketing forces' argument to the next level by focusing on the root causes of the anxiety aroused by media and marketing images directed towards kids?

To test this perverse notion that the anti-marketing activists and the polling guy might be on the same track, I ask Dr. Allen Kanner and Dr. Susan Linn, the SCEC activists, to comment on the idea that the media/marketing images they campaign against are perhaps just symbolic of a greater and more pervasive problem and that the real enemy is an inadequately restrained economic system that's placed excessive demands on parents, leaving many children virtual orphans in the care of the tube, the Internet, and the video console.

Dr. Linn rejects that proposition, partly, it seems, on tactical grounds. She suggests that if the issue were refocused as a question of how much time parents spend with their children, the marketing industry could easily slide out of its responsibility not to use images of violence and irresponsible sex to sell things to kids. For her, those practices are not just symbolic of a larger problem, but are themselves an evil with clearly negative consequences in the lives of kids.

"Does the fact that poor parents have to work—and forget about upper- and middle-class parents who are making a choice about values—does that give the media the right to exploit their children?" she asks. "I don't think so. I think that as a society we have a responsibility towards our children. It's that whole thing about 'it takes a village.'"

When pressed, Dr. Linn concedes that more concrete supports for families, like funding for better daycare, more parental leave, and public support for amenities like arts programs and public libraries, might provide some counterbalance to the influence of commercial media culture. But she insists that the onslaught of marketing aimed at kids would still be a formidable foe. And she remains dead set against any attempt to refocus the debate about media and kids on questions of parental oversight, the struggle between workplace and family commitments, and the public responsibility to support working families. In the current climate, she suggests, any attempt to shift the emphasis away from companies and onto families would become just another opportunity to blame the victim.

"It's like, with kids who joined gangs, people used to blame the parents in poor neighbourhoods. Sure, maybe there were some parents who just didn't care. But the culture was too compelling ... Families where kids have less support are probably more vulnerable, although I don't think that one family, no matter how intact, can combat the intensive marketing. Families can't work in isolation."

I get a more positive response when I propose to Dr. Kanner that marketing is simply the lightning rod for deeper-seated discomfort about the role of an accelerated, globalized economy in tearing apart the bonds of family and community.

"Well gosh, I'm writing an article about this right now," he responds. "I think what I'm really fighting is globalization. That is, the whole corporate culture that has been created and continually expands worldwide and promotes these plans and processes. I myself am very concerned about these larger issues."

But lest it seem that Kanner, the activist, and Silsbee, the pollster, are reading from the same script, it's important to point out that they disagree, big time, over the role of advertising and marketing in either promoting or mitigating the effects of this heartless global culture that places economic considerations above social ones.

For Dr. Kanner, marketing that promises happiness, salvation, or escape through the purchase of products is a primary agent that fuels the culture of consumerism and convinces humans to stay on the treadmill in pursuit of more possessions. The illusion that's being peddled, he says, is that more products will make you feel good. And so far, few people have woken up to the truth.

"I'm wondering why more and more people are buying more and more stuff," he says, "while every single study on happiness of the last fifty years shows that people are unhappier than they used to be. What's going on? I can't help thinking that they are being kept in this consumeristic frenzy by advertising—that's a big part of it—as well as by the materialistic values that permeate our society."

Silsbee, not surprisingly, takes a different approach. He believes that consumer products function as a balm for our psychic wounds, providing a surrogate sense of meaning in a modern world where traditional ways of finding meaning have been lost. People, kids especially, want to buy things, see movies, play with toys, because those things do make them feel good by giving them a sense of control and the illusion that their world makes sense.

"The products that kids really like—that everybody really likes—are the kind of things that define known universes," he says. "You know, like Disneyland is a known universe: you go to Disneyland and you know it has a certain ideology and there are different rides—different rides express different parts of this ideology—and somehow you relax inside of this because everything is planned for you. There are thrills and chills and action, but it's a safe scare, and you trust that everything is going to work out fine. It's not so easy in our normal lives when we are pulled in so many different directions."

So the icons of consumer culture provide stability and a sense of order in a rapidly changing, disorderly world. This idea that products have become the basis for many people's sense of self parallels the suggestion, made by psychologist Jeffrey Goldstein in Chapter 4, that in a world where identity is no longer formed through association with great causes, religious faith, or nationalism, people need to define themselves through the purchase of goods that have been invested with some deeper symbolic significance. Silsbee adds, however, that they do more than that. In a society that tends to "disenchant" its members (for example, through education system reforms that strive to remake kids in the image of computers), consumer goods provide a kind of synthetic experience of joy.

"When kids go to the mall and respond to a brand," Silsbee says, "I think they are reaching towards enchantment. I think enchantment might previously have been located in the church. Now it's located in some really terrific entertainment property, in the sense that it enchants kids' lives. I have a four year old daughter, and she thinks she's a Powerpuff Girl. She's constantly striking poses and telling me that I must die. But I realize it is all play—in my day it was cops and robbers or World War Two."

Comfort, meaning, a sense of place—these are qualities that our society has lost over the centuries. Borrowing an analogy from Neil Postman, Silsbee likens life in a traditional society to possessing a deck of cards "where you know that if you are dealt the two of clubs and then the two of hearts, you will probably get the two of spades and then the two of diamonds. You know what order the cards are in and what is going to be dealt to you. But with modernity, it's all mixed up. You don't know what's going to be dealt to you. So it makes our lives very complex and difficult."

Ultimately, says Silsbee, the fatal flaw in the anti–kid-marketing argument is its failure to accept that children themselves are willing participants in this process. Kids are thrilled to be enlisted in market research, he relates, because they like it when adults value their opinions. But more than that, they love toys. He recalls being in the same position a few decades ago. "When I was growing up in the 50s in America," he recalls, "you'd have these just horrendous commercials, that were very effective, from the Wham-o corporation, showing us hula hoops and Frisbees. And they looked great! They were going to revolutionize our lives, and they were so cheap. We were sitting ducks, but I can't say I didn't really enjoy my Frisbee, and I can't say I really didn't enjoy my hula hoop. I think it's always problematic to assign moral value to a consumer purchase because, if it's giving us some fun, is that bad?"

Of course, the trait that Silsbee cites as evidence of the benign nature of marketing to kids—i.e., that the kids themselves enjoy it—is, to the industry's detractors, proof of its insidiousness. Marketers' ability to activate the "nag factor," to stoke kids' dreams and desires and turn them loose against their weary, hapless parents, is perhaps the aspect of kid marketing that infuriates its critics the most.

In "Kiddie Capitalism," his highly nuanced summary of the history of marketing to children, University of Illinois sociology professor Dan Cook looks at the scope and limitations of these two opposing arguments, which describe kids, in the first case, as self-aware, "empowered" participants in this tango with the mass-marketing industry, and, in the second, as manipulated, propagandized dupes.[10] Cook expresses some sympathy for the critics' viewpoint that marketing to kids can involve trickery and can lead to deeper human values being replaced by a cult of commercial idolatry.

Yet at the same time, he gives a nod to the idea, hinted at by Silsbee, that today's parents are being a tad hypocritical in decrying the rampant commercialism that surrounds their children, while looking back at their own childhood ensnarement in the world of manufactured images and trinkets through a sticky lens of nostalgia. "Our memories, our sense of personal history," Cook writes, "are, to some extent, tied to the commercial culture of our youth: an old lunchbox with television characters on it; a doll, a comic book, or a brand of cereal; a sports hero, perhaps; certainly music of one sort or another." While today's parents may be alarmed by their kids' obsession with having the latest cool toy, they are, at the same time, inclined to explain the totems of their own youth as "benign artifacts of a fading past, harmless enough, slated to wind up as pieces of nostalgia at junk shops and yard sales."

All of which implies that: (a) marketers have targeted kids for a long time, and (b) the process has not entirely destroyed the moral fibre of preceding generations. Cook traces the origins of a distinct children's market back to around 1915. Before then, working-class children (mostly boys) worked as factory labourers, shoeshine boys, or newsies and spent their money on things like restaurant meals, candy, or pool halls and nickelodeons. But with the rise of the "bourgeois child"—who stayed in school longer to attain the skills demanded by a more complex economy, and whose life was romanticized by adults as an island of serenity, removed from the concerns of the world—marketers began pitching specific children's products that could be found in specific children's sections of stores. (Before then, children's clothes, for example, would have been sold in the men's or women's department—sorted by size, but not distinguished by style.)

At first, the new products for children were pitched to the mothers who controlled the family purse strings. But it wasn't long before the marketing gurus of the day realized the value of getting the kids onside. Department stores introduced "'floors for youth' complete with child-size fixtures, mirrors, and eye-level views of the merchandise," writes Cook. "Merchants hoped to provide children with a sense of proprietorship over the shop or area by visually, acoustically and commercially demonstrating that it was a space designed with them in mind." One strategy was to place the older children's products towards the entrance to the floor, with the younger children's merchandise placed farther in towards the inside walls. Cook cites a 1939 issue of the *Bulletin of the National Retail Dry Goods Association*, in which a designer of one such floor explains the rationale for this arrangement: it leads the smaller kids on a tour through their bigger brothers' and sisters' terrain. "The younger children are delighted to see the older children shopping as they go through these departments," the unnamed designer elucidates, "for all children want to be older than they are. The little boy and little girl seeing the big boys and big girls buying will long for the day when he too can come to these departments and buy."

If the statement "All children want to be older than they are" seems curiously familiar, it's because this logic was invoked in Chapter 3 as a possible explanation why Britney Spears has been marketed to preadolescent girls so successfully. In strategic terms, at least, little seems to have changed in close to seventy years. Certainly, it is nothing new that marketing to kids relies on the active participation, the partnership, of the kids themselves. The fact that kids are involved in the process leads some commentators to think that the anti–child-marketing forces are shortchanging kids by portraying them as passive, programmable receptacles for marketing hype. In reality, they protest, kids are more than that: they are discriminating, self-interested players with their own agendas.

"One strain of academic thought," explains Cook, "asserts that media and consumer products are just cultural materials, and children are free to use them as they will, imparting their own meanings to cartoons, toys, games, etc." Cook makes it clear that this viewpoint makes some sense to him: "There's little doubt that children creatively interpret their surroundings, including consumer goods. They colour outside the lines, make up rules to games, invent their own stories and make imaginary cars fly. If we lose sight of children's ability to exercise personal agency and to transform the meanings imposed on them by advertising (as well as those imparted by parents), we will forever be stuck in the belief structure which grants near omnipotence to the corporate realm."

Yet Cook believes this argument about "personal agency" has its limits, and this is where he parts company with Silsbee. For the academic sees something more sinister piggybacking in on this noble idea that kids' personal autonomy should be recognized. A self-serving marketing industry, he believes, has used this notion that kids are in control to launch an end run around parents' natural skepticism. Kids may want to manipulate the spectacles and durable goods that companies sell them, reshaping them in the image of their own imaginary worlds. But companies also want to manipulate kids.

"Children's commercial culture," he writes, "has quite successfully usurped kids' boundless creativity and personal agency, selling them back to them—and us—as 'empowerment,' a term that appeases parents while shielding marketers." But that applies as much to adults who grew up surrounded by marketing images as it does to today's kids, who are bombarded by Britney and Pokémon. The solution, Cook believes, lies in being able to make distinctions. Kid culture is neither wholly benign or completely bad, and kids and adults have to learn to read how it functions in their world.

"We have to incite children to adopt a critical posture toward media and consumption," he advises. " ... The mere autocratic vetoing of children's requests will only result in anti-adult rebellion. The challenge facing us all—as relatives, teachers, friends, or even not-so-innocent bystanders—is to find ways to affirm children's personal agency and their membership in a community of peers while insisting that they make the distinction between self-worth and owning a Barbie or a Pokémon card. Or anything, for that matter."

†

Placing too much emphasis on the role of media and marketing in harming kids—going beyond mere skepticism to demonize the marketing machine as the prime source of kids' problems—brings with it considerable risk. For one, it distracts us from factors operating within the sphere of real life that may make far greater contributions to the problems that concern us. It's probable, for instance, that the brilliant marketing campaigns that made McDonald's a global phenomenon (partly through its toy giveaways and the Disney-like atmosphere in its eateries) have played some role in the rise in obesity and the declining physical health of some North American children. But there were surely other factors at play, many of them more deeply embedded in the culture—and more difficult to root out—than the ubiquitous burger-marketing campaigns with the annoying jingles that make them such easy targets for public wrath.

You can ban fast-food marketing in the schools. But how do you deal with the systemic factors that have been fingered as causes of kids' declining measures of physical health? One important contributor, for instance, is the layout of our residential communities, which discourages exercise. The car-friendly, scattered design of the suburban communities where many North American children grow up has created a situation where walking to school or to the park has been replaced, for many kids, by minivan rides between home, school, and organized activities. This is a lifestyle with quantifiably negative health effects.[11] A pervasive unease about kids spending time in public places has also kept kids indoors and contributed to the sedentary lifestyle that packs on the pounds and elevates the blood pressure. True, fast-food consumption has increased as routine physical activity has declined. But what are the social roots of that trend? Fast food is an institution that reflects the deeper economic imperatives shaping our lives; the market for fast food was not created by advertising alone. Fast-food restaurants meet the expectations of our fast-moving, hyper-charged society. For people in a culture where time is always money, the ability to grab a bite on the run is a bigger selling point than the food's nutrition or even its taste. Convenience—drive-through everything—is a natural fit for a society that can't afford to sit still for too long. An entire system of food preparation, transport, and storage has been developed to satisfy the economic ideals that underlie almost everything we do: that we should get the largest quantity for the lowest cost, and that products should be ready quickly so as not to disrupt our busy schedules.

Blaming mass media and mass marketing as the cause of stress on families may similarly function as a counterproductive distraction from events in real life. You don't have to be a fan of the entertainment most kids consume to believe that there may be more important factors ripping the fabric of family life and undermining parental authority than TV and video games. Dr. Benjamin Spock, the granddaddy of North American childcare experts—whose liberal-mindedness was exemplified by his exhortation, during the Vietnam War, that young men should burn their draft cards—was one advocate of an expansive, multifaceted approach to making modern life more family friendly. In his final book, *A Better World for Our Children* (published in 1994), Dr. Spock lamented the exposure of children to seamy and brutal spectacles on television and in movies, but his recipe for the restoration of "American family values" dealt much more with the inner workings of families and the role of the social institutions that support them than with kids' media diet.[12] In agreement with the anti–child-marketing crusaders of today, Dr. Spock believed that children in millennial-era North America are raised to be overly competitive and materialistic, without a guiding ethic of compassion. But he saw the solution arising mostly from home and school rather than from network boardrooms. Parents can foster a more generous social ethic in their kids, he counselled, by setting an example of selflessness and social concern and by raising their children "not ... with the major aim of getting ahead in the world financially, as many are raised today. Instead, they should be raised from the age of two through adolescence with the ideals of helpfulness, kindness, and service to others." Spock also believed that educational institutions need radical reform in order to encourage the development of more kind-spirited kids. "I urge schools and universities to stop judging students solely on their grades—to do away with the conventional grading system altogether," he wrote. "The drive to get high scores distorts the real purpose of education."

Addressing the time crunch that makes it difficult for many parents to form close bonds with their kids, Spock saw much of the responsibility resting on the shoulders of corporations and governments, institutions that have the power both to increase the availability and improve the quality of daycare, and to provide flexible work arrangements and subsidies for parents who want to stay home with their kids. These were the concrete policy options Spock believed were necessary to counteract what he saw—concurring with several media critics we've heard from in this book—as a crisis in modern family life. "We have the means to save our society—enough funds to subsidize mothers or fathers who want to stay home to care for their preschool children, to subsidize better daycare centres and schools," he wrote.

It appears to me a telling sign that the battle over the effects of advertising and entertainment images on kids rages at a much higher intensity in precisely the geographical areas where the social supports that Dr. Spock wrote about are in shorter supply. In Canada, where income equalization policies and social services have not been eroded as dramatically as in the United States, media effects on kids have been only a minor focus of public debate. Yet south of the border—home of the laissez-faire revolution, where reasonable parental leave policies and subsidized, well-regulated daycare programs are off the political map, where statistics indicate that families are required to move more often to meet the needs of corporations—the media and kids debate has been conducted at a high decibel level. Is this an example of McLuhan's "referred pain," of desperately searching in the wrong places for an answer to a critical problem?

There are a couple of possible explanations why Americans may be more inclined to blame cultural inputs for social problems than their counterparts in other countries are. One is that American families are more stressed than their counterparts in countries with more comprehensive social safety nets, and lashing out at the mass media is a reaction to that. Another possible explanation is that the political right in the United States has more effectively promoted cultural issues as a smokescreen to obscure the obvious deficiency in social supports for families. The latter idea fits with the view — supported by the mea culpas of right-wing cultural warrior David Brock, who has renounced his former occupation as political character assassin[13]—that the American right's obsession with reframing social issues as issues of personal morality was intended primarily as a way of pre-empting serious debate on social and economic policies.

And therein lies a vexing question for liberals who would hold commercial interests responsible for the erosion of family cohesion and traditional values. Are they not being absorbed as junior partners in the "culture wars" strategy promoted by powerful right-wing forces? If the stresses on families do have at least as much to do with concrete issues like access to quality daycare, tax and economic policies that provide a break for poor families, and labour laws and workplace policies that favour families over corporations, isn't it ultimately counterproductive for social liberals to form coalitions with powerful forces that come out on the wrong side of all those policy issues?

Advancing a critique with clear echoes of Dr. Spock's prescription in *A Better World for Our Children*, historian and sociologist Stephanie Coontz argues that pro-family social policies, available to families of all descriptions, are essential to combat the havoc that's been created on the domestic scene by runaway economic reform. The author of the acclaimed *The Way We Really Are*, which explores the tension between work and family life, Coontz is clear that the problems facing most contemporary families are concrete, not cultural.

"What we need is a major new campaign," she says in an interview, "much along the lines of the Progressive Movement's campaign, at the turn of the [nineteenth] century, to make family issues a health and safety issue in terms of national regulation, guidelines, and investment ... We should have laws that prohibit forced overtime, where you can sue an employer who prevents you from taking time off. We should have laws such as Sweden's that allow any caregiver (not just parents, but caretakers of people with Alzheimer's) to drop down to three-quarters time—with a cut in pay, of course, but not to lose health benefits and not to lose seniority. We have to do something about our ludicrous family leave policy—it covers less than 50 percent of the workers, and it is unpaid. It is for wealthy people only, and for those who work for big corporations only. The maximum leave you are allowed under the act is smaller than the minimum amount of leave in all of our European counterparts. And we have to invest in quality childcare. Childcare is not good. We must make it better. That should be a major campaign, unless you think that kids are less important than inspecting meat and regulating airline safety."[14]

Of course, right-wing forces in the United States, especially fundamentalist Christian outfits, don't see it that way. To them, the sorry state of families is the outgrowth of immoral media influences, from *Murphy Brown* to *Will and Grace*, undermining public respect for the nuclear family, the bedrock unit upon which the economic viability and social harmony of the nation has been based. However, Coontz, the historian, points out that this idealized image of the family was only dominant for a brief period in history and is certainly not the norm in American life today. As long as society continues to embrace the modern concept of marriage as an institution based on love, companionship, and personal fulfillment, rather than as the economic or political arrangement between families that it once was, she believes that single-parent families, blended families, and non-traditional family forms like same-sex partnerships will account for a large percentage of the arrangements in which children are raised. And all of those family forms are deserving of sanction and support so that they might survive and prosper.[15]

Yet the kind of pro-family policies that are needed "are being talked about too timidly," Coontz complains. She is especially concerned that "the failure of liberals to confront these issues head-on has left the right wing in charge of not just the dialogue, but the very language" that is used to discuss issues of family and social policy.[16]

In a political sense, then, the excesses of the kid-media/marketing machine have served as a red herring, distracting the public from the pressing need for social supports to keep families viable. But they've been equally effective as a kind of Trojan Horse, allowing many organizations, particularly the fundamentalist Christian lobby, to channel public and parental distaste for Marilyn Manson, gangsta rap, and South Park into support for a broader, less visible agenda that includes the demonization of gay people and the promotion of regressive ideas about male/female relations, which—based on the idealization of a fictitious 1950s norm—would have working fathers serve as lords and masters of subdivisions filled with stay-at-home moms.

I asked Dr. Allen Kanner and Dr. Susan Linn, the SCEC advocates quoted earlier, whether their tight focus on marketing's effects on families might be used to advance an agenda that's alien to their own thinking. Kanner acknowledged that this is a serious concern. He told me he's careful to choose which right-leaning groups he'll work with and which ones he'll stay away from, and he always makes it clear to whatever audience he's addressing that the real target of his wrath is unchecked corporate power (a view you won't hear expressed by the soapbox moralizers of the right). On the opposite coast, Linn was adamant that what distinguishes her approach from that of the hellfire theocrats of the right is that she's a firm defender of the First Amendment right to free speech. She's only in favour of legislative restrictions on marketing products to kids; there should be no interference with entertainment content or artistic expression.

But that's a distinction that's sometimes been lost on liberal U.S. politicians, who have been more than willing to join the conservative crusade against cultural corruption—often by taking aim at artistic expression just as much as at the designs of marketers. In those cases, the standard liberal declarations about the need to protect civil liberties have done little to prevent the erosion of those liberties. The mid-1980s U.S. Senate hearings on rock music lyrics, for instance, attempted to balance First Amendment guarantees against the committee's disdain for the lyrical stylings of the so-called hair metal bands of the day (Def Leppard, W.A.S.P., Motley Crue, etc.)

by introducing parental advisory labels for albums that contained "offensive lyrics" (these labels were dubbed "Tipper stickers" after Tipper Gore, wife of then-senator Al, whose Parents Music Resource Center had pushed for the hearings). Yet Ithaca College politics professor Thomas Shevory notes that these stickers "became a focus around which other forms of censorship began to coalesce."[17] The first censorious spinoff from the Tipper stickers came when stores like Wal-Mart and Woolworths refused to stock labelled albums or insisted upon new versions of songs with changed lyrics. Various states subsequently introduced bills that would have banned the sale of recordings that appealed to the "prurient interest of minors in sex" or were seen as glamorizing violence, deviant sex, or "the illegal use of drugs or alcohol." With this pro-censorship movement gathering steam and broadening focus, Florida's legislature passed a bill denying state funds to a public radio outlet, based on one state senator's dissatisfaction with the station for airing "positive comments about Kurt Cobain and the playing of folk singer Iris Dement's 'Wasteland of the Free,' a song which protests economic inequality in the U.S." Yet while radio stations may have been punished for political commentary, attempts to stifle rock music fell short of achieving their primary purpose. The act of censorship, Shevory notes, has often given rock music a renewed sense of authenticity during periods of decline, and the Tipper stickers appeared to increase the sales of records lucky enough to receive this parental stamp of disapproval.

The mid-1980s hearings may themselves have been something of a turning point in that they presented a valuable opportunity for otherwise liberal politicians—impressed by the "can't lose" political optics and populist appeal of the issue—to jump on a traditionally conservative bandwagon. Shevory saw the Senate's hearings into music lyrics as part of a tradition of "right wing attacks against rock" that dated back to the 1950s, when the emergence of Elvis Presley and his form of rock 'n' roll were perceived by the establishment in the southern U.S. to be promoting "race mixing," i.e., relationships between blacks and whites. In the 1980s, concerns about popular music re-emerged when rising rates of teen suicide, teen pregnancies, and rape and other forms of violence were becoming linked in the public mind with the messages in rock music.

Shevory points out, however, that the hair-metal heyday was also a period of painful social dislocation, as traditional industry in North America headed into a sharp decline. Perhaps significantly, the bombastic, distorted guitar riffs and the plaintive, harsh lyrics offered by the metal bands under scrutiny by the committee struck a chord primarily with the young working-class males who would be most directly affected by that economic decline—possibly providing them a sense of catharsis.

This time around it wasn't the old-time Bible-thumpers and rednecks who made the most political hay from the frenzy over outlaw rock 'n' rollers. Much of the agitating that led to the committee hearings and the sticker campaign was done by Tipper Gore, whose husband Al, a member of the committee, got to play a latter-day Joe McCarthy, firing rhetorical questions at big-haired stadium rockers about the precise meaning of their lyrics and their impact upon the impressionable youth of America. Some of the most memorable moments of the committee's hearings came in exchanges between Gore and singer Dee Snider of Twisted Sister, whose overblown anthems like "We're Not Going to Take It" have been immortalized on video with obvious, tongue-in-cheek self-mockery. "Are you going to tell me you're a big fan of my music?" Snider goaded Gore when the senator took the microphone. Later, after Snider confirmed that the group's fan club is known as "Sick Muther Fucking Fans of Twisted Sister," Gore asked, "Is that a Christian group?"[18] (In an odd postscript to this episode, during the 2000 election campaign, Snider—who had since embarked on a post-Twisted second career as a DJ in Hartford, Connecticut—told the press he would be supporting Gore in his bid to become president. Snider was willing to bury his animosity because of Gore's pro-environmentalist stance, even though, he said, "I don't trust the guy as far as I can throw him.")[19]

Indeed, some commentators believe that Gore's involvement with music censorship was merely an opportunistic, profile-building manoeuvre on the long road to his turn-of-the-millennium presidential run. Cleaning up the cultural pollution to which kids are exposed was a surefire method for an ambitious political moderate to shore up his right flank and repel the standard barbs about liberals being unconcerned by, or at worst aiding and abetting, the country's moral decline. Since then it's become de rigueur for liberal Democrats to use the issue to reach out to middle America. And if they have to share the stage with conservative theocrats, so be it.

In 1998, for instance, Gore's future vice-presidential running mate Joe Lieberman joined with former Reagan education secretary William Bennett—America's leading figurehead in the crusade to restore moral rectitude to the land—to announce they were awarding the "Silver Sewer" prize to Seagram Inc. for producing the *Jerry Springer Show* and distributing music by Marilyn Manson. "Nearly three years ago, Bill Bennett and I formed a partnership based on our shared concern that the rising tide of sex, violence and vulgarity in the entertainment media had coarsened our culture, weakened our values and hurt our children," Lieberman told the National Press Club in Washington.[20]

At the grassroots level, as well, the attack on corporate purveyors of perversion and sickness has involved significant contact between progressives and the troops of the Christian right. Gary Ruskin, who runs the anti–kid-marketing lobby Commercial Alert under the aegis of former Green presidential candidate Ralph Nader, has been described by the *Village Voice* as a "definitely non-partisan but assuredly leftwing ... lynchpin in a coalition of progressives and Christian conservatives who agree on one thing: that laissez faire corporate America needs to be reined in as its denizens find, by turns, ever more insidious ways to peddle their wares, especially by targeting the young." Amongst Ruskin's allies, the *Voice* reports, are "right wing luminaries such as James Dobson and Donald Wildmon." When Ruskin presented research purportedly showing that the gambling industry was trying to lure young people by putting the visages of the Pink Panther and Spiderman on slot machines, the signatures of officials of the religious right were prominent on the letter of complaint that was sent to Congress. (The American Gaming Association denied that putting the cartoon characters on their devices meant that they were producing "slots for tots." Kids, they told the *Voice*, are not allowed into casinos—the machines were made for adults feeling nostalgic for their own childhoods.)[21]

For his part, Ruskin acknowledges that his work against "commercial exploitation" necessitates a coalition with the religious right, but he's not embarrassed by that. He doesn't want to join them, but to transcend them. Ruskin's organization describes its raison d'être as an attempt to break down the "semi-permanent trench warfare" wherein liberals are unable to recognize that "there is degradation in our culture," and conservatives are unwilling to admit the role of private enterprises in creating that situation. Commercial Alert's stated goal, which appears on its website, is to recruit to its cause citizens from all points on the political spectrum by opposing "the invasion of everything-for-sale, anything-for-profit values, with special attention to the harmful effects on children and the social and public health costs of the advertising of alcohol, tobacco, junk food, fast food, violent entertainment and gambling."[22]

But how much clout can a group like Commercial Alert—described by the *Village Voice* as a one-person operation, working out of a cramped office that Ruskin shares with an independent author—exercise in a partnership with a large and well-heeled outfit like Focus on the Family (whose high-ranking officials endorsed Ruskin's anti-slots letter)? Whose agenda is advanced the most through this kind of coalition? And are children really the beneficiaries if these campaigns ultimately wind up feeding a political program that wants to return American family life to a state of old-time authoritarianism, where parental will is enforced through strict discipline and kids aren't encouraged to think for themselves?

The point of these campaigns against rampant commercialism is ostensibly to protect kids—protect them from violence, from the harm that comes from junk food, booze, and gambling, from their own bad decisions. In the next chapter we'll look in detail at the debate about the respective contributions of media images and real-life situations in encouraging youth violence. For now, suffice it to say that conservative "pro-family" organizations have taken a rather paradoxical stand on issues of violence and kids. Conservative Christian outfits like Focus on the Family believe, as do many people of liberal and secular mindsets, that watching images of brutality is not good for kids. But the organization and its founder, James Dobson, are also strong proponents of the use of corporal punishment.

Does this protect children from violence? Or does it help create a climate in which violence against children can be justified? Do incidents where young children are injured after being "disciplined" by parents and adult caregivers, for example, have anything to do with the well-publicized position of pious childcare "experts" that hitting children is not only acceptable, but should be encouraged?

This acceptance of corporal punishment flows from the Christian right's broader commitment that authority is to be obeyed, not questioned. James Dobson has stated that parents serve the same role for their families as God does for human society: their word is absolute, to be taken as the truth and the law.[23] There is reason to fear that Dobson would apply the same authoritarian creed to society as a whole. In his bitter memoir *James Dobson's War on America*, former Dobson lieutenant Gil Alexander-Moegerle portrays his exboss as an autocrat who is "out of step with the American way and even, at times, dangerous to great principles of democracy such as diversity, tolerance, and compromise"—a man who would take away the hard-won rights of women, who has helped inspire a climate of fear and hatred against homosexuals, and who would force children from families of whatever belief system to participate in Christian education in the public school system.[24]

A scan through the film and television reviews presented on Focus on the Family's website reveals how Dobson's organization uses the soft sell to peddle his particular brand of Christian authoritarianism. On the surface, these reviews provide parents with a heads-up about movies with content—violence, horror, frightening situations, sex, bad language—that they may want to shelter their children from. This is accomplished using a kind of metric format. Each review contains standard subtitles such as "spiritual content," "sexual content," "violent content," "crude and profane language," "drug and alcohol content," which form sidebars within which the reviewer presents a careful tabulation of the number of times the "f-word" or the "s-word" are uttered, when "God's name is misused," and precisely what kinds of conflict, coupling, or imbibing take place or are hinted at, and how many times. Occasionally this cinematic accounting exercise becomes comic in its determination that no invitation to sin should go unnoticed. In FOTF's review of

Bridget Jones' Diary (incidentally, an R-rated movie), the reviewer notes that "several female characters show cleavage." Generally, though, the intent of this exercise seems to be in step with mainstream preoccupations, serving a kind of friendly neighbour role by whispering in parents' ears about which films contain which kinds of content they might be uncomfortable taking their children to see. Last time I was on the site, movies with uplifting moral messages and happy endings were marked with happy faces.

It's after reading a cross-section of these reviews that one notices the persistent presence of Dobson's political preoccupations, even though they are hidden beneath some personable prose and broad-based concerns about exposing children to images of violence, coarse language, and sex. Reinforcing Alexander-Moegerle's disquiet about Dobson's anti-democratic bent, numerous reviews suggest that the cardinal sin for FOTF is not presenting characters who have a potty mouth or a runaway libido, but rather undermining the idea that authority—especially parental authority—should be absolute and unchallenged. *Malcolm in the Middle* is condemned as a TV program that "ridicules organized religion, endorses bad behavior and ultimately reinforces TV's modern family mantra: *parents are stupid.*" A more forgiving, good-humoured assessment of *Malcolm in the Middle* is that it presents its parents as sometimes confused, anxious, or ineffectual, with foibles and hang-ups that make them objects of affection as well as the butt of jokes—and these qualities make them, ultimately, more *human*. Since they are not dishing out earnest moral lessons in the style of the Cleavers or the Nelsons, however, they don't cut it as TV parents.

Similarly, questions of authority are at the center of the FOTF reviewer's quarrel with the film *Harry Potter and the Prisoner of Azkaban*. The whole Harry Potter series has been divisive for conservative Christians, and FOTF has devoted a fair amount of space to airing the debate (debate being a rare commodity in this forum) between the camp that likes Harry Potter because it champions good over evil, and the camp that feels using a supernatural setting "glorifies that which is born in the pits of Hell." The review of *The Prisoner of Azkaban* mostly sidesteps those issues and finds plenty of positive things to say about Harry's loyalty and his sense of self-sacrifice. But the reviewer turns near apoplectic when contemplating the film's message that, in order to serve the cause of good, one will often have to define and follow one's one conscience, and that will sometimes put one at loggerheads with established authority. "Harry continues to disregard the instructions of the adult authority figures in his life," complains the reviewer. " ... A more subtle ill here is the way these *caring* adults are portrayed. His relatives can't stand him and subsequently treat him like dirt. Kids will instinctively understand that that's a bad scenario. The greater danger is portraying Harry's well-meaning — cool — teachers as ultra-tolerant. Throughout the film they wink at his misdeeds and look the other way as he defies them. He loves them for it, and everything works out marvelously in the end ... [And the portrayal of his unloving step-parents] may make some attentive young minds innately suspicious of authority figures. A good thing when it comes to strangers on the street; a terrible thing when it comes to teachers, pastors and parents."

What's curious about the selection of films reviewed by Focus on the Family is that a large proportion of them are adult-oriented films that no sane person would ever dream of taking a child to see. That makes me wonder about an ulterior motive: do the arbiters of taste and decency at Focus on the Family give parents and other adults as little credit for being able to think for themselves as they give to children? In the same way that Dobson's group thinks children should not be exposed through media to spectacles like permissive parents and well-adjusted, happy gay people (FOTF has campaigned against *Will and Grace* and supported a boycott of Disney, partly because of its gay-positive hiring policies), is it also their goal to sanitize the portrayal of the world that adults are exposed to? Take the FOTF review of Michael Moore's documentary *Fahrenheit 9/11*. Predictably, the reviewer dismisses Moore's criticism of the war in Iraq and the Bush administration's reasons for going to war as a pack of liberal lies. More interestingly, the reviewer instructs his audience not to watch the graphic, obscenity-laced footage from the battlefield, which Moore has used to show the reality of war on the ground. "Families trying to decide if wading into Moore's political swamp might prove a stimulating intellectual exercise in the art of debunking should be aware that one sequence features

American soldiers using the f-word and playing an obscenely titled heavy metal CD. The film also shows many images of war dead and wounded, some of them quite gruesome. (One boy is nude)." The problem for the reviewer is not in the reality of U.S. soldiers gleefully cranking up that song with the refrain "Burn, Motherfucker, Burn" as they ride their tank, shooting up Iraqi civilians' homes and killing and maiming the occupants. The problem isn't that children lie dead on the street. The problem is that it is in such bad taste to show that kind of thing.

Ultimately, what's most fascinating about many of these reviews (of both kids' and grown-ups' fare) is their tremendous capacity, while concentrating on those checklists of cuss words and cleavage, to completely miss the point. A critique of the teen cheerleader flick Bring It On laments that the film promotes a sexualized image of cheerleaders (a criticism that also appears elsewhere), which undermines its chances of "successfully promoting cheerleading as a serious sport." What the reviewer never once mentions is that Bring It On is a morality tale about class and race in the United States. The plot centres on a cheerleading squad from a white, upper-middle-class school that advances to the state finals after ripping off routines from a squad at a black school that can't afford to go to the championships. In the same vein, FOTF's review of American Beauty catalogues the film's portrayal of sex, violence, and middle-class angst and arrives at the conclusion that "just about everything in American Beauty—from drugs and sex to hatred and death—is sick, ugly and repulsive." What this reviewer never addresses, or even hints at, is the fact that American Beauty is intended as a biting commentary on the sadness of American middle-class life, with its materialism, hypocrisy, and lack of ideals, and the sordid results that all these things produce. Dealing honestly with themes like these, however, would require some analytical skills and a spirit of intellectual openness and self-revelation—qualities that might not mesh well with the authoritarian utopia envisioned by the religious right, where parents and pastors have all the answers, and unpleasantness of any kind must be kept away from the eyes and ears of kids and adults alike.[25]

Honest discussion might also tarnish the image of some of the prominent crusaders for a more sanitized media environment. Take, for instance, William Bennett, former Reagan education secretary, author of a series of bestselling books on cultivating "virtue," and blue-chip lecturer on the same topic. A campaigner against bad examples for kids in media, Bennett has been a big booster of the idea that adults should rehabilitate the American moral climate by pushing the right music, the right books, and the right TV, and by being virtuous in their own lives. The news, as pundit Michael Kinsley expressed it, that "Bennett's $50,000 sermons and best-selling moral instruction manuals have financed a multi-million dollar gambling habit" reinforced his detractors' view that people like Bennett have rather elastic standards about how, when, and to whom their moral edicts should be applied—and to what political effect.[26]

Bennett's work as a crusader against violence involves a similar double standard. In 1999, Bennett appeared before the Senate Committee on Commerce to speak about "marketing violence to children," at which time he pilloried Edgar Bronfman Jr., part owner of Interscope Records, for promoting singer Marilyn Manson, author of such works as "Irresponsible Hate Anthem," which Bennett claims encouraged a climate of violence amongst the young. It turns out, however, that Bennett is not against all violence—just violence that does not serve the right political purpose. When he wants to get behind state-sponsored violence on an immense scale, Bennett is much more direct and clear than the shock rockers, whose songs are sure to be interpreted as satire by some. Following the 2003 invasion of Iraq, Bennett travelled to college campuses across the United States, encouraging students to support the war and occupation. He spoke as a senior advisor to Americans for Victory over Terrorism, an offshoot of another Bennett-run organization called Empower America.[27]

What you see is not necessarily what you get.

PART TWO

The Roadrunner
Made Me Do It

CHAPTER 8

The Culture of Killing?

In September 1999 the U.S. Senate Committee on the Judiciary released a report entitled *Children, Violence and the Media*. With Utah senator Orrin Hatch (the committee's Republican chairman) at the helm, the committee purported to offer a cogent synopsis of the best scientific research on what violent media does to kids, leading to a list of suggestions for how parents and policy makers could help steer the nation out of what was apparently a profound state of crisis.

The dramatic news footage flooding the national airwaves suggested that all was not well with America's kids. Six months earlier two heavily armed students had walked into Columbine High School in Littleton, Colorado, and committed the largest ever massacre at an American school—murdering twelve students and one teacher, but failing in their plot to reduce the school to rubble with high explosives. Coming close on the heels of similar schoolyard massacres in Paducah, Kentucky, and Jonesboro, Arkansas, the Columbine tragedy confirmed—in the minds of most of the public—that the nation was in the midst of an epidemic of grotesque, unfathomable violence being committed by youngsters.

The country, of course, was frantic in its search for clues that might explain why this was happening. Media reports suggested that one common denominator amongst the young murderers was a love of graphically violent video games; much was made, for instance, of the revelation that the Columbine killers were devotees of the video splatter-fests *Quake* and *Doom*. This revelation prompted a new wave of questions about what media violence does to impressionable young minds. Parents started to ask themselves if their own kids—or their kids' classmates—were being turned into murderous zombies by the media products running on their rec room video-game console or the family VCR. Could the kid next door—or even the kid downstairs—be the next high school mass murderer in training?

One purpose of the Senate committee report, clearly, was to express the government's solidarity with a confused and horrified populace desperate to know that the root causes of the school massacres had been identified and that future Columbines, Paducahs, and Jonesboros would be prevented. Written in a tone of outrage and moral certainty, the report mirrors the public's mood of high anxiety and confirms that Something Must Be Done—now was not the time for equivocation or overly nuanced debate. It also contains several unequivocal statements about who's to blame for all this schoolyard mayhem. When the word "entertainment" is used to describe media products containing violence, for instance, it is placed in quotation marks—a subtle statement of disdain, signalling to American voters that "We're just as angry as you are." There are also veiled threats to the entertainment company executives, who are now assumed, by much of the public, to dwell on the same moral plane as drug pushers. Ominously, the committee warns that "the entertainment industries should not persist in using [their voluntary] ratings systems as an excuse for failing to take additional steps to reduce media violence." The ratings systems, it seemed, had done little to keep kids away from gruesome screen violence. Now it was up to the industry to stop peddling these images of mayhem—a step the politicians were confident would stem the bloodletting in the schoolyard—or feel the heavy hand of government.

Despite its bluster, however, the committee was conspicuously mild-mannered in its prescription of public policy remedies. Constrained by U.S. First Amendment guarantees to free speech, the committee steered away from recommending direct government pressure on the targeted industries, save for its instructions to the Federal Trade Commission and the Attorney General's office to monitor the marketing practices of entertainment companies. In regard to what parents can do, much of the committee's advice seemed to be of the common-sense, right-under-your-nose variety: know what the entertainment ratings systems mean and enforce them in your home; don't make television the focal point of family life; limit the number of hours your kids watch TV; unplug the video-game machine if your kid refuses to do his homework or starts to prefer gaming to socializing with friends ...

What's curious about all these measures is that they are decidedly half-hearted responses to what the committee insists is the definitive, indisputably proven cause of one of the gravest problems facing the United States. Calling media depictions of violent behaviour "one of the principal causes of youth violence," the committee baldly states that "television alone is responsible for 10 per cent of youth violence." In addition, it speculates that video games probably play a greater role in fostering youth violence than television. The report also repeats as proven fact the statement by University of Washington epidemiologist Brandon Centerwall that "[if], hypothetically, television technology had never been developed, there would be 10,000 fewer homicides each year in the United States, 70,000 fewer rapes, and 700,000 fewer injurious assaults. Violent crime would be half what it is." There is no mention of any dissenting viewpoints that would contradict statements such as Centerwall's. "The effect of media violence on our children is no longer open to debate," the report concludes. "Countless studies have shown that a steady diet of television, movie, music, video game and Internet violence plays a significant role in the disheartening number of violent acts committed by America's youth."[1]

That's a stunningly definitive conclusion to a debate that's baffled Western society's best minds for thousands of years. Consider, for example, the survey by psychiatry/psychology professor Richard Tremblay, which appeared a year after the Senate report and traces the controversy over the impact of culture on violence back at least 1,600 years.[2] That's when St. Augustine of Thagaste advanced the idea that aggressive behaviour is innate—a clear contrast to the dominant notion amongst modern-day commentators (including those who contributed to the Senate judiciary report) that violent behaviour is largely a product of cultural influences such as television and music. When St. Augustine wrote that "it is not the infant's will that is harmless, but the weakness of infant limbs," Tremblay says he was suggesting that aggression is a factor in human behaviour long before the child is able to interpret and learn from the culture that surrounds him.

This idea of aggression as a product of biology, not society, was reasserted a thousand years later by Thomas Hobbes, who characterized young, unsocialized children as "selfish machines striving for pleasure and power," according to Tremblay's paraphrase. Hobbes believed it was essential that humans, who were born "unfit for society," be trained from a young age to overcome their aggressive, selfish natures so that peace and order might exist in society.

All of this was turned on its head, however, by the philosopher Rousseau. Rousseau's more romantic worldview had it that "everything is good as it leaves the hands of the Author of things; everything degenerates in the hands of man." His conviction that an impure human world corrupts the inherent, innocent goodness of the child led Rousseau to advise that children be kept away from books and peers until adolescence and that they live as much as possible within nature to preserve their purity of spirit. Tremblay believes that Rousseau's idea of the child as innately pro-social has had an enduring impact, providing much of the philosophical foundation for the practice of social science in the twentieth century. He hears strong echoes of Rousseau, for instance, in the words of Albert Bandura, a leading theorist of the "social learning" movement (and a researcher who in the 1960s designed experiments to measure the impact of television violence on children's aggression). In his 1971 book *Aggression*, Bandura wrote that "people are not born with preformed repertoires of aggressive behaviour; they must learn them in one way or another"—a statement of philosophical commitment that, although less ornate than Rousseau's pronouncements, is virtually identical in intent.

Tremblay, chair of child psychology at the University of Montreal, believes that fundamental philosophical convictions such as this act as a powerful, if invisible force in the laboratories of contemporary social scientists and in the offices of policy makers. He is convinced, for instance, that the key assumption that children start out pure and learn their aggressive behaviour slowly over time has skewed the research agenda, leading researchers to skip over the question of how the experiences of preschoolers shape their future behaviour, and to focus inordinately on teenagers and their cultural environments. "A lack of attention to physical aggression during the early years appears to be the result of a long-held belief that physical aggression appears during late childhood and early adolescence as a result of bad peer influence, television violence and increased levels of male hormones," Tremblay writes.

But Tremblay says there is reason to doubt this bedrock set of assumptions. The small quantity of research on aggression that does include preschoolers, he writes, appears to contradict that idea of a "late onset" of aggressive behaviour. Tremblay cites one longitudinal study showing that physical aggression peaks at age four and declines steadily from there, and another one (which he co-authored) that was unable to locate any subset of subjects whose aggressive behaviour started later than the age of six. Indeed, some research suggests aggressive behaviour takes root much earlier than this. Tremblay refers to a study which "showed that language skills between 18 and 24 months were a good predictor of adult criminality in a Swedish sample of males followed from birth to adulthood. In fact," he continues, "numerous studies have shown an inverse correlation of verbal skills with impulsivity and criminal behaviour." Although he acknowledges that the "mechanisms underlying these associations" between language skills, aggression, and later criminality are currently unknown, Tremblay concludes from the research he cites that those associations "are clearly operating in the first two years of life."

Though he doesn't comment directly on the research examining the relationship between media violence and violent behaviour, the idea that factors predicting violent or criminal behaviour show up at a very early age—well before a child would be inclined to join the Marilyn Manson fan club or dedicate her spare time to playing *Doom*—has real significance for the debate on the cultural roots of teen violence. If children are set on the course towards later violence in their early preschool years, then preventing youngsters from growing into violence-prone teenagers and adults will surely be a more complicated process than simply turning off the TV or installing a v-chip, and will require earlier intervention. Tremblay himself favours a greater emphasis on early childhood education. It is imperative that children "learn alternatives to physical aggression during the pre-school years," he writes. The link between early language deficits and the inability to control aggressive urges suggests that one particularly crucial skill is the capacity to negotiate situations of conflict verbally. And so, contrary to Rousseau's prescription that children be left alone, sheltered from the corrupting influences of "the arts, sciences and civilization in general," during the tender years of youth, Tremblay is convinced that society must intervene early to help children manage their aggressive impulses, which spring from somewhere within the children themselves.

All of this does not disprove the idea that mass media messages might play some role in encouraging aggressive behaviour later in life. Still, Tremblay's reconstruction of the ancient debate does provide a useful reminder that establishing the link between cultural artifacts and criminal acts has long confounded great scholars, and that even today's social scientists—with their cold, numerical conclusions and flat, clinical vocabulary—are not immune to being swayed, in subtle ways, by their own personal convictions. In complex matters of human behaviour, there are few obvious conclusions, and often ample room for dissent.

Dissent was in short supply in the aftermath of the Columbine tragedy, however, when a mood of shock and sorrow made it possible for legislators, researchers, and assorted commentators to pronounce, without fear of contradiction, that the case was now closed: there could be no doubt that the steady diet of bloodletting coursing through all that electronic circuitry and into kids' brains was turning at least some of them into monstrous killers.

One such commentator, unequivocal in his conviction that media violence has unleashed an epidemic of brutality amongst American youth, was retired U.S. Army colonel David Grossman. Grossman is co-author (with media literacy activist Gloria DeGaetano) of the influential book *Stop Teaching Our Kids to Kill: A Call to Action Against TV, Movie and Video Game Violence*. Although he had not been involved with any of the academic research into the impact of media violence, Grossman's credentials as a psychology instructor at the famed West Point military academy—an institution where the unflinching application of lethal force is a key element of the curriculum—made him a frequently cited expert in the media and elsewhere. *Time* magazine's coverage of the atrocity at Columbine, for instance, included a sidebar in which Grossman explained the video-game connection. He was also apparently a popular speaker in high schools and on college campuses.

In 1999 I conducted a lengthy telephone interview with Colonel Grossman while researching an article on video-game violence for a Canadian parenting magazine. Grossman proved to be the kind of interview who makes the jobs of deadline-driven freelance journalists like me a lot easier. His frequent references to studies by organizations like the American Medical Association and the office of the U.S. Surgeon General give him the requisite air of authority by association. Grossman's advantage over those august bodies, however, is that he can be a lot less measured and a lot more colourful in his choice of language. With Grossman on the other end of the line, a journalist can forget about having to reframe an academic argument in terms that will resonate with the lay reader—the colonel obliges with his own ready-made supply of homespun homilies and clever metaphors. His description of violent video games as "murder simulators," for example, is a simple analogy that aims to demolish most parents' conception of those games as mere toys. "We have flight simulators that will teach you to fly without ever touching a real plane," Grossman elaborates during our conversation, without the slightest trace of weariness in his voice at having to replay this stock sound bite for the umpteenth time. "And we have murder simulators that will teach you how to commit a murder, to rehearse the act of murder, without ever touching a gun. That's what we're talking about here." To diffuse the obvious questions about why some kids can play violent games and never behave violently, Grossman introduces his idea that people have a "violence immune system"—a natural aversion to hurting other people—which he claims can be short-circuited by constant exposure to violent images. "We all know that AIDS doesn't kill people; it leaves them vulnerable to being killed by other things," says Grossman, extending his metaphor. "If your immune system is destroyed, now the cold or flu that shouldn't kill you, will kill you. In the same way, if your violence immune system is destroyed, now the things that shouldn't result in death, will result in death. Like breaking up with your girlfriend, child abuse, gangs, drugs—variables which as a rule of thumb don't result in death, now have a far higher propensity to result in violence."

This is indeed a clever and well-crafted pitch, calculated to minimize the logical doubts that will occur to most people when presented with this idea that entertainment is a dominant determinant of kids' behaviour. His use of AIDS as a metaphor for violent entertainment has a chilling impact on two levels. For one, it undermines the complacency that many parents feel if they have decided that, although Junior likes to play shoot-'em-up in the rec room, he's still a basically good kid who hasn't shown any sign of wanting to hurt people. Don't believe what you see, Grossman is suggesting. Millions of outwardly placid kids like these are being primed to go postal as soon as they encounter some commonplace emotional stress. There's a virus lurking in their system that's just waiting for its chance to wreak havoc. The other way in which the AIDS metaphor works to overcome resistance to Grossman's overall thesis is by minimizing the obvious reality that there are a wide range of compelling factors—poor parenting, child abuse, social neglect, bad peer influences, etc.—that can lead kids to violent behaviour. Comparing violent entertainment to AIDS allows Grossman to acknowledge those factors but to place them within a new hierarchy of importance. Sure, those other conditions play some role, he's saying, but violent media imagery is the lynchpin, the trigger, the smouldering fuse that can transform the contents of a kid's psyche into an inferno of violent rage.

Like any good motivational speaker, Grossman salts his cauldron of dire prophecy with some down-home warmth and the occasional humorous aside. To explain why kids fantasizing mayhem at the video arcade is more destructive than the "controlled" processes of military training, for instance, Grossman comments that "the army can take the fun out of everything. They can take the fun out of sex, I tell you. When you're out there on the [rifle] range, it's no doggone fun." Mostly, though, his tone is one of restrained contempt. "This industry is horrendously liable," he says of video-game manufacturers, vowing that they will face the same fate as Big Tobacco — hounded in the courts until they are forced to pay big settlements and curtail their marketing.

During the course of our interview, there are occasional indications that this lawyer for the prosecution is willing to stretch an outrageous distance to draw a link between real-life tragedies and the influence of video-game manufacturers. "In Liberia," he tells me, "the last place that had power was a bar where the thugs could come and drink and play violent video games and then go out and replicate that behaviour." Violence immune system or not, it's unlikely that many rational people would see the carnage and social chaos played out on the streets of Monrovia as having its roots in the boardrooms of Nintendo or Sony. I suspect, however, that most reporters would be willing to overlook Colonel Grossman's rhetorical excesses on the grounds that his personal experiences have stoked a passion that periodically overcomes prudent speech. When the massacre at Jonesboro took place a short distance from Grossman's Arkansas home, the retired officer tells me, he was enlisted as "the lead trainer of mental health professionals the night of the shootings."

Which brings us to another reason why Grossman got lots of ink and airtime in the aftermath of Columbine: a personal connection always humanizes an issue, making a Karen Silkwood or Erin Brockovich — someone who's come face to face with the evil they're crusading against — a much more likely media star than some detached egghead in a lab coat. Indeed, Grossman has used his public profile to good effect. It seems that a critical factor in the renewed interest in the media violence debate was the publication of *Stop Teaching Our Kids to Kill*, by Grossman and DeGaetano. Much like Grossman himself in conversation, this book is passionate and populist—heavy on declarative statements supported largely by anecdotal evidence (it includes unreferenced stories, for instance, about a preschool-aged boy terrified of a man on a bus whom he thought looked like *Nightmare on Elm Street* killer Freddy Krueger, and another about a child who developed a fear of black people after seeing a black man whipped on the dramatic TV miniseries *Roots*. The child's reasoning, apparently, was that the man must have been bad because people are not punished without reason).[3] The authors cite some of the best-known scholarly work purporting to show a link between media violence and its real-life counterpart (for instance, studies by Centerwall and by University of Michigan professor L. Rowell Huesmann), but mostly they offer statistics without citation or contextual support. Grossman and DeGaetano write, for instance, that "since 1982 television violence has increased 780 per cent and in that same time period teachers have reported a nearly 800 per cent increase in aggressive acts on the playground." The statement raises obvious questions—including, for example, how were those aggressive acts defined? Were they reported as part of a formal study in which the definitions and reporting methods remained constant? What's included under the rubric "television violence"? Who was responsible for calculating either of the statistics cited?—that are never addressed.

It's clearly Grossman and DeGaetano's intention to avoid having the populist force of their argument blunted by footnotes, and despite its flaws the book seems—to the deadline-driven scribe, at least—to have a certain ring of plausibility. The circumstantial aspect of their case is intriguing: rising worldwide levels of social violence, they state, appear to have started around the same time that television first brought spectacles of mayhem into people's homes, and real-world violence has continued to increase as TV violence has become more explicit and more pervasive. To support this part of their argument, the authors return to the early days of television, when the network executives allegedly decided to use violence as a way of attracting and maintaining the attention of audiences for their new medium. Grossman and DeGaetano recall, with a certain sense of fuzzy, soft-focus nostalgia, that in the more innocent era of the early 1950s, programs were "designed specifically to inspire as well as entertain." But providing intellectually stimulating fare was no way to run a business. When broadcasters realized that such "quality programming" inspired viewers to turn off their sets to discuss what they had just watched, they began to develop programs like The Untouchables and Gunsmoke, predicated upon a "violence formula" that assumed "the more graphic and gratuitous the violence, the more viewers will watch." The problem was that audiences quickly became jaded, so broadcasters, the authors maintain, had to keep upping the ante—depicting violence more vividly and serving it in ever-greater quantities.

The authors believe it is no coincidence that levels of violent crime began an upwards trajectory around the same time that Elliot Ness and Marshall Dillon found a home on the small screen. "What's the big picture of crime in America?" they ponder. "From 1960 through 1991 the U.S. population increased by 40 per cent, yet violent crime increased by 500 per cent; murders increased by 170 per cent, rapes 520 per cent and aggravated assaults 600 per cent." They claim that similar rises occurred in other Western nations during part of the same time frame. "According to InterPol, between 1977 and 1993 the per capita 'serious assault' rate increased: nearly fivefold in Norway and Greece; approximately fourfold in Australia and New Zealand; it tripled in Sweden; and approximately doubled in Belgium, Denmark, England-Wales, France, Hungary, Netherlands, and Scotland. In Canada, per capita assaults increased almost fivefold between 1964 and 1993."

It is a great leap to assume that a rise in violent crime in society and the increasingly routine depiction of bloodletting on television are bound together by anything more than coincidence, but for the past several decades a small cadre of social scientists has been on a mission to find the theoretical missing link that draws those two phenomena into a common equation. In some cases, these researchers have studied smaller groups of people in an attempt to ascertain whether television influences the way they interact—that is, do populations suddenly exposed to television become more aggressive or prone to violence? Grossman and DeGaetano describe a study by University of British Columbia researcher Tannis Mac-Beth Williams, released in 1986, which tracked the behaviour of adults and children in three towns: two that had long had access to television, and one where television was about to be introduced. Williams' researchers noted a rise in physical aggression amongst children in the formerly TV-free community (dubbed "Notel") in the two years after television was introduced there, although levels remained constant in the communities where television had been available during the whole period. Some critics of media violence claim such studies confirm the relationship between fictionalized television violence and its real-life counterpart. If television can make people act more aggressively in the small communities that are placed under the microscopes of social scientists, they say, isn't it reasonable to think that entire countries would feel the same impact, and that this would drive up the national indices of violent crime?

Other research has focused on the biological and/or behavioural effects of violent imagery on individual kids or adults. The thinking here is that if scientists can prove acts of cinematic brutality affect the viewer's behaviour the way the ingredients in foods, say, affect the consumer's physical health, it becomes less of a leap to imagine some cumulative social impact—an impact that would show up in national crime statistics just as the consumption of junk food might be reflected in national figures on heart disease or diabetes. Numerous clinical studies conducted since the 1960s have sought to determine, in a laboratory setting, how violent imagery affects the individual's behaviour. The studies commonly cited by critics of media violence are said to support one or more of the following conclusions: that depictions of violence put the viewer in a state of emotional arousal or excitement; that they desensitise kids to the impact of real violence; and that, as a consequence, media violence increases kids' level of aggression and makes them more prone to using violence in play.

Besides cataloguing the most commonly mentioned social science research, Grossman and DeGaetano's unique contribution has been to create their own über-theory about how media violence can flick the off-switch on a kid's "violence immune system." This idea appears to be the product of dozens of fragments of research, combined with some breathtaking rhetorical flourishes and considerable moxie.

"We attest that, due to overexposure to gratuitous violent imagery," Grossman and DeGaetano write, "our children undergo a systematic conditioning process that alters their cognitive, emotional and social development in such ways as to embed in them a conditioned reflex to act out violently without remorse." To support this premise, they begin with the idea—the subject of numerous clinical studies—that media violence has a stimulating effect on children. "Screen violence can increase the reactivity of the brain stem," they précis the research. "Children's hearts race, their eyes bug out, their breathing comes in gasps as they munch on snacks and watch the body count soar. The brain's alarm network, known as the 'fight or flight mechanism,' sits at the base of the brain and sends out noradrenaline pathways to other brain centers that control heart-rate, breathing, blood pressure, emotions and motivation." This chemical response, they claim, sidelines the brain's prefrontal cortex—the part that's responsible for thinking—and casts the kid into some kind of primordial autopilot state in which she is primed to behave violently and impulsively. The authors liken aspects of this state of arousal to drug addiction: kids who experience this kind of adrenalin rush will seek out repeated and more intense exposure to violent imagery in order to keep the juices flowing.

Meanwhile, this interaction between chemicals and grey matter, so their theory goes, facilitates a learning process in which the child's brain is "imprinted" with the message that violence is a good and logical way to behave. The pair describe this process as analogous to the conditioning that affects children who witness or experience domestic abuse. In such cases, the child may be "two, three, four or five years old and he despises this behavior and he hates his father. But if he is not careful, twenty years later, when he is under stress and he has a wife and kids, what is he likely to do? He will do the same thing he saw his father do ... He, of all people should understand how despicable this behaviour is, how much his children will hate him. How much he will hate himself. But he can't help it—it was burned into his system at an early age ..." The point the authors are making is that this type of violent behaviour is largely involuntary, the product of childhood conditioning, which functions outside the realm of reason. They suggest that violent media images have a similarly paradoxical impact on children: casting a powerful spell over kids who may simultaneously find this imagery frightening and repulsive. Kids who are victims of violence may be especially drawn to violent programming—despite being scared and repulsed—because it helps explain their violent world. "Research indicates that children may be deliberately trying to conquer their fears of vulnerability and victimization by desensitising themselves through repeated exposure to horror movies," write Grossman and DeGaetano, exhibiting their typical disdain for the citations that would explain exactly which research they are referring to (and how the research was conducted).

Parts of Grossman and DeGaetano's argument seem almost self-evident, so much a matter of common sense that they hardly need to be proved with formal experiments. That violent entertainment has a stimulating effect, for instance, appears obvious given the popularity of violent fare with the viewing public and the entertainment industry's continual willingness to invest large sums in products with a high violence quotient. That blood sells is beyond doubt. But what diminishes one's faith in the authors' ability to discern larger truths behind the truisms is the creeping realization that their main means of arguing their case is to string together a multitude of research findings, personal observations, and hunches that are often only marginally related.

Grossman and DeGaetano, it seems, have never met a negative statement about mass media that they didn't like. No theory about why mass media is bad for kids seems insubstantial enough to warrant a little critical scrutiny or perhaps a contrary interpretation. Take the authors' insistence, for instance, that video gaming leads kids into an unhealthy world of solitary, antisocial obsession: "As children and youth are playing these games for ten or more hours a week, they are not solving and negotiating conflicts with their peers, and they are missing priceless opportunities to gain needed co-operative and social skills." This becomes a downward spiral, the end point of which, it is implied, may be the creation of more dangerous loners like the ones who in recent years have shot up their school cafeterias. "The more they become inept at dealing effectively with real-world people and situations, the more likely it is that they will lose themselves in the video games, particularly violent ones that ensure feelings of control, mastery and exhilaration," the authors warn.

Well, sure, maybe some kids will use video games to escape from difficult social situations (in the same way that other kids might retreat from the world by becoming bookworms or getting lost in, say, astronomy or model making). But the idea that video games are making kids antisocial en masse seems doubtful when tested against day-to-day experience. Most people who live in close proximity to a kid will possibly have noticed that electronic games are among the top social activities for today's youngsters. They are a facilitator of social interaction. Kids in my neighbourhood can be observed huddling together over a Game Boy in the school playground at recess, eager to see how the kid at the controls is going to advance to the next level of the game. Those same kids will call each other up on the phone at night to share strategies and ask for help. Often the object of this interaction is for one kid to help another advance in his game. There's a distinct sense of collegiality surrounding this pursuit. One could argue, credibly, that electronic games can be a far more cooperative pastime than traditionally venerated activities such as team sports, where the goal is generally domination of one group of kids over another, and losing can sometimes lead to feelings of inadequacy or exclusion. Perhaps the unhappy sight of one kid playing endless video games alone is not a product of the technology itself, but an outgrowth of some other contextual factor: conditions in that individual kid's life, for example, or perhaps the broader social tendency for North Americans to live in privatized isolation, cut off from neighbours and communities.

The authors' argument about kids being conditioned by media is also undermined by their noticeable tendency to inflate any statistic that appears to provide only modest support for their thesis. Take, for instance, their assessment of just how much more violent American society has become since the era when TV was a novelty. As they acknowledge, the murder rate is often taken as the definitive measure of general social violence. This is because murders are almost always reported ("as a society we don't allow dead bodies to lie around uninvestigated," they slyly remark) and because death is not measured by degrees—meaning that, unlike assault and various forms of harassment, the seriousness of the crime can never be in dispute. Still, the rise in the murder rate since the late 1950s doesn't appear as dramatic as the rise in the number of reported cases of other types of crime, especially when these sets of figures are represented on a graph (as they are in the book). While the line depicting the number of murders is relatively flat—starting off well below 25 per 100,000 citizens in the 1950s and still remaining well below 25 per 100,000 in the mid-1990s—increases in the rates of assaults and imprisonment are represented by lines that make a quick, almost vertical ascent towards the top of the page. Aggravated assaults shot up from 75 per 100,000 people in the late 1950s to almost 450 in the early 1990s, and the number of people incarcerated in the United States rose by a similar order of magnitude over that time period.

For a crusading author, therefore, using the murder rate as a measure of the explosion of violence since the 1950s might be problematic. Simply stated, the increase does not look that big. Which may explain why Grossman and his collaborator insist that the rate of aggravated assault provides a more accurate reflection of the rising climate of social violence. Why? Because, they state, improvements in medical technologies have led to a rise in the number of people who have been stabbed or shot but still survive. This means that the murder rate can be dismissed as merely "a measure of how successful we are at killing each other," rather than a gauge of how often we try it—which they say is more accurately captured by the figures on aggravated assault.

Expert opinion seems to support this idea, but only to a limited degree. The New York Times recently reported on a study by University of Massachusetts criminologist Anthony Harris, which examined the impact on the U.S. murder rate of innovations such as the 911 system, paramedics in ambulances, and hospital trauma teams. Harris concluded that the murder rate in 1999 might have been four times higher were it not for those improvements in the response to serious assaults.[4] Meanwhile, author Richard Rhodes cites FBI stats from 1998 to show that major injuries rarely resulted from violent crimes—there were just over 20,000 such injuries out of 1.5 million violent crimes—which means that, although the murder rate had the potential to double if those injuries led to death, this year's violent crime rate cannot simply be taken as equivalent to what the murder rate would have been if medical technology had not improved.[5]

Harris, the University of Massachusetts researcher, also notes contradictory factors that Grossman and DeGaetano fail to mention, such as the fact that police today are reporting assaults that would previously not have been noticed. Before 1985, for instance, spousal assaults rarely became part of the crime statistics, although "they can be every bit as deadly as assaults on the street."[6] So the exponential rise in the rate of assault may signify, paradoxically, a rising social sensitivity to issues of violence, rather than providing the most accurate reading of how much violence has increased since the late 1950s. Although it's true that the murder rate could have risen more noticeably if medical care had not improved, those fearsome-looking graphs in *Stop Teaching Our Kids to Kill* hardly provide a realistic view of the increase in crime.

Grossman and DeGaetano really test the reader's credulity, however, when they suggest that any rise in crime rates has come despite social trends that should have led to a drop in criminal acts during the past forty years. For example, they say, removing unprecedented numbers of people from the general population by sentencing them to long prison terms would logically result in fewer criminal types being around to create mayhem. Similarly, the "progressive social initiatives reducing malnutrition and confronting child abuse," which the authors hold up as a defining trait of the post-1950s era, could be expected to have the same effect. Ergo, there is no other place to look to explain escalating levels of social violence: bloodletting in the media must be responsible. If you accept this argument, you're likely in step with Grossman and DeGaetano's conclusion that the power of images of violence in the media is almost impossible to overestimate. They have been strong enough not only to increase crime rates, but also to reverse the impact of other social trends that should have been leading us into a golden era of civic calm and social harmony.

Of course there are a lot of big assumptions in all this, stated alarmingly casually and with a startling lack of evidence, and based on very particular readings of social trends that can certainly be disputed. For example, in response to the authors' flat assertion about "progressive social initiatives reducing malnutrition and confronting child abuse," one can obviously raise the issue of how America (and Canada, to a lesser extent), at least since the early 1980s, has seen an unprecedented polarization between rich and poor, symptoms of which are the numbers of children growing up in homeless shelters, the emergence and institutionalization of food banks, and the decay of inner-city public schools. The word "underclass" was hardly a common part of the lexicon in the 1950s. Still, none of these developments—nor any other of the twentieth century's much-lamented social stressors, like the increasing economic demands on the post-1950s two-income family, the rising rates of family breakup, the increasing requirement for a mobile labour force and the consequent diminution of social connectedness in North America, etc.—stand in the way of the author's blanket declaration that progressive social policies enacted in recent history should have reduced levels of violent crime.

There are other key assertions in *Stop Teaching Our Kids to Kill* that start to crumble when scrutinized in the light of a less sentimental view of history. Take the statement that bloodshed in media became commonplace after the adoption of a "violence formula" that brought *The Untouchables* and *Gunsmoke* to the small screen in the late 1950s. How do the authors square this with the fact that shoot-'em-up cowboy flicks had been a mainstay of Hollywood for decades before, or that Jimmy Cagney gangster movies had been standard fare for kids with a nickel to spend at the Saturday morning picture show throughout the 1930s and '40s? Why didn't obviously violent entertainment in the pre-Second World War era lead to a rise in social violence similar to the one that authors say resulted from television?

This is not to say that there isn't some good advice contained in Grossman and DeGaetano's book. One of the best is essentially a paraphrase of that old "Have you hugged your child today?" bumper sticker. "An enlightened, intelligent, and loved child," they write, "is our best defense against rising youth crime rates." And their recurrent exhortation for parents to be aware of what their kids do and watch, and who they hang out with—which is obviously something that didn't happen at Littleton, since the Columbine killers were reportedly making bombs and assembling a huge arsenal right under their parents' noses—makes thorough sense at multiple levels. But these commonsense commandments have just about nothing to do with the authors' theorizing about how and why media violence has contributed to a jump in juvenile crime since the time when the Cleavers ruled suburbia, and their inclusion in this book is something of a non sequitur. Certainly, many experts and average folks would endorse the general principle that parents should be involved in their kids' lives, which would include being concerned about the messages kids take out of media and being prepared to intervene if those kids developed an unhealthy obsession with images of mayhem. But it's a long leap from accepting this general precept to accepting the more specific and controversial ideas about media images being time bombs that lie hidden deep in the psyches of an entire generation, ready to be detonated by emotional stress.

How receptive you are to the ideas of Dave Grossman, Brandon Centerwall, William Bennett, and others who propose that media imagery is a chief cause of social violence and the generalized malaise of youth may depend on what social landscape you're sitting in, and how that social setting helps form your priorities and preoccupations. Those ideas emphasizing the influence of media on kids seem to have been much more warmly received in the United States, for instance, than they have been north of the border in Canada.

During the two years I was working as a columnist for a Canadian parenting magazine, for instance, it became apparent to me that there's more general skepticism in my country over the question of what television does to kids. When I raised this topic with child psychologists or media specialists, they invariably emphasized how the family experience intersects with mass media to influence a child's social development—they didn't focus on what visual media do to a child's brain. For instance, Dr. Steven Kline, a leading social psychologist and children's culture specialist at the University of British Columbia, stresses that it's important for parents to let their kids know what media products they object to, not so much because those products are objectively harmful, but because opening up such a discussion is one more way parents can communicate and explain the values they hold. As far as violent programming is concerned, Kline says there is "some evidence that people who talk to their kids about scariness are helping them deal with it." In short, the programming content doesn't seem as important as the social, familial context in which kids absorb it. Kids will learn more from their parents' reaction to media images than from the images themselves, although this is far from the only way in which parents teach by example. "The real problem," according to Kline, "is that we are modelling behaviours for kids, modelling ways of doing stuff all the time — whether it's playing or just chatting with them or having them help us around the house, and that is much more important than the time they spend in front of the TV."

Montreal child psychologist and McGill University psychology professor Jeffery Deverensky agrees that family context can be a more powerful influence on children's behaviour than the broadcast or cinematic images themselves. Some research shows that "you can actually inhibit aggressive behaviour when a parent is sitting there watching with the kids, telling them that this is inappropriate behaviour." As for the rest of the research examining the link between violent media and violent kids, Deverensky is much more restrained than, for example, the authors of that U.S. Senate report in his assessment of what those studies prove. Prior studies indicate "a slight positive relationship" between fantasy violence and aggressive kids, he says. And in contrast to Grossman's assertion that violent images have a long-term conditioning impact, Deverensky believes the effect wears off over time. "For kids who watch wrestling, and then they grab their little sister and put her in a chokehold, that's pretty clear. When you watch violent TV, you tend to be more aggressive during that period of time or immediately after. If the kid watches wrestling at seven at night and then goes to school the next day, is he going to put a kid in a chokehold because of what he saw? The answer is that he's less likely."

Of course, there are also commentators in the United States who are skeptical that violent media is a psychic time bomb, impervious to the influences of family and community. These skeptics range from left-wing pundit Alexander Cockburn to John Stossel, the resident libertarian on ABC TV's 20/20 newsmagazine program, whose regular shtick is to target government agencies and self-righteous officials, whom he sees as conspiring to remove individual Americans' right to make their own decisions. Motivated by his concern that the censorious, meddling forces of "political correctness" had found another stooge to help them chip away at personal liberties, Stossel took a shot at Grossman, finding his critique suspiciously self-referential and his research flawed. Stossel pointed out that many of Grossman's own statements about the impact of violence on kids' minds have been cited by other organizations, which Grossman has in turn cited to bolster his own position. One example of this circular citation exercise involves the U.S. Surgeon General's office. Grossman cites a study by the Surgeon General supporting a link between media violence and the real stuff, but Stossel remarks that this research is almost three decades old. When asked to provide more up-to-date research, the Surgeon General's office tells Stossel that the Marines have used the video game *Doom* to desensitize recruits to the impact of violence, an example they got from Grossman. Meanwhile, the Marines deny Grossman's allegation, telling Stossel "they used a version of the software to teach hand/eye co-ordination and team work," not to desensitize members to violence.[7]

Overall, though, Grossman's view that violent media is a powerful force that "programs" kids' behaviour has won much more mainstream acceptance in the United States than in Canada and Europe—witness the platform he was given by the Senate Judiciary Committee. Perhaps there are social reasons for this. Perhaps the psychological effects of media have become the focus of much more intense scrutiny in the United States because electronic media have taken on a more prominent role in daily life as other longstanding social institutions have been eroded. The relentless onslaught of technological change, and Americans' resolute unwillingness to rein in economic forces in order to serve social goals (see Chapter 6), has put immense pressure on families. Given these new circumstances, with many kids cloistered in their wired bedrooms while their parents work overtime or are stuck on the freeway, perhaps it is not surprising that U.S. society in particular is deeply concerned about what kind of job the entertainment industry is doing in raising the next generation.

There are others who feel the reason the media-violence hypothesis has been so readily endorsed in the United States is that it provides a convenient excuse to not talk about more obvious contributors to social violence: old-fashioned preoccupations like poverty and social disadvantage.

"One of the reasons America remains such an intractably high-risk society, suffering from rampant dangers other Western nations better control," the American author Mike Males writes in his book *Kids and Guns: How Politicians, Experts, and the Press Fabricate Fear of Youth*, "is the habit of American politicians and institutions to blame social problems on easy scapegoats and specious 'cultural' influences rather than facing difficult issues like poverty and adult norms. Just as the mass shootings of the late 1990s promised to bring about a true national debate over gun violence, in stepped the president and quotable authorities to throw the debate off-track by trivializing the real menaces facing kids at the same time they demonized kids and their cultural influences."[8]

What vexes Males most about the politicians' singular fixation on kids' cultural influences is the underlying assumption that violence is a *youth* problem that flows from some mysterious, dark wellspring within the disturbing, indecipherable world that young people inhabit. A careful reading of the crime statistics, he writes, debunks that idea, despite the horrific spectacles of Columbine and Paducah. Males, who lectures in sociology at the University of California Santa Cruz, cites FBI and Department of Justice crime figures showing that high schools are much safer than most other places and that teenagers are more likely to be victims of violence at the hands of older people than the perpetrators of violent crime. Violent acts committed by adults, he reports, accounted for 95 percent of murdered children and 70 percent of murdered teens between 1980 and 1997. And despite the predictions of Grossman and others that the advent of graphic video games and increasingly explicit violence on TV would lead to soaring violent crime rates in the 1990s, Males counters that during that period there has been a decline in violent crime committed by all groups, but especially by young people. Between 1994 and 1999, young people's contribution to the mayhem in U.S. society has dropped precipitously. The percentage of homicides committed by people under eighteen fell from 10.5 percent to 6.3 percent.

Furthermore, the most noteworthy and horrific of violent crimes committed by youth—the high school massacres—cannot be considered indicative of youth culture, Males argues, because they are invariably committed by alienated outsiders with little contact with their peers. Instead, these remarkable but rare incidents in which kids shoot up schools strongly resemble the other "rage killings" or "rampage killings"—the by-now commonplace multiple killings unleashed by a single shooter as a kind of grotesque public ritual—which are most often committed by middle-aged men. In a ten-month period in the same year (1999) that the Columbine massacre took place, Males says that at least fifteen other rampage killings occurred in the United States, each of them with multiple victims, which were all but ignored by the press.

The characteristics that link these events with the school killings make up what Males refers to as "dissed suburban male phenomenon." He writes: "Clearly, massacres are not a 'youth' phenomenon. The middle-aged mass killer motives were strangely akin to those of the schoolboy shooters from Pearl to Columbine. The gunners felt rejected by employers, co-workers, wives, girlfriends, saw themselves as failures, harbored racism, accumulated massive gun and bomb arsenals." In addition, Males asserts that, contrary to the fixations of the news media, "very few of the rampagers patronized violent media; practically none harbored occult or satanic interests." Instead, the fact that half the rampage killers had been diagnosed with conditions such as schizophrenia and depression points to a strong correlation, not between entertainment and violence, but between violence and mental illness.

As for the more common types of murder and other forms of violence committed by youth, Males says these differ from the rampages (which have been committed by white and typically affluent suburban kids) in that they are strongly correlated with low socioeconomic status. In California, for example, "just 10% of California's zip codes accounted for five-sixths of the gun murders among persons under age 20 in 1997, while four-fifths of California's zip codes had zero gun deaths among children and youths." Contracted to prepare a report on juvenile gun violence for the California attorney-general in 1999, Males compared the economic status of youth, which varied dramatically from county to county, with the likelihood of experiencing violence. "As poverty rates increase nine-fold from the richest white youths to the poorest youths of colour, murder rates jump 700%, gun death rates triple, and gun homicides leap nine-fold. Middle-income white and nonwhite youth are in between," he writes. With the poorest youth ten times more likely to be involved in gun killings than their wealthy counterparts, Males concludes that society's remedial lessons should focus not on the influence of film, TV, and video games (pastimes enjoyed by affluent kids, who are at a comparatively low risk of experiencing violence), but on the impact of poverty (which is strongly associated with the experience of violence). "If the murder difference between high- and low-risk youth populations were, say, 30%, some plausible alternatives to socioeconomic inequality would make sense to explore," states Males. "But a difference of 1,000% means that fixation on causal factors unrelated to economic disadvantage is escapist and diversionary."

Males is not the only observer to see the furor over media violence as a distraction from other issues that should occupy a higher place on the public agenda. What are some of the other concerns that get overlooked? The celebrated (and reviled) filmmaker Michael Moore, in his film *Bowling for Columbine*, argues that fear, social distrust, and a creeping sense of paranoia are among the scourges fundamentally responsible for Americans' habit of pumping bullets into their fellow citizens. If this is correct, the practical implications are distressing in a country that went on high alert after September 11, 2001, and hasn't yet come down. Consider the observation, made by Nicholas D. Kristof in his *New York Times* commentary "Chicks With Guns," that in the six months following the World

Trade Center attacks, the FBI conducted 455,000 more background checks for handgun ownership than in the corresponding period the previous year, and that a new phenomenon—associations of female gun owners opening branches on college campuses—sprang up.[9]

What should college women in the United States be most afraid of: sharing a dorm room with a fan of Marilyn Manson or Eminem, or having a roommate who packs a .45? For Kristof, the answer is clear: fear kills. "While we don't know whether more Americans will be killed by anthrax," he wrote, "we can be quite confident that plenty of us will be killed by these additional handguns ... We should worry about the fallout from 9/11 on gun ownership. Already, since the beginning of September, more than four times as many Americans have fallen to guns as to terrorism, but quietly, one by one, with no one noticing."

Others believe that the fuss about media violence is a functional fiction used to distract people from the pernicious psychological effects of living in a society where militarism—the systematic use of massive, state-sanctioned violence as a means of achieving political goals—is rampant and generally unquestioned. This position is advanced by the leftist pundit Alexander Cockburn. "There's no evidence that blood splattered on celluloid and videotape raises the level of actual violence in our society," he writes. "There is on the other hand plenty of evidence that state violence, most notably in the form of war, is real violence's prime sponsor." Cockburn's Exhibit A is Timothy McVeigh, the Oklahoma City bomber responsible for the mass murder of 168 people, including 19 children. Cockburn found it telling that public memorials to the victims of the Oklahoma federal building bombing do not mention that McVeigh was a decorated veteran of the first Iraq war. Unaccomplished and unexceptional before joining the military, McVeigh found a raison d'être and a method for his madness while serving overseas. In Cockburn's view, it is nonsensical to obsessively ask whether some mass murderers honed their skills with video games, while ignoring the question of whether McVeigh's murderous ways were related to his military training.[10]

This paradox—that a nation that accepts massive military violence in the pursuit of national goals should get so upset over fictional screen violence at home—nagged at me during my interview with Colonel Dave Grossman. The colonel seemed to embody some of that paradox. Here was a guy wringing his hands over what video games were doing to kids in the schoolyard, sounding the alarm about an impending epidemic of killings amongst kids, but whose job had been to take raw recruits off the street and teach them how to kill. So I asked him if he had any misgivings about his military career, hinting that there was some irony in the fact that a crusader for a more peaceful United States had earned his living teaching soldiers how to turn off their "violence immune systems."

"No, no," came Grossman's answer without hesitation. "Number one, we do it [military training] to adults. Number two, we do it with safeguards." And then, without prompting, he invoked McVeigh. "I was called as an expert witness in the McVeigh trial, the Oklahoma City bombing trial. The defence was trying to claim that McVeigh's military training, his military experience, would help explain what he did, would be a matter of mitigation to try to dodge the death penalty. And I was able to pull out the Bureau of Justice data stating that the returning veteran is a superior member of society—less likely to be incarcerated than a non-veteran of the same age."

But didn't he have, given his anguish over violence at home, any misgivings, any regrets? No way. "I am proud to be a soldier. I'm proud of the service that our guys have provided across the centuries, around the world—and they need those skills as much as they need an M-16. As much as they need a state-of-the-art rifle, they need state-of-the-art training. But what is horrifying is the knowledge that the same state-of-the-art training is being given to children."

Some academics have studied the question of the effects a country's military posture has on its rate of civil violence, and while some of their findings provide a limited endorsement of Grossman's view, for the most part they contradict him. In an article entitled "Peacetime casualties: The effects of war on the violent behavior of noncombatants," sociologists Dane Archer and Rosemary Gartner move slightly towards Grossman's camp when they state that there is little evidence to support the popular notion that returning veterans are responsible for a spike in violent crime rates after a war. Although each war in the United States seems to have a produced a few celebrated soldiers-turned-criminals—Jesse and Frank James and the Younger brothers, for example, launched their criminal careers after returning from the Civil War—Archer and Gartner insist that there is insufficient data to support the idea that returning soldiers are, as a group, more violent than the general population. In addition, postwar violent crime surges occur amongst both men and women, and within all age groups, which makes it difficult to single out returning soldiers as the particular locus of any increase in civil violence.[11]

In the big picture, however, Archer and Gartner's analysis indicates that it is unwise to ignore the connection between foreign military adventures and the violent crime rate at home. Published in the late 1970s, their work drew on a huge database comparing the prewar and postwar homicide levels of about fifty nations on either side of the two World Wars, the Vietnam War, and eleven other wars. Nations that had taken part in wars were compared to a control group of nations that had been neutral during those wars. They concluded from this comparison that "warring nations were more likely to experience homicide rate increases than nations not involved in war. A majority of the combatant nations experienced homicide rate increases of at least 10 per cent, while a majority of the uninvolved nations experienced homicide rate decreases of greater than 10 per cent. Many of the homicide rate increases were very large; in several cases the nation's prewar homicide rate more than doubled." The sociologists also note that these figures likely understate the real impact of war in raising the violent crime rate, since the young male population (which is normally associated with a large proportion of violent crime in civilian society) would have been greatly reduced in the aftermath of war in most countries, while postwar baby booms would mean that a greater proportion of the overall population would have been too young to be counted in crime statistics tabulated immediately after the war. This suggests that the experience of living through a war has a disproportionately large impact on people old enough to commit crimes who wouldn't, in other circumstances, be expected to participate in violent crime.

Archer and Gartner's explanation for this clear rise in homicides in postwar societies is that governments' promotion of war communicates a message to populations that violence is an acceptable means of resolving conflicts. "Wars, after all," they write, "carry the full authority and prestige of the State, and wars reward killing in the sense that war 'heroes' are decorated and lionized in direct proportion to the number of their wartime homicides ... What all wars have in common—when they are stripped of their idiosyncratic circumstances—is the unmistakable moral lesson that homicide is an acceptable, even praiseworthy, means to a certain end."

It's worth noting that the basic assumptions underlying the sociologists' statistical experiment are identical to those which underpin attempts to prove the negative impact of media violence: that is, the idea that behaviour is "modeled" by influential forces and that people (young people in particular) are more inclined to imitate a behaviour if it is condoned or congratulated or rewarded (a process referred to as "social learning"). Yet Archer and Gartner found it curious that official violence—the massive violence of warfare, invested with all the prestige and sanctity that national governments can bestow on it—has been neglected as a subject of study. They speculated that this might be because social scientists are themselves swayed by the dominant social ethic that says official violence is "legitimate," not really violence at all, or because funders have steered researchers away from this topic in order to avoid political controversy.

Whatever the reason, the fact that fantasy violence is scrutinized far out of proportion to its real-world counterpart remains, to this day, a striking feature of the debate about what causes kids to act violently.

CHAPTER 9

Can This Many Experts Be Wrong?

Psychologist Jonathan Freedman has been dubbed "the anti-Grossman." Since that tag appeared on a website devoted to video gaming, it should probably be considered a term of endearment. It is also one that well describes both Freedman's views of media violence and his personal style. While Grossman is quick with a quip or a pithy sound bite, Freedman is more ponderous, unspooling the logic behind his position slowly and with little panache. And while Grossman draws from the academic research only fleetingly, as it serves his purposes, Freedman's contribution to the field of media violence has been to examine, in meticulous detail, some two hundred studies focusing on various aspects of the subject. His interpretation of what those studies actually prove is contained in his book *Media Violence and Its Effect on Aggression: Assessing the Scientific Evidence.* In Freedman's view, scholarship on the impact of media violence on human behaviour is so inconsistent and so contradictory—with some oft-cited studies indicating a link, but the vast majority, according to Freedman, showing no connection at all—that cumulatively they prove nothing.

When I interviewed the Harvard- and Yale-educated New Yorker just before the release of his book, he was serving as head of the

University of Toronto's psychology department, a position that comes with prime real estate in the form of a spacious, sunlit corner office looking out onto the pastoral campus below. Freedman was casual and somewhat rumpled, on the greyer side of fifty, with a worn leather jacket hanging from his office coat rack. Despite his prestigious position and Ivy League credentials, Freedman is a controversial figure in some circles. Partly that's because he's stood virtually alone amongst academics in saying that the American Medical Association, the Surgeon General, the Senate, and other august bodies in the United States have got it all wrong when they tell the public that the effect of violent media on kids' behaviour has been scientifically established. Mostly, though, the controversy that surrounds Freedman has to do with his acceptance of funds from the Motion Picture Association of America, an obviously partisan player in this story. (Indeed, MPAA monarch Jack Valenti has used Freedman's work when publicly pleading the Hollywood lobby's case that entertainment is not responsible for the way kids behave.) Freedman's association with the MPAA has led his opponents to hint that he's little better than those experts-for-hire trotted out by the tobacco industry to deny the link between smoking and cancer, advancing arguments that involve a spurious methodological nitpicking designed to obscure an obvious truth.

In his book, Freedman returns fire to those who equate his research into media violence with that which examines the impact of smoking. He does agree with his critics that for both tobacco smoking and violence viewing it is impossible to design a perfect study that will definitively prove a causal connection between exposure to that substance/imagery and some suspected ill effect. His critics are therefore correct, he writes, to assert that scientists must look at numerous other types of evidence—some of it circumstantial—to determine whether smoking/media violence create the damage they are suspected of creating.[1]

But Freedman protests he has never demanded that the impact of fantasy violence be nailed down by the perfect experiment or that causality be proven beyond any doubt—only that the evidence used to assess the issue is convincing and consistent. In this respect, Freedman believes research into smoking and research into screen violence are not at all alike. For scientific studies to provide a reliable basis for public policy, he writes, their results must show more than a marginal impact and be replicable from study to study. Clinical inquiries into the effects of tobacco smoke generally meet those criteria: animals exposed to smoke in the laboratory "have developed cancers ... in virtually every experiment. The effects are dramatic, recognizable and deadly; they are also consistent and replicable." By contrast, most of the laboratory experiments involving exposure to media violence have shown no increase in the subjects' aggression, and those that did indicated only a small increase. This aggression, however, is defined and measured by the researchers. None of these experiments involve violence in real-life settings (unlike the tobacco studies, which involve real illnesses). And none of them correlate exposure to fictional violence with serious criminal acts.

Meanwhile, longitudinal studies that use statistical tracking (rather than clinical experiments) to determine the impact of media violence over a period of time are similarly much weaker than those studies that seek to statistically evaluate the link between lung cancer and smoking. Statistical analysis clearly shows that the risks of smoking "are huge," writes Freedman. "The National Cancer Institute says the risk of dying of lung cancer is 22 times higher for male smokers and 12 times higher for female smokers than for people who have never smoked ... In addition, the more people smoke, the higher the risk; the longer they smoke, the higher the risk; and if they stop smoking, the risk goes down. This dose-response relationship is crucial for the argument and is powerful evidence that smoking is the cause of lung cancer." By contrast, "the most favourable findings [from statistical correlations of violent-media exposure and aggression] have been that those who watch a lot of media violence early in life have a slight tendency to be more aggressive later than those who watch less ... and more studies fail to find this than find it."

Still, you might expect that someone on the payroll of the Forces of Darkness would have an interest in misrepresenting the evidence, right? In conversation, Freedman himself concedes that you could reasonably suspect the motion-picture producers had influenced his conclusions if his position on media violence changed after he took their money—but it didn't. "I published my first article on this in 1984 and have been saying the same thing ever since then," he tells me during the interview in his U of T office. He initially came to the subject when he was preparing to teach a graduate seminar and was searching for "a topic on which lots of research had been done that would also be inherently interesting." His graduate students would track down existing research studies on the topic and compare the results. Once his graduate students began reviewing the research, Freedman remembers, "I was amazed that the results [of the studies] weren't the way people said they were—and we actually read a fair amount of research."

It was only in 1999—fifteen years after this first foray—that Freedman accepted the film lobby as his new benefactor, well aware that the MPAA had its own political interests at heart when it decided to pony up. "Obviously," he says, "they picked me because they thought I would agree with them." But he says the money came without strings, and Freedman insisted that his funders would have no input into how he reviewed the literature and no right to alter his conclusions, even if he did a sudden about-face and recanted his longstanding view that the dangers of media violence remain unproven. The MPAA's support of his research, Freedman says, is just a simple case of converging interests; the professor needed financial backing for his study from somewhere, and the producers, aware of his prior work, could confidently bet that the conclusions of his next project would support their point of view. As for his personal stake in the issue, Freedman reports that he has one son (who was twelve at the time of our interview), but the boy's media intake was never a major parental concern. "It [media violence] is not an issue that I care profoundly about," offers Freedman, "except that I think we shouldn't lie to the public."

In print, Freedman deals extensively with the kind of arcane methodological issues that social scientists can spend years furiously debating among themselves: Did researchers communicate their own biases and expectations to children in the laboratory? How can scientists measure aggression? Does aggression in play necessarily reflect a tendency towards aggression or violence in real life, or is it something the child can confine to his or her fantasy life?

In conversation, however, Freedman dwells on simpler, more fundamental questions, mostly related to the social and historical contexts that critics of media violence have constructed to frame the topic. Take the idea, promoted by Grossman and others, that a rise in the rates of social violence occurred at the same time as—or more pointedly, as a result of—the introduction of television. Freedman insists that the broad strokes used to make this argument are eminently open to challenge; the numbers its proponents use just don't stand up when viewed in the larger context.

It is true, says Freedman, that crime rates began to rise in 1965, and that this trend was sustained for over two decades, with the result that violence was much more a defining factor of life in the late 1980s than it was in the late 1950s. It is also true that this all began roughly in sync with the adoption of the television set as the most common appliance in the North American home—with the result that by 1965, when crime rates began to take off, most members of the middle class were able to watch *Gunsmoke* or *Bonanza* in the comfort of their own living rooms. Yet the longer historical view, says Freedman, seems to undermine the idea that the presence of television and rising crime rates are directly related. There was, for instance, a similarly dramatic rise in the crime rate fifty years prior, in the early part of the twentieth century, well before television was invented. This suggests to Freedman that "maybe these things go in cycles and we just don't understand them."

And if it was the violent content of television that caused crime rates to start spiralling upwards, how does one explain the sudden reversal of this trend? In the 1990s, precisely when Grossman and others were predicting graphic advances that produced more realistic gore in video games would intensify the climate of violence, leading to more carnage in the playground and on the street, the rate of violent crimes committed by both youths and adults fell dramatically.

"Since 1990," Freedman recounts, "we have had just as much violent television and lots of other violent images in video games and music, but the crime rate has been dropping so that it is now lower than it was before television was introduced. So that makes it very implausible that the increase was originally due to television."

The irony is that a marked decline in juvenile violence occurred at the same time as North Americans were witnessing mass killings like the ones at Columbine and Paducah. "Although there has been an increase in multiple killings in American schools over the past ten years," Freedman says, "there has been a dramatic drop in the numbers of students killed. And so American schools, despite these horrendous killings and the publicity they've generated, are now safer than they have been for decades." Obviously the mass killings are horrific events, but they don't shed much light on the more general situation.

What accounts for this unexpected, and generally unrecognized, decline in social violence? "I don't know—it's a mystery," Freedman replies. One reason that's often cited is the decline in the percentage of young males (the social group most likely to commit crimes) in the general population. But this would only explain a small part of the overall drop and would not account for lower crime rates within the younger age groups. Another common explanation is that the 1990s saw a run of economic growth and prosperity, but there have been other eras—like the 1960s—when living standards rose and crime continued to climb. The fall in the use of crack cocaine has also been cited as a moderating factor. While that might help explain lower crime rates in the United States, it says nothing about the fact that crime rates in Canada—where the crack epidemic never took hold—mirrored the same downward trajectory. Similarly, the claim of some politicians that society is safer because there are more police on the street doesn't address the drop in domestic violence, which generally takes place away from the watchful gaze of the local beat cop. Freedman admits he's baffled about what caused crime to fall in the 1990s, just as he has no one answer for why crime shot up early in the twentieth century and again in the 1960s. He is convinced, however, that "when there is a major change in something like the rate of violent crime, it is almost certain that it is due to major causes, huge causes, huge changes in society rather than anything minor, like the introduction of television."

Comparing crime rates and entertainment preferences in different cultures is another exercise that Freedman says discredits the idea that media violence causes social violence. If media was really a cause of violence in society, one would expect the countries with the most violent media to have the highest crime rates. But that's not the case. Although Japanese television is more explicitly violent than American TV, for instance, the crime rate has traditionally been much lower in Japan than in the United States. Canada and the United States provide an even more striking comparison. On either side of the Canada-U.S. border, the television programming available to viewers is virtually identical. In terms of real-life crime, though, Canadians and Americans "live in different worlds," says Freedman. "The homicide rate is not even comparable. Toronto, for example, with three million people has about fifty to sixty murders a year. Detroit has a lot fewer people than that, and it has six hundred to eight hundred murders a year." Freedman's obvious point is that if media content does influence the crime rate, its effect must be infinitesimal compared to that of the ingrained social and cultural factors, or major economic or political factors. Social cohesion, disparities in wealth distribution, the pace of economic and technological change, differing stresses on the family, neighbourhoods, individuals—these are more logical places to look to determine why two neighbouring countries that share an almost identical media environment experience very different levels of violent crime.

Still, despite the fact that it's unable to pass these logical litmus tests, the notion that violent media make violent people is widely accepted. This is partly because the idea seems to make intuitive sense, Freedman writes in his book. After all, kids who commit crimes have to get the idea from somewhere. Yet in several sensational cases where television has been cited as a factor in young people's crime, the link has turned out to be false. In his book, Freedman revisits the horrific Bulger case in Britain in 1993, where two ten year old boys murdered a two year old they had abducted from a shopping mall. Although the judge in the case remarked that the boys had imitated a TV program involving kidnapping and murder, the police report was clear that the boys had not seen the television program, did not watch much TV, and that television had not been a factor in the murder. Similarly, in an October 1992 case of an American boy who set a fire that killed a girl, there were reports that the arsonist had been inspired by a television program broadcast a few days before, but these reports proved to be false. The program was presented on cable TV, which neither the boy's parents nor anyone else in the trailer park where he lived was hooked up to. The boy did not see the program.

Freedman also writes that influential and respected institutions have fostered public acceptance of the theory that media images are a major cause of crime by telling people there is a large body of scientific study proving it. Yet "although they have all made unequivocal statements about the effects of media violence," Freedman continues, "it is almost certain that not one of these organizations conducted a thorough review of the research." Freedman charges that this makes organizations like the American Medical Association, the Canadian Psychological Association, and the American Academy of Pediatrics "guilty of the worst kind of irresponsible behaviour."

The most obvious sign that these organizations did not have an accurate understanding of the prior research, writes Freedman, is the wild variance in their statements about how many studies have been conducted. After methodically searching for studies on the impact of media violence since the mid-1980s, it was clear to him that there have been no more than two hundred such studies conducted. But the medical and professional associations—without ever having published literature reviews that contain an accounting of the number of studies they've consulted—cite figures many times greater than that. Referring to earlier work conducted by the Surgeon General and the National Institute of Mental Health,[2] the American Psychological Association points vaguely to "hundreds of studies" that lead to "the irrefutable conclusion that viewing violence increases violence." Meanwhile, the American Academy of Pediatrics stated in 1999 that "more than 1,000 scientific studies and reviews" have shown the negative effects of media violence. In 2001 the AAP revised its estimate, claiming that "more than 3,500 research studies have examined the relationship between media violence and violent behaviour," with all but eighteen concluding that media violence has an adverse impact on behaviour. Freedman is adamant that "there have not been 3,500 or even 1,000 scientific studies on this topic." The AAP's citation of those figures, he writes, should have the same damaging effect on that body's credibility as would occur if "an organization of economists asserted that there were serious economic problems in over 150 American states ... If they were so sloppy as to think there were that many states, who could possibly trust the rest of their statement?"

Freedman is similarly scathing about the professional organizations' assessment of what the research into media violence does prove. In some cases, he writes, the fault lies with the third parties, whose public references to social scientists' experiments or surveys involve either a misinterpretation or misrepresentation of the works' conclusions. For example, in testimony before the U.S. Senate, an American Psychological Association official referred to a 1973 study by Lynette Friedrich and Aletha Stein, which the official claimed had "found that youngsters who watched Batman and Superman cartoons were more likely to hit their playmates, start arguments, disobey the teacher, and be more impatient." Freedman insists that the study shows nothing of the kind. Having concluded, after looking at their group of subjects in aggregate, that "there were no effects of this type of programming on the children's physical, verbal, object or fantasy aggression nor on a measure called interpersonal aggression, which combines physical and verbal aggression" (that's Freedman's description of what the study says), the authors re-examined their material by "conducting a complex internal analysis" that divided the children into those who began the experiment high in aggression and those who had low aggression. While the low-aggression children did become more aggressive after watching action cartoons, the high-aggression children became more passive—results that Freedman believes can be attributed to an "obvious regression effect," which suggests that subjects with an especially high or low quotient of a particular behaviour can be expected to score more moderately on a test. This is hardly the definitive conclusion that the APA official cited; in fact, Freedman's analysis is that the experiment *disproves* the idea that superhero cartoons foster aggression.

In other instances, Freedman takes exception to the way the researchers themselves (whom he believes can be influenced by their personal convictions or by the centrality of the issue to their careers and funding prospects) have structured their experiments or interpreted the data they've collected. Though it's impossible here to précis all the studies Freedman catalogues and dissects in his book, it's worth noting that several of the studies he singles out as failing to prove the media/violence link are those most frequently cited as accomplishing just that. The following three summaries of examples from *Media Violence and Its Effect on Aggression* highlight some of the key instances in which, according to Freedman, commonly cited research falls short of proving a clear connection between media violence and children's behaviour.

1. While Freedman says that laboratory-centred experiments have produced some of the strongest evidence that there may be a causal link between viewing violence and aggression,[3] he also maintains that several of the most prominent examples of this type of inquiry have been undermined by (a) researchers neglecting to distinguish between the effects of media violence and other arousing aspects of the film or TV presentations, and (b) the failure to offset "demand factors" (that is the tendency for subjects to behave the way they think the researchers want them to behave). On the first score—the failure to distinguish between different forms of arousal—Freedman explains that it is important to ensure that aggressive behaviour observed after subjects have viewed violent films is specifically related to the violence and not to some other arousing element of the film. After all, violent movies often contain other aspects—e.g., a suspenseful plotline, disturbing characters, a sense of threat, tension between good and evil—that can also produce arousal. And whatever the source of this arousal, "it is well known that when people are aroused, they tend to act more forcefully and strongly," Freedman writes. "Given the opportunity to be aggressive, they will be more aggressive than if they were less aroused." Therefore, if researchers are to be certain that their subjects' aggression is related to the violent content and not to other exciting, arousing, or angering content, they must make sure that the control group sees films that, despite containing no violence, have the same elements of suspense, controversy, or emotional tension that are woven into the violent

film. Though it's impossible to match films exactly, Freedman points out that researchers could show the control group action/adventure films that don't contain violence or show them nonviolent but tense and arousing sporting events. Yet some researchers have done just the opposite, juxtaposing the responses of viewers of violent films with the responses of people shown slow-moving and innocuous films or, in some cases, with the responses of a control group that has been shown no film at all. "Perhaps the most extreme [example] was a study that compared the effect of a film of a violent, bloody prizefight, with that of a film of canal boats in England," writes Freedman. He also notes that several researchers who conducted such studies have themselves attributed the varying aggression levels "to differences in arousal rather than to the presence of violence in the film," although third parties have cited these studies as proof of the effects of visual violence.

To explain the second contaminant that has allegedly tainted some lab experiments—"demand factors" or "experimenter or situational demand"—Freedman employs the analogy of a child visiting a friend's family. When "young Fred, eight years old, goes to dinner at Sally's house," explains Freedman, he can pretty soon clue into whether Sally's parents expect children "to sit quietly, to eat carefully, and generally to behave in a grown-up, serious manner," or whether they're more relaxed about kids talking over each other, eating with their fingers, etc. How Fred perceives the adults' rules will likely determine how he behaves at the dinner table. Freedman believes the same is true in a laboratory setting. Children who are shown aggressive films will interpret this as adult permission to engage in aggressive play; those who are shown non-aggressive films will take the opposite cue. "This is especially true in experiments in which young children are shown films of people interacting with Bobo dolls or other such toys," Freedman elaborates. "In these studies, usually children are told nothing about why they are watching the films. They watch a film of an adult kicking or hugging a Bobo doll in a room that contains various other toys, and they are then taken to the very same room, which contains the Bobo doll and the other toys. Surely even quite young children will infer that they were shown the film as an indication of how they should behave in the room. What other possible reason could there be?"

Freedman also takes issue with the logical extrapolations that have been drawn from this sort of experiment. For example, a 1963 study by Albert Bandura and colleagues involved experiments in which children were shown films of adults behaving aggressively towards other adults. In the first film, when a man became aggressive, a second man tried to retaliate but was overpowered. The second film "began the same way, but the second adult turned the tables, sat on the first adult, and spanked him." A third film showed non-aggressive behaviour between the adults. When the children were allowed to play after watching the films, the children who watched an adult's aggressive behaviour go unpunished behaved more aggressively than the other children. The children who saw the aggressive man get punished for his behaviour acted no more aggressively than the children who had watched the non-aggressive film. A common interpretation of this study is that it shows that watching violence will be particularly harmful for children if they do not see the aggression being punished—that is, if they don't see the consequences of aggression. Freedman, however, believes that this study is fundamentally a vindication of most of the screen violence that children are exposed to. In the study, he points out, the adult punishing the aggressor behaved at least as violently as the instigator did, if not more so. But his actions conform to the general plotline of the majority of violent programs, like superhero cartoons or cop shows, that children watch: the heroes often resort to using violence, but it is in retaliation against some kind of evil force. Therefore, Bandura's experiment showing no rise in children's aggression when the aggression they've been watching is punished seems "to show that typical plots in violent films and television either have no effect on aggression or even reduce it ... If one were to accept this result as indicative of the true state of affairs, it would mean that we should stop worrying about the Power Rangers and Batman and other heroes' aggressive behaviour," Freedman concludes.

2. One of the most pointed and sensational statements to be amplified by the U.S. Senate's committee on media violence was epidemiologist Brandon Centerwall's observation that if "television technology had never been developed, there would be 10,000 fewer homicides each year in the United States." Centerwall produced those statistics by extrapolating from his comparison of crime rates in the United States and Canada (where television became commonplace in the 1950s and 1960s) with those in South Africa (where television was banned by the government during the same period). Since Canadian and U.S. crime rates rose dramatically in that time but remained static in South Africa, Centerwall's conclusion was that television promoted crime.

Freedman's first criticism of Centerwall's study is that comparing North American and South African crime rates is a bizarre and meaningless exercise given how little data is available describing South Africa in that period, and given how different those societies were from one another. While North America was experiencing dramatic social change on many fronts, change was almost non-existent in South Africa. Under the apartheid system, South Africa was a highly repressive police state. Preventing the arrival of television was only one of the milder measures that the government was prepared to take to ensure the status quo was not challenged and that citizens stayed in line. It would have been much more appropriate to compare Canada and the United States with other industrialized liberal democracies, and Freedman relates that this is precisely the comparison that two violent crime experts, Franklin Zimring and Gordon Hawkings, did undertake—with results that directly contradicted Centerwall's. Zimring and Hawkins correlated television ownership and homicide rates in France, Germany, Italy, and Japan and found that while TV ownership increased dramatically between 1955 and 1975, those countries did not experience a rise in the rate of violent crime similar to that which occurred in North America beginning in the 1960s. The pair explicitly state that their findings disprove the theory of a causal relationship between television and violence.

Freedman also insists that Centerwall's analysis of the data that appears in his own study is flawed. Although 25 percent of American homes had television by 1952, he relates, the "homicide rates actually dropped slightly between 1947 and 1957," a period when, if Centerwall's reasoning were applied consistently, a significant exposure to television should have manifested itself in significantly more violent behaviour. Freedman adds that any reliable study linking a major social trend with television use would have attempted to control for a number of other key factors normally linked by social scientists to criminality. Centerwall looked at two variables— age distribution and economic conditions—and concluded that neither of these were responsible for the rise in crime in North America. However, Freedman blasts Centerwall for ignoring several other huge social trends that clearly would have had an impact on the quality of the home environment experienced by North American children, especially since criminologists and sociologists commonly consider home life and parenting practice determinants of whether children are "at risk for becoming aggressive and committing crimes." Divorce rates and the number of women working outside the home, for example, soared during the time frame that Centerwall examines. Freedman makes it clear that neither of these two trends should in themselves be considered negative. However, the various ways in which different societies deal with these changes may lead to differing degrees of social stress that could provide some explanation for the differing crime rates in the U.S. and Europe. There is evidence, for instance, that being a child of divorce "is no worse and perhaps better than living in a home in which the parents do not get along." Yet negative feelings (stress and a sense of deprivation) may arise from the subsidiary economic effects of divorce, given that "typically, the wife earns less than the husband, does not receive adequate financial support from him after the divorce, and finds herself in greatly reduced circumstances." A similarly huge social shift was the entry of more women into the workforce, but North American society made few efforts to adjust to this change. Again, Freedman notes that "mothers who hold jobs outside the home may, on average, have higher self-esteem than those who do not hold such jobs, and this may have positive effects on their children." However, the lack of support for quality daycare could be seen as damaging to children, since most experts in the field believe that "children do not do so well when ... they are in low-quality daycare or informal daycare arrangements (e.g., the neighbour takes care of them) ... Also, children who come home to an empty house ('latch key children') are generally experiencing less-than-ideal childcare." While Freedman notes that factors such as the rising divorce rate are more closely correlated, chronologically, to the rising crime rate, he is baffled that Centerwall saw no reason to control for these major social changes before concluding that television alone was responsible for increases in crime.

3. Similar in approach to Centerwall's study is the oft-cited comparison by the University of British Columbia's Tannis MacBeth Williams of three Canadian communities: one that had been receiving multiple television stations (dubbed "Multitel"), one that received only one station ("Unitel"), and one where television was absent but soon to be introduced ("Notel"). The researchers visited all three communities and recorded aggression levels in each, measured in three ways: what teachers said about the children, what children said about their peers, and what the researchers observed directly. They returned later, after television had been introduced to Notel, and repeated the exercise. While aggression levels had been the same in all three communities during the first round of experiments, they increased dramatically in Notel after television had been introduced, but only according to one of the three measures—the observation of the researchers. According to teachers and the children themselves, there had been no change. This rise in aggression noted by the researchers led them to conclude that television does indeed make children more aggressive.

Freedman argues that there are a number of critical flaws in the study. For one, there is no indication whether any other social change could have accounted for the change in children's behaviour. Also, Freedman finds it curious that the one station Notel received was a Canadian Broadcasting Corporation outlet, which would have had a far lower quotient of violent and action-oriented programs than the stations that had been available over a longer time frame in Multitel. He is also convinced, given the extraordinary rate of aggression recorded in post-TV Notel, where kids were said to be committing one aggressive act every minute, that researchers mistook aggressive play (which is of little concern to most psychologists) for real aggression (which is of great concern). This reading, writes Freedman, tends to be supported by the fact that neither the children nor their teachers reported any increase in levels of aggression. Freedman also believes that the statistical content of the report itself directly contradicts the conclusion that researchers drew from it. If television has such a profound effect on aggression levels, why had the communities with none, one, and multiple television channels scored equally on levels of aggression in the first phase of the study? "You can't have it both ways," writes Freedman. "If television is such an important factor, Notel should have had less aggression in Phase 1." The fact that it didn't suggests that television is of no importance in priming kids to behave violently.

Although the complaints of Freedman and a handful of other contrarians were just cries in the wilderness around the time of Columbine, by the dawn of the new millennium there was a new team on the field that firmly embraced the view that the prior consensus on what the research says about media and violence was flawed and dangerous. Late in 2001, for example, a group of media scholars—under the banner of the National Coalition Against Censorship (NCC)—wrote to the American Academy of Pediatrics asking it to withdraw statements to the effect that media violence created violent kids. "Laboratory experiments that are designed to test causation rely on substitutes for aggression, some quite far fetched," their letter read. "Punching Bobo dolls, pushing buzzers, and recognizing 'aggressive words' on a computer screen are a far cry from real-world aggression. Researchers have also manipulated data to achieve 'statistically significant' results."[4] The NCC is a coalition of just over four dozen organizations, including the American Civil Liberties Union, the American Federation of Teachers, the American Library Association, the Children's Literature Association, the Screen Actors' Guild, the Directors' Guild, the Writers' Guild, and the National Education Association.

Still, researchers who back the media-violence link have stuck to their guns. University of Michigan psychology professor L. Rowell Huesmann, who told a Senate committee in 1999 that "widespread portrayal of violence in [the] media is having an insidious effect on increasing violence in society,"[5] has been defending himself against elements of Freedman's critique since the mid-1990s. Writing in *The Harvard Mental Health Letter* in 1996, Huesmann and colleague Jessica Moise accuse Freedman of using nitpicking methodological criticisms to discredit essentially sound research. "Dr. Freedman's highly selective reading of the research minimizes overwhelming evidence," they write. The two respond to Freedman by arguing that "more than 100 ... studies over the last 40 years have shown at least some children exposed to visual depictions of dramatic violence behave more aggressively afterward both toward inanimate objects and toward other children" and that these results are consistent across different countries, ages, races, and intelligence levels, and among both boys and girls. They deny that researchers consistently mistake harmless pounding of Bobo dolls and other innocuous measures of "aggression" for real violence, citing a Finnish study in which children shown a violent film "were more likely to hit other children, scream at them, threaten them and intentionally destroy their toys." The Michigan researchers also discount Freedman's claim that demand factors influence research outcomes as "extremely implausible, considering the wide variety of experiments conducted in different countries by researchers with different points of view."[6]

The debate heated up considerably in the following decade, with Huesmann duelling ferociously with another disbeliever, the Pulitzer-prize-winning author Richard Rhodes. On the website of the American Booksellers' Foundation for Free Expression (www.abffe.com), the two men traded conflicting views of the research, charges of dishonesty, and allegations of bias. Rhodes, for instance, used the word "fraud" after stating that Huesmann tried to conceal the sample size of a study much ballyhooed in the halls of government. Meanwhile, Huesmann claimed that Rhodes' revelation elsewhere that he grew up in a violent home proves that the author has an axe to grind and a personal stake in his view of the issue.

The opening salvo in that conflict was ABFFE's posting of Rhodes' *Rolling Stone* essay "The Media Violence Myth" on its website.[7] In the article, Rhodes critiques the laboratory experiments and the famous Centerwall study much as Freedman did. He goes further, however, and offers his own hypothesis as to why research into the links between media and social violence came to exert such influence over American politicians and social commentators. Rhodes starts this story by returning to the early research into childhood aggression, begun in the early 1960s by Huesmann's colleague Leonard Eron, which looked at television viewing as one small variable contributing to violent behaviour. According to Rhodes' account, Eron's initial findings on television and violence were weak and contradictory. In a study that examined 875 third graders in upstate New York, the researchers found a correlation between some boys' aggression and the amount of violence they watched on TV, although the finding did not extend to girls. The study also found that kids who watched the most television overall were the least aggressive of the group. These results weren't considered worth exploring further at the time, but in the early 1970s some law makers' interest in the effects of television prompted the National Institute of Mental Health to give Eron and his colleagues (now including Huesmann) a grant to find as many of the 875 third graders as possible and correlate their later experience of crime and violence with their earlier records of TV viewing (more on the results of this experiment later).

Rhodes speculates that this blossoming political interest in television and violence was driven not just by a need to distract the public from other pressing issues, but also by a deep-seated social desire to strike back at an entertainment industry whose influence had grown dramatically as traditionally powerful institutions like the church began to lose authority. In short, this is a question of "social control," and in a time of social upheaval, "blaming the media for criminal violence is one campaign in an ongoing turf war." Rhodes believes that this largely unconscious process gave funding agencies and partisan academics a political reason to amplify findings like those of Eron and Huesmann and also a reason to suppress results that ran against the grain. Rhodes comments that there has been little notice, for example, of a study by sociologist Steven Messner that correlated violent television programs (as classified by the National Coalition on Television Violence) with Nielson ratings and with FBI figures for violent crimes and robbery in order to determine whether areas with high rates of violence viewing are afflicted by higher crime rates. (The result? Messner found, counterintuitively, that metropolitan areas "in which large audiences are attracted to violent television programming tend to exhibit low rates of violent crime.") For another study, a psychologist named Seymour Feshbach divided four hundred boys in three private schools and four boys' homes into two groups: one group could watch only violent programming, and the other could watch only non-aggressive programming. Feshback reported that although there was no difference in behaviour among boys in the private schools, the incarcerated boys who watched the most violent programming were less aggressive.

On the other hand, Rhodes says Huesmann's longitudinal study—the one that began with 875 third graders in upstate New York—has been given too much weight. Huesmann, Rhodes recounts, presented his data to Congress in the form of a bar graph, which showed that boys who preferred violent entertainment at age eight were almost twice as likely to have serious criminal convictions as boys who preferred nonviolent entertainment. But Rhodes says this conclusion is fatally flawed because it extrapolates from only three subjects who were involved in serious violent acts as adults—far too few to draw general lessons from.

Huesmann, in a joint rebuttal with Leonard Eron, confirms that the bar graph figure does indeed hinge on the experience of only three boys, but he insists the sample size is just fine. "There were 145 boys in that study on whom we had data about how violent was the TV they watched at age 8 and how aggressive and criminal they were at age 30 ... When we looked at serious violent crimes we found that 3 of the 145 boys had been arrested for such crimes. This is about typical in this country—not many people are arrested for serious violent crimes. To our great concern we found that all three of those boys who had been arrested for serious violent crimes were in the highest 40 per cent of childhood violence viewers and 2 were in the highest 20 per cent."[8] Huesmann and Eron also argue that this research is supported by other work the Michigan group has undertaken. For example, Huesmann conducted another longitudinal study, looking at schoolgirls in Oak Park, Illinois, which is said to show that of girls who watched a lot of *Charlie's Angels* and *Wonder Woman* in the 1970s, "59 per cent were involved in more than the average number of such aggressive incidents [confrontations, shoving matches, chokings, and knifings] later in life."[9]

For Huesmann, such figures are proof of a causal relationship between media violence and real violence. This is consistent with the idea, advanced by many advocates of a media-violence link, that impressionable children (for instance, those between the ages of six and eight) use media to create "scripts" that they will file away for use later in life. However, opponents such as Rhodes don't buy that. Rhodes notes that most social scientists would assume that any impact on behaviour produced by outside influences such as watching screen violence would wear off with time. If this assumption is true, then Eron and Huessman's upstate New York study makes no sense. The longitudinal tracking records a small relation between violence viewing and aggression in third graders, which appears to disappear entirely at age thirteen, but somehow returns with even greater force at age eighteen.[10]

Critics like Freedman, far from seeing causality in these figures, say that if the findings are correct, they indicate only a mild correlation between viewing violent media and acting aggressively. And that correlation, says Freedman, merely proves what psychologists have known all along: that aggressive people tend to gravitate towards violent entertainment. Freedman insists that there are several possible explanations for such a correlation—the idea that violent images promote violence is only one of those possibilities. Equally plausible is the suggestion that aggressive people use violent media as a calming or cathartic agent. In his book, Freedman explains the logic of correlation with an analogy about heart disease and carrots. If statistics reveal that people who eat lots of carrots have lower rates of heart disease, this is not proof that carrots prevent heart disease. Rather, the connection may be a step or two removed, with the correlation explained by the fact that people who eat lots of carrots also exercise more and have generally healthier lifestyles.

It's the same with violent entertainment—any correlation with real aggression may point to a third common factor. So to base public policy on the assumption that one phenomenon causes another is to risk both missing the real root of the problem (say, continuing to smoke heavily while upping one's daily intake of carrots) and adopting policies that are destined to fail. Banning violent entertainment will do nothing if a love of such fare is merely indicative of a frame of mind and not its cause. "If kids are born with aggressive personalities that tend to like violent video games and like violent television and like to be aggressive," Freedman told me, "there's no legislation that's going to change their personalities."

I wanted to get a better sense of how this unresolved debate about the media's role in promoting violence has influenced the work of other researchers looking more broadly at violent kids. So I contacted Jennifer Connolly, a professor of psychology and director of the LaMarch Centre on Violence at York University, in the suburban hinterlands of Toronto, who has been conducting research on kids and aggression. One of her recent projects was a study of high school students' experience of bullying, dating violence, and sexual harassment. Connolly seems less sanguine about the current climate in schools than those who take comfort in that one key marker: the falling levels of homicide in U.S. educational institutions. She cites statistics that show one in five students is the victim of some form of harassment or bullying (a snapshot that remains consistent across class lines and even across national boundaries, she says), with the numbers rising to one in two when the specific issue is some kind of sexual harassment in high schools. Connolly stresses that research into schoolyard intimidation hasn't been conducted for long enough to allow researchers to determine whether the situation has improved or worsened over the years. Still, if the number of kids on the receiving end of these forms of abuse really does hover around the 20 percent mark, there's obvious cause to be concerned about the wellbeing of kids in school.

Although Connolly insists, "I'm not a communications researcher; I'm a teenager and relationships researcher" with only a peripheral interest in mass media, her study has been collecting data on what kind of media kids use and how it relates to the rest of their lives. The students are asked to rank how much aggression is communicated through the videos, games and music that they consume, just as they are asked to rank how aggressive they are in their interpersonal dealings. On the basis of that, "we can say that there is a link," reports Connolly. "The more aggressive the content that you view or listen to, the more likely you are to report [being the perpetrator of] bullying and dating violence and sexual harassment."

But what does this link actually signify? That violent media inspires interpersonal aggression? That it helps kids justify their behaviour? That it merely mirrors existing personality traits? Or is it simply coincidental? Connolly's answer seems to echo some of the skepticism expressed by Freedman. She believes it's unlikely that violent media is the one key factor that drives kids to violence, and she cautions that establishing a causal link "is very difficult in this field of research." Instead, she advances an alternate paradigm that talks of a "funnelling effect," where film, TV, and especially music help consolidate the bonds between groups of teenagers who already share common attitudes and outlooks. "Kids self-select certain types of media that they use," the psychologist explains, "particularly music, video games, internet—and that creates a base for a lot of kids' peer group interaction, and it's through these peer groups that a lot of these media effects come into play. So not all kids are heavily influenced by very aggressive media; only some kids are, and it's most often when it's that media that forms the context for their peer interaction."

Connolly differs from Freedman in the degree to which she distances herself from the idea (advanced by the U.S. Senate committee and pundits like Grossman) that media violence has a significant role in creating civil violence. While Freedman proposes that media violence is neutral in its social effects—possibly having the power to push certain aggressive personalities towards violent acts, but also with the potential to diffuse other individuals' violent impulses by providing an experience of catharsis—Connolly insists that "media is certainly not cathartic." Connolly also differs from Freedman by subscribing to the hypothesis that, although violent media probably doesn't have the far-reaching powers that crusaders like Grossman ascribe to it, electronic violence likely does reinforce negative behaviour when the group dynamics are right. "It's our view," she says, "that kids' attitudes and behaviours are shaped at least in part by the media and that then becomes a feature of themselves around which they join other kids. Particularly music is very defining, and kids connect with other kids through these kind of shared similarities."

There are clearly policy implications to a statement like that. If music, for instance, can solidify the antisocial attitudes of a group of teenagers, then perhaps politicians from various jurisdictions who have proposed shutting down Eminem's local concert appearances are on the right track. Yet Connolly is evasive when it comes to the policy implications of her work. "I'm not a policy person," she says. "Other people are more comfortable with that. My sense is that when there's a collective will, and enough people take this seriously, then things will happen."

Meanwhile, Freedman believes that the evidence in support of a link between violent images and violent acts is so weak that any public policy solutions would be useless or counterproductive. This doesn't mean that, at a household level, Freedman would advise parents to let their six year olds watch *Friday the 13th*. "That depends on the child," says Freedman. "Some children are scared by it [horror movies or screen violence] and some children think of it as nothing. But certainly the parents have a right and indeed an obligation to make sure their kids don't get traumatized or scared or upset. My guess is that images of September 11 were pretty upsetting to most kids, as they were for most adults. You probably don't want to sanitize the world for them, but you do want to shield them, sure. But that's a different issue from whether these images are going to turn them into bad people. The possibility that it would make them unhappy people is something parents need to pay attention to."

Freedman's invocation of the World Trade Centre attack is a telling one, raising the question of whether there is any difference between the impact of media images drawn from real life and those drawn from imagination. Since there has been a huge fuss about fictional violence in media, why has there been none about disturbing non-fiction images? I asked Freedman if he saw a distinction between fictional violence and a violent sporting event such as a hockey game or a boxing match.

"There I have a totally different view," he responded. "My guess is—and there have been studies that show this, but very few—that watching violent hockey games will cause kids to play a violent hockey game. I think the same is true of any real behaviour; I think kids are affected by real behaviour. They say, 'Here is this hockey player who earns $5 million a year, here is what he does, this is how he plays.' I suspect they know the difference between that and the fact that when the Power Rangers kick somebody, or Bruce Willis shoots somebody, that is fiction. There's no reason to imitate fiction—or there are lots of reasons to not imitate fiction. But one of the reasons kids watch hockey is to learn how to play hockey."

Though he stresses that there's been no definitive proof of how real-life media images affect kids' behaviour (partly because there's been little academic interest in this field, and partly because such research is difficult to conduct), Freedman ventures that it's more plausible to suggest that programs featuring people who are not actors will pack a greater wallop when they collide with young craniums. "Watching a talk show [like Jerry Springer] where real people are behaving uncivilly and being unpleasant—and there certainly is an awful lot of that—I can see that that says to everyone who's watching, 'Well, civility is no longer necessary,' or at least that the boundaries have been moved," he says. "Real-life cop shows, where you have somebody travelling with the cops in their car," are another instance where Freedman believes, though there is no evidence at this point to prove or disprove it, that the context may be telling kids that a particular behaviour is worth imitating. This notion that children are more likely to take their behavioural cues from the images that have been extracted from reality becomes particularly problematic, however, when one considers the network newscasts. Given that images of destruction and violence, and stories of aggression, greed, and deceit, are the mainstays of television news, should parents consider filtering out CNN or Newsnet when the kids are near the tube?

In turn, those questions about what the nightly news teaches children, and people in general, about the way the world operates lead to a deeper set of queries about the lessons that leaders of society are sending to the public when they exercise the authority of their office in full public view, from the podium the news media affords them. Particularly in the United States, says Freedman, government exerts its will in both foreign and domestic policy arenas through the calculated use of violence. It also crows about these deeds at press conferences and in news briefings. So if children can indeed distinguish between what's fantasy and what's reality, the message they are sure to pick up from the world's most powerful leaders—via the serene TV news anchor—is that might makes right, that violence is a legitimate tool for achieving one's goals.

"The real problem," says Freedman, "is that American society in particular is a very aggressive society, not just at the individual level, but at the governmental level. I am appalled when I see American generals and politicians gloating over military victories. I'm not saying they shouldn't use that power—that's a much more complicated issue—but it strikes me as perfectly straightforward that every time the most powerful country in the world kills somebody, rather than gloating they should apologize. It's the same thing with executions, where the state is using its power to kill somebody. First of all, I don't think they should do it—remember, the United States is the only country in the industrialized world that still executes people—but when they do, they should apologize: 'We regret this, this is a terrible thing that life has put this person on earth who did such a terrible act that we feel forced to execute him.' But they don't do it like that. They gloat over these executions; they thrive on them. I don't know what that does, but it can't do any good." In short, Freedman sees non-fiction violence and fictional violence as having different functions: while the former can be instructional, the latter is largely escapist.

There's another school of thought that extends this idea that fictional mayhem and real-world conflict have distinct roles in relation to one another. This view holds that violent, aggressive stories—rather than reinforcing life's cruel, brutal lessons—help kids come to terms with, cope with, and move beyond the real terrors that exist in real life. Proponents of this idea reckon that violent entertainment—no matter what the laboratory experiments and statistical extrapolations might say—can actually be *good* for kids.

Jack Zipes, a University of Minnesota German professor and an authority on the history of fairy tales, says that gory, unpleasant bedtime stories have always been a staple for small children. In the beginning, stories for tiny tots had a violence quotient that rivalled the worst of today's video games: the earliest version of "Little Red Riding Hood," published in 1697, ended with the decided downer of Grandma being eaten by the Wolf; in the Grimm Brothers' version of "Cinderella," meanwhile, the wicked sisters' eyes are pecked out, and blood drips onto the glass slipper. But that's okay, says Zipes, because all these gruesome fables contain a hidden message about strong-willed people overcoming the nastiness of a hostile world—and overcoming the brutality that lurks within them.

"Violence in fairy tales is not pernicious," he says, "because it enables children to work through violence they feel in themselves: the anger, frustration, needs and desires that they have. The authors of these works are trying to show that it is possible to overcome, to survive, to understand these drives and feelings. These fairy tales are linked to the way children experience the world. And the world is not a nonviolent place. The world is not clean and tidy."[11]

Screenwriter, comic book author, and pop-culture commentator Gerard Jones, noting that the famed child psychiatrist Bruno Bettelheim saw fairy tales aiding children's development by enabling them to better understand the menace they saw both within themselves and in the broader world, believes this lesson also applies to the so-called junk culture of today. In his book *Killing Monsters: Why Children Need Fantasy, Super Heroes, and Make-Believe Violence*, Jones insists that the often disparaged phenomena noted in the subtitle of his book all help children make aggression a central element of their play. And that's a good thing because although "one of the functions of stories and games is to help children rehearse for what they'll be later in life, … anthropologists and psychologists who study play … have shown that there are many other functions as well—one of which is to enable children to pretend to be just what they know they'll *never* be. Exploring, in a safe and controlled context, what is impossible or too dangerous or forbidden to them is a crucial tool to accepting the limits of reality. Playing with rage is a valuable way to reduce its power. Being evil and destructive in imagination is a vital compensation for the wildness we all have to surrender on our way to being good people."[12] One can see how useful an exercise such as this might be if one accepts Dr. Richard Tremblay's idea (described in Chapter 8) that aggression is innate and needs to be mastered and controlled—an idea that contrasts with the "social learning" framework within which most media violence studies have operated.

Children will gravitate towards violent themes in play and in the culture they consume, says Jones, when events in the outside world communicate to them that their environment is dangerous or filled with violence. Just after the September 11, 2001, attacks, for example, at a time when adults wanted to clamp down on the sales of violent toys, kids' demand for those toys went through the roof. The Columbine massacre also apparently triggered a resurgent interest amongst kids in the violent video games and movies that adults had identified as at least partly responsible for the problem of teen violence. What this indicates, Jones theorizes, is that kids are acutely anxious about the violence which they know has infected the world they live in—and seeing that violence on a screen, sometimes repeatedly and obsessively, allows them to bring their unacknowledged fears into the open in an attempt to understand them better.

Not that Jones claims that fantasy violence is always a useful thing and that the childish obsession with it is uniformly a cause for rejoicing. A kid may become fascinated with violent media because he's got underlying issues to deal with—maybe it's something in the broader environment, maybe it's something in his own life—but that doesn't mean he will successfully deal with what's bothering him and be able to move on. Jones believes it's important for the significant adults in a kid's life to find out what feelings are behind that kid's obsession and to try to play a positive role in helping the kid move to the next plateau. He is convinced, however, that seeing a child's appetite for superhero fantasies or shoot-'em-up video games as the evil in itself will do more harm than good. That merely closes up a means of self-expression, burying the problem deeper in the kid's psyche and allowing it to fester.

Jones corrals a few statements in support of his point of view from people within the medical establishment. He quotes forensic psychologist Dr. Helen Smith, author of *The Scarred Heart: Understanding and Identifying Kids Who Kill*, who says, "Not one young person in my experience has ever been made violent by media influence. Young people who are already inclined to be violent do feel that violent media speak to them. Some of them do get dangerous ideas from it. But more of them find it a way to deal with their rage." We get a similar line from University of Chicago pediatric psychiatrist Dr. Edwin Cook, who remarks that "entertainment has the power to overexcite or present a distorted worldview to some children. But for other children, the right aggressive entertainment might be the best thing they can see."

The mainstay of Jones' book, however, are the testimonials from people who confess a taste for dark tales and who remain defiantly convinced these things have been good for them. He tells his own story of growing up an unhappy kid, discovering comic books, and turning into a well-adjusted adult who makes his living as a pop-culture historian, writer of comic books, and the guy who helped adapt Pokémon for the North American marketplace. He talks to colleagues in the business who say that the power fantasies of superheroes helped them overcome feelings of resignation that came from growing up in poverty. He relays the words of teenage Goths, who were drawn to the dark imagery of that subculture, so they say, because it introduced them to a community of like-minded people who allowed them to recognize the negative feelings they had grown up with, to acknowledge where the events of their lives had brought them, and to recognize who they felt they were as people. Jones also ventures inside classrooms and doctors' offices, talking to teachers and physicians who are committed to the idea that kids should be encouraged to express their aggression through art and play—the better to bring it out into the open and use it as a platform for discussion.

This pastiche of stories, of course, is at odds with the scientific method that's led to the controlled beating of Bobo dolls and the correlation of watching *Charlie's Angels* with later spousal conflict and motor vehicle offenses—but for Gerard Jones that's just fine. The focus of laboratory science, he says, is far too narrow to ever be able to quantify the impacts of art. "The research on violent entertainment," he wrote in an article for *KidScreen* magazine, "has limited the whole dialogue by clinging to a 'cause and effect' model that fails to consider the complexity of stories and our individual, emotional, interpretive relationship with them ... Would we dream of applying such a reductionist medical approach to understanding the power of fairy tales, love songs or French Impressionism?"[13] He borrows a theory from an Irish television producer, who saw this difference in approaches stemming from two entirely separate ways of dealing with the world. Jones describes one methodological mindset as "*lyricism*, which formed the central thread of Celtic and Catholic civilization, seeking truth through art and emotion more than through externalities." Its opposite is "*literalism*, a more Protestant thread, which seeks a single, objective reality to the world. Shakespeare and cartoons are lyrical. Barney is literal. Psychiatrists who explore dreams and understand the value of hidden fantasy are lyrical. Psychologists who quantify media effects are literal."[14]

It strikes me that living lyrically (especially when that involves dealing with children) is much more difficult than living literally. With no one key to unlock the truth, no one, unassailable research finding on which to base one's life, no hard and fast rules, everything is open to interpretation. Even the possibility that there are two legitimate ways of looking at a vexing issue like violence in media, and that each paradigm stems from a respectable tradition and can be justified in its own way, adds to the uncertainty and the need to constantly reexamine individual situations to find the explanation that makes most intuitive sense. In the end, this idea—that the lyrical and literal worldviews are both legitimate and might possibly form two halves of a reasonable discussion—suggests that a problem that has baffled philosophers throughout the ages remains an open question in the age of modern science. Are cultural artifacts an incitement to violence or merely a diversion? Does "social learning" explain how attitudes form, or do the mass media merely hold a mirror to what kids already have inside them? Those are puzzles put to the test each day in living rooms, cinemas and video arcades everywhere, with no clear and satisfactory resolution.

Epilogue

This has been a captivating journey for me. It began at that kid marketing conference, where the accelerated quest to find new ways of pushing product to kids, to snare kids as lifelong brand loyalists, struck me as a cold, calculating, and cynical exercise and more than a trifle annoying. The unnerving suspicion that this line of work could actually be dangerous to kids was something we explored by looking at early exposés of the marketing biz—from the 1950s phenomenon that was Vance Packard's *The Hidden Persuaders* to more audacious theories like subliminal suggestion, which was popular in the psychedelic sixties. Along the way we've looked at how ideas about the impact of marketing intersect with events in the real world—a line of inquiry that led us to the subject of media violence and real-life violence, an area where variations on Packard's ideas about subconscious manipulation and Manchurian Candidate-style programming have come to the fore.

What's clear from more recent history, however, is that the political context within which those ideas are played out has changed completely. While many past attempts to save childhood from the psychological pressure applied by marketers were spearheaded by social liberals (people who want to give children the opportunity to define themselves, without scripts imposed by commercial interests), the conservatives who are now in the vanguard of this debate are pushing quite a different agenda. They object to the media/marketing establishment because it encourages an individualism that stands in the way of their authoritarian project. In particular, the campaign to reduce the issue of "youth violence" to a cultural question—to blame it on the marketing of video games and horror movies—seems at least partly designed to forestall questions about more relevant social issues and calls for meaningful public policy changes.

You may have detected an attitude of ambivalence in the preceding pages. Let me try to be a bit clearer: I still find the people rushing around trying to infiltrate kids' culture, hoping to sell them things they really don't need and probably wouldn't want if the big marketing push weren't there, fairly annoying. But I find the agendas of some the people who bash the kind of youth culture promoted by the media/marketing establishment—the people who oppose that culture because it represents a challenge to the authority of church, state, and old-style controlling parents—genuinely frightening.

If it strikes you that this ambivalence is anathema to any kind of constructive action, perhaps I can suggest a pragmatic approach to addressing the issue. You can look at our current media-centered world as a house of mirrors. Everywhere in this house there are reflections of ourselves—distorted, reconstituted images of who we are—that are so ubiquitous and distracting that it becomes difficult to know what's real, which way is forward, and which way is back. These images are meaningful in that they change our sense of the room we occupy and of what we look like. But those images don't just rely upon mirrors. There have to be real people walking through the house in order for us to see these images. And so perhaps what's important is not just that we keep talking about what these twisted reflections—what the marketing campaigns that fill our media-defined society—are doing to us, but also that we examine what they reflect back to us about events and things in the real world, and how those images and the real people wandering through the house interact and intersect. We should see those images as having a significance beyond themselves. They should help move us back into a concrete world, to focus us again on what is real, what is here and now, to answer our questions about who we are and how we should act.

Notes

CHAPTER 1

1. Patrick Allossery, "Growing focus on impact of advertising on children," *National Post*, September 25, 2000.
2. Rebecca A. Clay, "Advertising to children: Is it ethical?" *Monitor on Psychology* 31, no. 8 (September 2000).
3. "Marketing to children harmful: Experts urge candidates to lead nation in setting limits" [press release]. Center for Media Education, Washington, DC, October 18, 2000.
4. James U. McNeal, *Kids as Customers: A Handbook of Marketing to Children* (New York: Lexington Books [an imprint of Macmillan], 1992), 3–8. McNeal writes that in the 1980s, parents began having fewer children and often postponed having them until they were in their thirties or beyond. Dual-income and single-parent families also became more the norm. The result in many dual-income families was that parents had more money but less time to spend with their children, and often parents would give their children money as a way of assuaging their own guilt. In single-parent families, meanwhile, children often became more like partners in running the household—meaning that they gained experience buying items for the home at an earlier age. The fact of fewer children per home, writes McNeal, also suggests that parents prized their children more than might have been the case before and were therefore willing to indulge them more, materially.

   McNeal traces the increasing recognition of children as customers in their own right, and consequently as the focus of attention for the marketing industry, throughout the post-Second World War period. A 50 percent increase in the number of kids between 1946 and 1951 corresponded with an increasingly individualistic ethic in the 1950s and the development of television advertising aimed at children.

By the middle of the 1960s, kids in the United States were spending over $2 billion of their own money and influencing exponentially more parental spending. In the 1970s, Ronald McDonald and the Toys "R" Us mascot, Geoffrey Giraffe, became American children's icons. In the 1980s, children's media like the Nickelodeon TV network and *Sports Illustrated for Kids* magazine established solid footholds in the marketplace.

5. Sources Diamond cites for these statistics are: the spring 1999 Teenage Research Unlimited's Marketing and Lifestyle Survey; U.S. Bureau of the Census; *Hollywood Reporter*; Spring 2000 Simmons Market Research.

6. McNeal, *Kids as Customers*, 5.

7. This quote, attributed to Nancy Shalek, then president of the Shalek Agency, has been widely cited by opponents of marketing to children. It originally appeared in an article by Ron Harris, "Children who dress for excess: Today's youngsters have become fixated with fashion. The right look isn't enough—it also has to be expensive," *Los Angeles Times*, November 12, 1989.

8. The World Wrestling Federation changed its name to World Wrestling Entertainment in 2002 after losing a court battle with the World Wildlife Fund over use of the acronym WWF.

9. These issues surfaced in a reported case at Stonington High School in Connecticut when the school invited McDonald's to a jobs fair, ostensibly to hold a workshop on how to prepare a job application. A fifteen year old student, who is a vegetarian and an animal rights advocate, became angry at having to attend the school event when a video was shown that, according to the student, dealt with "how great it is to work for McDonald's." The student told one of the hamburger chain's representatives, "I hate large corporations like McDonald's," and made negative comments about the company's alleged misrepresentation of its french fries as vegetarian (they contain beef tallow). After the student was disciplined for being "an embarrassment to the school," a controversy erupted over the apparent compromise of free speech and honest intellectual inquiry. "Schools, we hope, are teaching critical thinking skills," remarked Emily Heath of the San Francisco-based Center for Commercial Free Public Education. "Advertising is antithetical to that. It teaches them to believe whatever is presented to them and to take what your school endorses." Source: Hank Hoffman, "McCensored: Student punished for criticizing McDonald's," *In These Times*, July 30, 2001. Posted on Alternet's *WireTap* magazine (www.wiretapmag.org).

Corporate sponsorships became a fact of school life in many parts of the United States in the 1990s, writes Paul Pellizzari, "when government cutbacks forced boards in many states to strike new kinds of school-business partnerships." For example, the District School Board of Colorado receives about $100,000 annually from advertising within the school system. Among the most controversial business enterprises to become a fixture in schools is Channel One (part of Primedia Inc.), which gives schools television and video equipment in exchange for the right to broadcast educational news programs to the students. For every ten minutes of broadcast programming, students watch two minutes of commercials. (A similar service called the Youth News Network—[YNN]—has been introduced in some Canadian schools.) Pellizzari says that advertisers hope to find a receptive audience in the school setting, since the purpose of attending school is to absorb information. Source: Paul Pellizzari, "Selling the classroom to save the school," posted on *www.straightgoods.com*, April 2, 2001.

10. Gregory Roberts, "Seattle schools may phase out controversial video service," *Seattle Post-Intelligencer*, October 25, 2001.

CHAPTER 2

1. Vance Packard, *The Hidden Persuaders*, rev. ed. (New York: Washington Square Books, 1957 and 1980). Quotations and examples from Packard throughout this chapter are drawn from this book, various pages.

2. Gary Ruskin, "Why they whine: How corporations prey on our children," *Mothering*, November/December 1999. Original citation: Joel Babbit's paper "Channel One Vision," presented at the On The Youth Market conference, Boston, May 5–6, 1994.

3. Wilson Bryan Key, *Subliminal Seduction: Ad Media's Manipulation of a Not So Innocent America* (New York: Signet, 1973). Quotations and examples from Key throughout this chapter are drawn from this book, various pages.

4. I characterize this as a credible theory because it doesn't require the reader to be in an altered state of consciousness to judge whether the author's suggestions have merit. You only have to look at the picture to see if Key's assertions make sense. My assessment, in this particular context, is that they do.

5. Kalle Lasn, *Culture Jam: How to Reverse America's Suicidal Consumer Binge — And Why We Must* (New York: Quill [an imprint of HarperCollins], 1999), 13. Subsequent quotations from Lasn are drawn from this book, various pages.

6. In "Why won't anyone say they are Jewish?" an article in the March/April 2004 *Adbusters*, Lasn writes: "We decided to tackle the issue head on and came up with a carefully researched list of who appears to be the 50 most influential neo-conservatives in the U.S ... What they all share is the view that the U.S. is a benevolent hyper-power that must protect itself by reshaping the rest of the world in its morally superior image. And half of them are Jewish." The list is presented below the text with stars appearing beside the Jewish names.

   The piece produced instant outrage. Quoted in the Toronto weekly *NOW*, anti-WTO activist and philosophy professor Klaus Jahn said, "Whether listing physicians who perform abortions in pro-life tracts, gays and lesbians in office memos, Communists ... under McCarthy, Jews in Central Europe under Naziism and so on, such list making has always produced pernicious consequences." Source: Kate Raynes-Golie, "Race baiting: *AdBuster's* listing of Jewish neo-cons the lastest wacko twist in lefty mag's remake," *NOW*, March 18–24, 2004.

   Michael Niman said that although the charge of anti-Semitism is sometimes falsely levelled against critics of Israeli policy, by focusing on Jews as an ethnic group, Lasn reveals that he "is the real article. He is an anti-Semite." Niman also notes that Lasn's "carefully researched" list is fixed: missing from the list are prominent non-Jewish neo-cons such as Newt Gingrich, John Ashcroft, Karl Rove, and many more. Source: Michael I. Niman, "Would you buy sneakers from an anti-Semite?" *ArtVoice*, reprinted at *www.mediastudy.com/articles/adbusters.html*.

7. Naomi Klein, *No Logo: Taking Aim at the Brand Bullies* (Toronto: Knopf Canada, 2000). Quotations from Klein throughout this section are drawn from this book, various pages.

8. Vance Packard noted in the 1950s (*Hidden Persuaders*, 90–91) that the current brand image of Marlboro cigarettes was not the original one. Marlboros were once a cigarette with red papers and a ivory tip that were marketed mostly to women. Since male smokers outnumbered women smokers, in 1956 Marlboro hired Louis Cheskin of the Color Research Institute to remake the brand as a man's cigarette with a rugged image. That led to the birth of the Marlboro man.

CHAPTER 3

1. Susan E. Linn and Alvin F. Poussaint, "The trouble with Teletubbies," *American Prospect* 10, no. 44 (May 1999).
2. "Researcher links TV wrestling, dating violence," Associated Press story in the *Charlotte (NC) Observer*, April 29, 2001; "Wrestling 'link to teen violence,'" BBC News, April 29, 2001 (*news.bbc.co.uk*).
3. "FTC releases report on the marketing of violent entertainment to children" [press release]. Federal Trade Commission, Washington, DC, September 11, 2000.
4. Christopher Stern, "Songs for grown-ups still aimed at kids," *Washington Post*, April 25, 2001.
5. Doreen Carvajal, "Major studios used children to test-market violent films," *New York Times*, September 27, 2000. The article quotes Jack Valenti, chairman of the Motion Picture Association of America, as saying that the practice of marketing movies to underage kids "is really not acceptable." A spokesperson for Disney said the company would stop using under-seventeens in focus groups for R-rated films.
6. Eric Schlosser, *Fast Food Nation: The Dark Side of the All-American Meal* (Boston: Houghton Mifflin, 2001), 42 and 47.
7. Allen D. Kanner and Mary E. Gomes, "The All-Consuming Self," in *Ecopsychology: Restoring the Earth, Healing the Mind*, eds. T. Rozak, M.E. Gomes, and A.D. Kanner (San Francisco: Sierra Club Books, 1995).

CHAPTER 4

1. As this book was going to press, the revised Television without Frontiers directive had not been made public.

2. Pascaline Dumont, "Temptation-free television for children?" *UNESCO Courier*, September 2001.

3. Dr. Reinhold Bergler, "The effects of commercial advertising on children," *Commercial Communications*, January 1999 (*europa.eu.int/comm/internal_market/comcon/newsletter/edition16-17/page41_en.htm*). Quotations from Bergler throughout this section are drawn from this report.

4. Dumont, "Temptation-free television for children?"

5. Jeffrey Goldstein, "Children and advertising – The research," *Commercial Communications*, July 1998 (*http://europa.eu.int/internal_market/comcom/newsletter/edition13/page04_en.htm*). Quotations from Goldstein throughout this chapter are drawn from this report.

6. Naomi Klein, *No Logo: Taking Aim at the Brand Bullies* (Toronto: Knopf Canada, 2000), 72–76.

7. Marketing companies have different answers to the question of whether reps are obligated to identify themselves when infiltrating their target audience's personal spaces. Marc Schiller, CEO of New York-based Electric Artists (EA)—a company credited with helping propel Christina Aguilera to superstar status with an Internet-based, buzz-stoking campaign—is quoted in *Shift* magazine as saying his employees must "always" tell fans who they are. What's at stake is the credibility of the campaign; marketers who are discovered trying to conceal their identities would bring disgrace to the band they are trying to promote, Schiller says.

   The classic strategy employed by EA (recognized as one of two leaders in the field, LA-based M80 Interactive being the other) is to identify a pop group's core fan base and to start mailing them things like news releases, advance copies of songs, T-shirts, and tickets to concerts in order to rev up their interest and get them communicating with friends about the band. All this begins with a process one EA employee calls "lurking." Employees silently observe the postings on Internet chat groups and start to join the conversation when they've located participants they believe will be receptive to their message. Those fans eventually become a volunteer sales force, sending e-mails to their friends (in their own words, so their memos don't look like spam), distributing comp tickets, or spray-painting hoardings with promotional messages. Source: Chris Turner, "Buzz, Inc.," *Shift*, November 2000.

   Other companies feel no duty to tell their targets that they are being marketed to by paid professionals. Jonathan Ressler, head of New York's Big Fat Promotions, which sends plants into public places to talk up products like Evian water and Nintendo games, says people can make up their own minds about whether the advice is useful. "People say you have to let them know that it's an advertisement," Ressler told the Canadian television program 21C. "Well, why? I mean, don't you think people are smart enough to know if they need something? So we give consumers credit and we don't think it's unethical at all. In fact, we think when we show people something, and we show them how it fits into their life, they should say thanks." Source: "The Marketing Game," 21C, episode 3, CTV television network, aired November, 2001. Videotapes available from Magic Lantern (*www.magiclantern.ca*).

8. From an interview conducted with Mark Crispin Miller for "Merchants of Cool," a documentary film originally broadcast on the PBS series *Frontline* on February 27, 2001. The broadcast transcript and the unedited interviews are available on the PBS website (*www.pbs.org/wgbh/pages/frontline/shows/cool/etc/script.html*).

CHAPTER 5

1. Ideation, a word that does not appear in my Webster's dictionary, roughly translates as the verb form corresponding to the phrase "focus group." As far as I can determine, "to ideate" is to search for meaning using the methods of market research.
2. Marshall McLuhan, "American Advertising," reprinted in *Essential McLuhan*, edited by Eric McLuhan and Frank Zingrone (Toronto: House of Anansi Press, 1995), 13.
3. Sarah Ferguson, "First tear gas, now bullets," *The Village Voice*, July 18–24, 2001.
4. Alicia Rebensdorf, "Nike and brand name bullies try to co-opt anti-sweatshop protests capitalizing on the anti-capitalist movement," *AlterNet*, August 7, 2001. Posted on the Organic Consumers website (*www.organicconsumers.org/Corp/nikeBully.cfm*). See also Ferguson, "First tear gas."
5. "Merchants of Cool," originally aired on PBS *Frontline*, February 27, 2001. Transcript available on PBS website (*www.pbs.org/wgbh/pages/frontline/shows/cool/etc/script.html*).
6. Vance Packard, *The Hidden Persuaders*, rev. ed. (New York: Washington Square Books, 1957 and 1980), 147.
7. Paul Knox, "Sudan threatens to boycott conference on children," *Globe and Mail*, September 15, 2000; Juan Forero, "A Child's Vision of War: Boy Guerrillas in Colombia," *New York Times*, December 20, 2000.
8. Peter Buitenhuis, *The Great War of Words: British, American, and Canadian Propaganda and Fiction, 1914–1933* (Vancouver: University of British Columbia Press, 1987). The following examples and quotations are drawn from this book, various pages.
9. Barbara Ehrenreich, *The Hearts of Men: American Dreams and the Flight from Commitment* (Garden City, NY: Anchor Press/Doubleday, 1983), 104. Subsequent quotations and examples from Ehrenreich are drawn from this book, various pages.
10. Quoted in Ehrenreich, *Hearts of Men*.
11. Douglas Rushkoff, *Playing the Future: What We Can Learn from Digital Kids* (New York: Riverhead Books, 1999). Quotations from Rushkoff throughout this section are drawn from this book, various pages.
12. David Brooks, "The next ruling class: Meet the Organization Kid," *Atlantic Monthly*, April 2001, pages 40–54.
13. Writer Charles McGrath, commenting on the notorious case in which a forty-four year old Massachusetts hockey father murdered his son's coach in front of a rink full of kids, ventured that the incident was at least partly an outgrowth of parents being too involved in their kids' recreation. Hockey, the traditional Canadian pastime that has recently become enormously popular in the U.S. (even the parts where it never snows), is so capital-intensive that parental input is de rigueur. "It is a game that

kids can no longer play by themselves—not unless they happen to be independently wealthy and live next door to the rink," writes McGrath. "Mom and Dad must now fork over the $400 or $500 it costs to outfit a young player (not to mention the hundreds, even thousands, more for ice time), and someone has to drive the kids to the rink, often at an ungodly hour, and then wait and drive them home."

McGrath calls organized kids' hockey "a kind of recipe for parental over-involvement—an extreme example of what is happening to youth sports in general." With its fast pace and element of violence, it's no wonder that parents get swept up in the emotion of the game—yelling from the stands, shouting orders to their kids, and sometimes threatening other parents or officials. McGrath believes that the tragedy in Massachusetts was at least partly due to the fact that hockey is so demanding of parents' time that it starts to consume the lives of those parents; the game becomes as much about the adults' feelings as the kids' fun. "Why, at a time of non-stop parental efforts to reduce risks to our kids, would we encourage them to play such a rough and aggressive game?" asks McGrath. "Could it be that we are asking our offspring to discharge the frustrations and aggressions that we no longer have any outlet for?" Source: Charles McGrath, "Ice Stürm: How youth hockey has unleashed a torrent of parental overinvolvement—and deadly rage," *New York Times Magazine*, January 20, 2002, pages 9–10.

14. The fact that the United States has gone to war since Brooks wrote his article has surely changed that climate.

15. Neil Howe and William Strauss, *Millennials Rising: The Next Great Generation* (New York: Vintage Books, 2000). Subsequent quotations from Howe and Strauss are drawn from *Millennials Rising* unless otherwise noted.

16. Brooks's biggest beef—and the one he states most directly—is that the millennials have replaced the traditional lexicon of good and evil with the kind of therapeutic language that implies bad deeds and antisocial attitudes are merely mechanical problems that can be engineered out of existence. This is a generation more inclined to label an antisocial person "sick" rather than "evil."

17. Interview with William Strauss and Neil Howe broadcast on C-SPAN's *Booknotes* program on April 14, 1991. A transcript is available at the *Booknotes* website (*www.booknotes.org/transcripts/10114.htm*).

18. Neil Howe and William Strauss, "Teens shun gross-out movie genre," *Los Angeles Times*, July 15, 2001.

CHAPTER 6

1. Peter Silsbee, "Jane and Joe Tweenager: New masters of time and space," (a PowerPoint version of this paper was presented at the Understanding Youth conference, Toronto, June 2001; a text version was posted on the Zyman Marketing Group website, *www.zmarketing.com*, though it's no longer available online).

2. To be fair, there were a few minor mea culpas from conference delegates who felt awkward about some of the more negative impacts of the kid-marketing/culture racket. One panellist expressed misgivings about the kind of messages young girls were receiving by being fed a steady diet of Britney Spears videos. A television VJ, meanwhile, took aim at the same target. He expressed regret for his role in pushing a pop icon with so little musical talent.

3. Juliet B. Schor, *Born to Buy: The Commercialized Child and the New Consumer Culture* (New York: Scribner, 2004), 10–11. Schor's account of the survey described in the following paragraphs is on pages 141–175.

4. Neil Postman, *The Disappearance of Childhood* (New York: Delacorte Press, 1982). Quotations from Postman throughout this section are drawn from this book, various pages.

5. *The Corruption of the American Child*, an O'Reilly Factor special, broadcast on the Fox network March 28, 2002. As the title suggests, the program clearly advocates the view that media product has corrupted kids, although it offers no proof in terms of statistics linking consumption of violent or otherwise offensive media with crime or antisocial behaviour. At one point, host Bill O'Reilly says: "Now, most stories have two sides. Not this one. American children are being corrupted at a rate never before seen in the world."

   Despite its tone of moral earnestness, however, the program makes use of an old trick of the tabloid press by playing both sides of the street; that is, it strenuously professes a moralistic, pro-law-and-order/family-values stance while at the same time revelling in the unseemly details of the subject matter under consideration. After each commercial break, the program is reintroduced with a collage of titillating visuals taken from adult websites, rap videos, and WWE spectacles. A guaranteed ratings booster.

6. The Family Research Council is the Washington lobbying arm of Dr. James Dobson's Colorado-based Christian parenting empire, Focus on the Family.

7. Lynn Smith, "Hollywood rediscovers the family film," *Los Angeles Times*, reprinted in the *Ottawa Citizen*, May 25, 2002.

8. Barbara Kantrowitz and Pat Wingert, "The parent trap," *Newsweek*, January 29, 2001, 53.

9. "Study says welfare switch slighted young," an Associated Press article reprinted in the *New York Times*, April 16, 2002. The study followed more than 700 families in California, Connecticut, and Florida.

10. Kantrowitz and Wingert, "The Parent Trap."

11. Marshall McLuhan and Quentin Fiore, *War and Peace in the Global Village* (New York: McGraw-Hill Book Company, 1968). Subsequent quotations and examples from McLuhan are drawn from this book, various pages.

12. From American Vision Online (*www.americanvision.com*).

CHAPTER 7

1. Alliance for Childhood, *Fool's Gold: A Critical Look at Computers and Childhood* (College Park, MD: The Alliance for Childhood, 2000), various pages. Available online (*www.allianceforchildhood.net*). The U.S. branch of the Alliance for Children—a children's rights group with eight other international offices—was founded in February 1999. The position statement that accompanied the release of *Fool's Gold* was endorsed by a blue-chip assembly of over seventy experts and advocates, including physicist Fritjof Capra, former American Education Research Association president Larry Cuban, primate researcher Jane Goodall, authors Jerry Mander, Bill McKibben, and Neil Postman, and the children's entertainer Raffi.

   Although I have used information from the Alliance report to suggest that the alleged crisis of values affecting youth and families has roots that are far deeper than the effect of media and marketing messages, the report itself was endorsed by some key players in the fight to restrict commercial messages aimed at kids, including Alvin Poussaint and Susan Linn from Judge Baker Children's Center, and Gary Ruskin, director of Commercial Alert.

2. "Once an idyll of graham crackers, fingerpainting and naps, the 'children's garden' has become a thicket of academic challenges, a result of increased state testing in the elementary grades that demands students know more, sooner," according to *New York Times* reporter Kate Zernike. In her article about the rise of "academic kindergartens," Zernike quotes Karen Lang, deputy superintendent of schools in Greenwich, Connecticut, as saying that "the notion that kindergarten is a place where kids come and play is an anachronism. The expectation by the professionals is that whatever children do, it's going to be time [sic] that leads to some kind of ultimate achievement." And for some parents and school districts, the "ultimate achievement" they're aiming at is getting their five year old on track for admission to a good college. "College admissions have become more competitive, and even that adds to the scurry," writes Zernike. "When Montgomery County, Md., revised its kindergarten curriculum last year, cutting out art as a separate subject and reducing time in physical education so schools could add more reading and math, one school official predicted that the district's SAT scores would 'skyrocket.'" Source: Kate Zernike, "No time for napping in today's kindergarten," *New York Times*, October 23, 2000.

3. "Homework overload may hit grades," BBC News Online, June 28, 2001 (*news.bbc.co.uk/hi/english/education/newsid_1410000/1410847.stm*).

4. Kate Zernike, "As homework load grows, one district says 'Enough,'" *New York Times*, October 6, 2000.

5. Amelia Hill, "Stressed students get ill to win good marks," *The Observer* (London), July 15, 2001.

6. Dawn Walton, "Kiddie coke," *Globe and Mail*, April 7, 2001, F4–F5. The story links the emergence of a large black market in Ritalin and Dexedrine to the alleged overprescription of those drugs to school children and the lack of monitoring of the use of those drugs by physicians. According to Dr. David Cohen, a Canadian

researcher and psychotherapist who chairs the doctoral program in social work at Miami's Florida International University, up to 90 percent of cases diagnosed as attention deficit disorder and treated with Dexedrine and Ritalin could be dealt with through less intrusive measures such as increased tutoring, smaller class sizes, and changes in sleep and eating habits.

7. Kate Zernike and Melody Petersen, "Schools' backing of behavior drugs comes under fire," New York Times, August 19, 2001, 1.

8. From an interview excerpted in "Generation Rx," a segment of the television series N3TV broadcast on Citytv, Toronto, in 2000. Beth Kaplanek, president of Children and Adults with Attention-Deficit/Hyperactivity Disorder (CHADD), in an open letter on the CHADD website in 2000, called Dr. Breggin "a controversial practitioner" and chastised the U.S. network ABC for "the irresponsible act of providing Peter Breggin a forum for his views" by inviting him to participate in an online chat on abcnews.com.

9. Dan Kindlon, Too Much of a Good Thing: Raising Children of Character in an Indulgent Age (New York: Hyperion, 2001). Subsequent quotations from Kindlon are drawn from this book, various pages.

10. Dan Cook, "Kiddie Capitalism: The History of the Child Consumer," posted on the PopPolitics.com website on December 5, 2001 (www.poppolitics.com). Now available in the site's archives.

11. A study by the Rand Corporation associated chronic health problems such as high blood pressure, arthritis, headaches, and breathing difficulties with metropolitan sprawl. Source: "Rand study finds first link between suburban sprawl and an increase in chronic health ailments" [press release]. Rand Corporation, September 27, 2004, available online (www.rand.org/news/press.04/09.27.html).

   Meanwhile, there is evidence that the design of, and social conditions that exist in, rundown inner-city neighourhoods have made children victims of diseases once only associated with the old. Source: Helen Epstein, "Enough to make you sick," New York Times Magazine, October 12, 2003.

12. Dr. Benjamin M. Spock, A Better World for Our Children: Rebuilding American Family Values (Bethesda, MD: National Press Books, 1994), various pages.

13. See, for instance, Frank Rich's article "Ding Dong, The Cultural Witch Hunt is Dead" in the New York Times Magazine, February 24, 2002. Rich's story—which draws from Brock's book Blinded by the Right: The Conscience of an Ex-Conservative—maintains that right-wing Republican warriors of the 1990s lacked the kind of coherent economic vision articulated by Reagan Republicans in the previous era and so resorted to mere smear campaigns and the creation of moral panics in order to divert attention from real issues.

14. Lori Leibovich, "Christ was quite anti-family—Stephanie Coontz on the way we weren't—and are," www.salon.com, May 1997.

15. Stephanie Coontz, "Nostalgia As Ideology," American Prospect 13, no. 7 (April 8, 2002). Available online (www.prospect.org). Coontz writes that the twentieth-century idea of marriage as a romantic union arose as institutions such as banks, schools, hospitals, unemployment insurance, and social security took over many of the economic and

political functions formerly handled within the family. By the 1920s, this new view of marriage had caused divorce rates to skyrocket, and commentators questioned whether "marriage was headed for extinction." The number of unwed mothers tripled between 1940 and 1948. By 1946, one in three marriages in the U.S. ended in divorce. Although the trend was reversed somewhat in the 1950s—a situation Coontz refers to as "an aberration stimulated by the most massive government subsidization of young families in American history"—even in the 1950s the number of working mothers grew by 400 percent, and by the late 1960s, divorce rates were on the rise again.

16. Leibovich, "Christ was quite anti-family."

17. Thomas Shevory, "Pop Goes the Censor: Law, Political Economy, and the Suppression of Popular Music" (paper delivered at the annual meeting of the Northeastern Political Science Association, Fall 1997). Subsequent quotations from Shevory are drawn from this paper.

18. Senate transcripts available online (www.freerepublic.com).

19. Wayne Parry, "'80s metal band Twisted Sister wants more Gore," Associated Press, April 8, 2000.

20. "Lieberman, former education secretary William Bennett present first 'Silver Sewer' award to Seagram, Inc." [Press release]. March 17, 1998.

21. Jason Vest, "Gary Ruskin's Christmas Present," The Village Voice, December 29, 1999–January 4, 2000.

22. See the Commercial Alert website (www.commercialalert.org/campaignsinfo.html).

23. Dobson is by no means the most extreme proponent of a revival of authoritarianism within family life. Perhaps the most bitterly criticized of the fundamentalist childrearing pundits are the husband-wife team of Gary and Anne Marie Ezzo, whose book Growing Kids God's Way uses scriptural quotation—for instance, a verse from the book of Matthew in which Jesus, on the cross, asks God, "Why have you forsaken me"—as justification for parents refusing to tend to a crying, distressed infant. The bestselling, secularized version of the book, On Becoming Babywise, has apparently become a big hit among busy professional parents who find that strictly regimented feedings and ignoring crying kids leads to more manageable offspring. This approach, however, has been roundly criticized by other experts (including Dobson) as promoting a form of child neglect with the potential to leave children profoundly damaged. Source: Nancy Hass, "The men and women who would be Spock," Offspring: The Magazine of Parenting, April/May 2000, 98–103.

24. Gil Alexander-Moegerle, James Dobson's War on America (Amherst, NY: Prometheus Books, 1997), various pages.

25. All the reviews noted here were (at the time of writing) archived on the Focus on the Family website (www.fotf.org or www.family.org).

26. Michael Kinsley, "Bill Bennett's Bad Bet," Slate, posted May 4, 2003 (slate.msn.com/id/2082526).

27. Michelle Loayza, "Former education chief endorses war on Iraq," Columbia Daily Spectator, February 13, 2003. Reprinted on www.avot.org (also available at www.columbiaspectator.com).

CHAPTER 8

1. Senate Committtee on the Judiciary, "Children, Violence and the Media: A Report for Parents and Policy Makers," September 14, 1999, available online (judiciary.senate. gov/oldsite/mediavio.htm).

2. Richard E. Tremblay, "The Origins of Youth Violence," Isuma, Canadian Journal of Policy Research 1, no. 2 (Autumn 2000): 19–23. Quotations throughout this section are from Tremblay's article.

3. Lt. Col. Dave Grossman and Gloria DeGaetano, Stop Teaching Our Kids to Kill: A Call to Action Against TV, Movie & Video Game Violence (New York: Crown Publishers, 1999). Quotations and examples from Grossman and DeGaetano throughout this section are from this book, various pages.

4. Anthony Ramirez, "One more reason you're less likely to be murdered," New York Times, "Week in Review," August 25, 2002, page 3.

5. Richard Rhodes, "The media violence myth," Rolling Stone, November 23, 2000. Reprinted on the website of the American Booksellers' Foundation for Free Expression (abffe.com/myth1.htm).

6. Ramirez, "One more reason you're less likely to be murdered."

7. "The Games Kids Play" originally broadcast on the ABC series 20/20, on March 22, 2000. ABC News is owned by the Disney Corporation, a major producer of film and television products, some of which contain violence. Some critics of media violence have blamed the cross-ownership of news companies and film studios as one reason why their campaign against violent images in entertainment has either been treated critically (as in the Stossel piece) or not given the amount of coverage they feel is warranted.

8. Mike A. Males, Kids and Guns: How Politicians, Experts, and the Press Fabricate Fear of Youth (Monroe, ME: Common Courage Press, 2001). An updated version (September 2004) is available on Mike Males' website (home.earthlink.net/~mmales/). Quotations from Males throughout this section are drawn from the book and website, various pages.

9. Nicholas D. Kristof, "Chicks with guns," New York Times, March 8, 2002.

10. Alexander Cockburn, "Real violence and Tim McVeigh," posted April 6, 2001 (www. antiwar.com/cockburn/c040601.html).

11. Dane Archer and Rosemary Gartner, "Peacetime casualties: The effects of war on the violent behaviour of noncombatants," in Readings About the Social Animal, 6th ed., edited by Elliot Aronson (New York: W.H. Freeman and Company, 1992). Quotations from Archer and Gartner throughout this section are drawn from this article.

CHAPTER 9

1. Jonathan L. Freedman, *Media Violence and Its Effect on Aggression: Assessing the Scientific Evidence* (Toronto: University of Toronto Press, 2002). Quotations from Freedman throughout the chapter are from the author's interview unless specifically identified as from Freedman's writing.

2. Freedman contends in his book that, rather than conducting the exhaustive literature review that would be needed to draw sweeping conclusions about what had been established about the relationship between media and violence, the NIMH commissioned four studies looking at smaller, specific aspects of the question. Freedman says none of these studies examined the conclusions of substantial numbers of previous studies, and some of the authors of the four studies were vocal supporters of the theory of a causal link between media violence and real violence.

3. Freedman says that he found eighty-seven laboratory experiments examining violent media and aggression. The essential format of this research is that one group of subjects is made to watch a violent film, while another group watches a nonviolent film. After they have watched the films, the behaviour of the two groups is compared. By Freedman's calculation, close to 40 percent of these experiments produced results that did not support the proposition that violent media fosters aggression; around 20 percent provided mixed results; and another near 40 percent supported the hypothesis. This is very different from the commonly held belief that the laboratory research overwhelmingly proves there is a causal link. Freedman believes this impression came about partly because the supportive studies are cited most often, while the studies that don't back the causal theory are generally ignored. Still, Freedman calculates that when you add the supportive and mixed results together, the majority of studies provide either complete or partial support for the notion that screen violence causes aggressive behaviour, which he says is a better result for the pro-causal forces than has been produced by the field work.

4. "Scholars ask American Academy of Pediatrics to Reconsider Misstatements about Media Violence" [press release]. National Coalition Against Censorship, New York: NCC, December 5, 2001. Available on the NCC website (*www.ncac.org/issues/aapviolenceltrpress.html*).

5. L. Rowell Huesmann, PhD, "Violent videos and violent video games: Why do they cause violence and why do they sell?" (testimony on May 4, 1999, before the Senate Committee on Commerce, Science and Transportation regarding "Marketing Violence To Children").

6. L. Rowell Huesmann and Jessica Moise, "Media violence: A demonstrated public health threat to children," *Harvard Mental Health Letter*, June, 1996.

7. Richard Rhodes, "The media violence myth," *Rolling Stone*, November 23, 2000. Available on the website of the American Booksellers' Foundation for Free Expression (*abffe.com/myth1.htm*).

8. Rowell Huesmann and Leonard Enron, "Rhodes is careening down the wrong road." Also available at the ABFFE site (*www.abffe.com/mythresponse.htm*).

9. Nathan Seppa, "Charlie's Angels made a negative, lasting impression," *The APA Monitor*, April 1996.

10. Rhodes, "Media violence myth."

11. "Q & A—Jack Zipes—An expert in children's literature says a little violence is okay for kids," *Offspring* magazine, December/January 2001, 42–43.

12. Gerard Jones, *Killing Monsters: Why Children Need Fantasy, Super Heroes, and Make-Believe Violence* (New York: Basic Books, 2002). Quotations and examples from Jones throughout this section are drawn from this book, various pages, unless otherwise noted.

13. Gerard Jones, "Why kids love what they love—a new dialogue on make-believe violence in kids entertainment," *KidScreen* magazine, September 2002.

14. Jones, *Killing Monsters*, 229–230.

Index